FASHION CRIMES

FASHION CRIMES

Dressing for Deviance

Edited by

JOANNE TURNEY

BLOOMSBURY VISUAL ARTS
LONDON • NEW YORK • OXFORD • NEW DELHI • SYDNEY

BLOOMSBURY VISUAL ARTS
Bloomsbury Publishing Plc
50 Bedford Square, London, WC1B 3DP, UK
1385 Broadway, New York, NY 10018, USA
29 Earlsfort Terrace, Dublin 2, Ireland

BLOOMSBURY, BLOOMSBURY VISUAL ARTS and the Diana logo are trademarks of
Bloomsbury Publishing Plc

First published in Great Britain 2019
This paperback edition published in 2021

Selection, editorial matter, Introduction and Chapters 2, 7, 10 and 14 © Joanne Turney, 2019
Individual chapters © the contributors, 2019

Joanne Turney has asserted her right under the Copyright, Designs and Patents Act, 1988,
to be identified as Editor of this work.

For legal purposes the Acknowledgements on p. ix constitute an extension of this
copyright page.

Cover design by Liron Gilenberg
Cover image © Sarah Hand from the series Walter Benjamin, 2008

A catalogue record for this book is available from the British Library.

A catalog record for this book is available from the Library of Congress.

ISBN: HB: 978-1-78076-698-0
PB: 978-1-35022-721-7
ePDF: 978-1-78831-563-0
eBook: 978-1-78831-564-7

Typeset by Deanta Global Publishing Services, Chennai, India

To find out more about our authors and books visit www.bloomsbury.com and
sign up for our newsletters.

CONTENTS

FIGURES

ACKNOWLEDGEMENTS

I would like to thank all of the contributors to this book, all of whom have added a particular viewpoint that has added richness and variety that demonstrate the depth and breadth of this subject.

I would also like to thank Philippa Brewster and colleagues at I.B. Tauris, and Yvonne Thouroude at Bloomsbury without whom there would be no book. Your support and guidance has been greatly appreciated. Likewise, I would like to thank the institutions (Bath Spa University and Winchester School of Art) that have supported this book from start to completion.

My sincere thanks go to all of the individuals, friends, family and colleagues who have personally supported me in the visualisation of this publication. These include John Armitage, Daniel Cid, Emmanuelle Dirix, David Dollery, Alex Franklin, Amanda Goode, Calum Kerr, Lyanne Holcombe, Alessandro Ludovico, Joanne Roberts, without whom nothing would be possible. Thank you all.

CONTRIBUTORS

Anne Cecil is Program Director, Design and Merchandising in the Westphal College of Art and Design at Drexel University, Philadelphia, PA, US. Her professional career is comprised of a bricolage of experience – retail, product design, fitness professional, speaker, award-winning artist and art/design educator. Currently Cecil conducts research and presents nationally and internationally on subcultural style and its intersection with music and fashion to form systems of identity. Cecil is area chair of *Punk Lifestyle!* for the Popular Culture Association of America (PCA) and the Exhibition Editor for the *Journal of the Popular Culture Association of Australia and New Zealand* (POPCAANZ).

Marilyn Cohen has a PhD in art history from the Institute of Fine Arts (NYU) and a master's degree in Decorative Arts, Design History and Material Culture from the Bard Graduate Center in New York City, US. She currently teaches in the Master's program in the History of Decorative Arts and Design at Parsons, The New School/Cooper-Hewitt National Design Museum. She has researched and published widely on fashion in film and television, including 'Breakfast at Tiffany's: Performing Identity in Public and Private', in *Performance, Fashion and the Modern Interior* (2011). She is author and curator of Reginald Marsh's New York, an exhibition at the Phillip Morris Branch of the Whitney Museum of American Art.

Jonathan Faiers is Professor of Fashion Thinking, Winchester School of Art, University of Southampton, UK. His research examines the interface between popular culture, textiles and dress. His publications include *Tartan* (2008) and *Dressing Dangerously* (2013), essays for *Alexander McQueen* (2015), *Developing Dress History* (2015) and *Colors in Fashion* (Bloomsbury 2016). He founded and edits the journal *Luxury: History, Culture, Consumption*. His current research includes a new history of *Fur* (2020).

Alex Franklin is Senior Lecturer in Visual Culture at the University of the West of England, Bristol. Her research interests span visual, material and popular cultures and gender studies.

Sharon Kinsella was awarded a PhD in Sociology from Oxford University in 1997 for her thesis on the manga industry, a version of which was published as the book *Adult Manga* (2000). Since the early 1990s, Kinsella has been researching cultural genres, fashion and cultural production in Japan, focusing on three overlapping areas: manga (comics); girls' culture, magazines and fashion performance and the journalistic discourse in male magazines about girls in art, film and news. Since 2000, she has taught at a number of institutions, including Yale, MIT and Oxford, and she currently holds a lecturing post in visual culture at the University of Manchester. She is completing a book about girls and men and the antiphonal and responsive style performances of young women.

Ingun Grimstad Klepp is Head of research at National Institute for Consumer Research in Oslo, Norway, and leads the technology and environment research group. She wrote her MA and PhD on leisure time and outdoor life at the University of Oslo. Her current field of research is sustainable fashion, clothing, laundry and leisure consumption. She has written numerous articles and books of these themes. For more information, please see homepage: http://www.sifo .no/page/Staff//10443/48249-10600.html

Katalin Medvedev is Associate Professor in the Department of Textiles, Merchandising and Interiors at the University of Georgia, Athens, GA, US. Her primary research interests include the construction and expression of cultural and gendered identity through dress in fashion peripheries. Her other research focuses on the social, political and gendered aspects of material culture. She has published book chapters in publications published by Berg, Pennsylvania University Press, Minnesota University Press, Purdue University Press and journal articles by dress, fashion practice and other related topics.

Holly Price Alford is Professor at Virginia Commonwealth University and historian specialising in twentieth-century fashion and African American fashion. She has presented her research and been quoted nationally and internationally. Her article entitled 'The zoot suit: Its history and influence' was published in *Fashion Theory* and reprinted in McNeil and Karaminas (eds), *The Men's Fashion Reader* (2009). She co-authored the fifth edition of *Who's Who in Fashion* (2010).

Stephanie Sadre-Orafai is Assistant Professor of Anthropology at the University of Cincinnati. Her research focuses on transformations in contemporary US racial thinking and visual culture through the lens of expert visions within and beyond the fashion industry. She has published essays on casting, model development and fashion reality television and is beginning work on a comparative project on image and knowledge production practices in fashion and criminal justice.

Joanne Turney is Associate Professor in Fashion at Winchester School of Art, University of Southampton. She is the author of *The Culture of Knitting* (2009), the co-author with Rosemary Harden of *Floral Frocks* (2007) and the co-editor with Æsa Sigurjónsdóttir and Michael A. Langkjær of *Images in Time* (2011). She has published widely on subjects as diverse as hand-knitting, antisocial behaviour and dress and vajazzling.

Philip Warkander born in 1978, received his MA in Ethnology at the University of Gothenburg, Sweden, in 2004. Since 2008 he has been employed as a PhD candidate at the Centre for Fashion Studies. He also teaches at Södertörn högskola and at the Beckmans College of Design, where he is also a member of the Fashion Department Board. In addition to this, he is part of a network of scholars, united by their interest in ethnographical research methods – the Wardrobe Network.

INTRODUCTION

Joanne Turney

If the devil wears Prada, what does God wear?

ANON

The relationship between clothing and behaviour as a site of social acceptance or rejection has long been discussed by fashion theorists,[1] particularly those adopting an anthropological approach to dress and how and why it's worn.[2] Likewise, notions of clothing as means of materialising the psyche or emotional self have been addressed by fashion theorists, adopting a psychoanalytical model.[3] This established discourse rarely overlaps, and one might conclude that the fusion of the personal, the social and the institutional offers a site for an investigation into the way clothing is recognised, used and worn, as expressions of wider sociocultural and political concerns in contemporary everyday life.[4]

Indeed, dress historians and fashion theorists acknowledge that clothing has a personal and social function, and although it may be difficult to create an absolute language of dress, clothing or its more glamorous sister, fashion, it is widely accepted that what one wears communicates something about the self either as projection or as reflection. This means that clothes are loaded with cultural meaning, and this makes them significant. Yet, frequently the clothes one wears are less communicative than the ways in which garments are worn, which leads us to suggest that clothing is performative. This fusion of communication as understood by the social group, when combined with the concept of clothing as a vehicle in which to perform the self (real or perceived), suggests that clothing is a form of costume; something worn to play a particular social role. We are all aware of this either consciously or subconsciously; we know what is socially acceptable through the unwritten rules of sartorial coding. So, one wouldn't wear a dirty tracksuit to a job interview in a bank or a white dress to a friend's wedding.

Much academic enquiry surrounding issues of dress and behaviour consider the means by which clothing can demonstrate conformity or nonconformity to social norms. This is best demonstrated by the literature of subcultural style, in which clothing is used as a means of differentiation, demonstrating a conscious resistance to normative society at a given time.[5] Conversely, discussions of uniformity in dress have equally considered individuals' desire to establish personal sartorial nuances in order to distance the self from the group, whilst still appearing to fit in. So, there is much written about clothing and social conformity and nonconformity, yet little is written about the way in which particular types of clothing can be and have been socially and culturally demonised, considered deviant and frightening, embodying or making solid social perception. *Fashion Crimes* will redress this by considering two everyday experiences and their interrelationship; dress and behaviour, specifically antisocial and criminal behaviours that could be considered as 'deviant'. Can clothing be criminal? Can wearing certain clothing affect behaviour or encourage others to literally 'follow suit'? This is the first book to address and discuss the relationship between clothing and deviant or criminal behaviour, and it aims to develop a new field of enquiry that considers representation, perception and behaviour within an overarching understanding of the dressed and undressed body. By privileging dress – and specifically fashionable dress – *Fashion Crimes* offers and demonstrates collaborative and interdisciplinary enquiry that expands the fields of dress history and fashion theory.

Crime trends

Scholars are divided on the actual meaning of the term 'crime' primarily because as a core element of contemporary society, crime goes beyond mere law-breaking; it has, as a concept, act and form of behaviour, moral, social and cultural implications that affect society as a whole and the foundations on which it is based. Studies in criminology, a discipline developed to understand and prevent criminality, are constantly questioning the nature and definition of the term, as prospective demarcations are frequently too broad or too narrow, too vague or too specific.[6] For example, the police force might focus on what they consider to be a major crime, such as murder, whereas minor crimes such as vandalism might consume little police time and resource, but be regarded as major by those living in a continually vandalised neighbourhood. Similarly, as crime is inherent within society and simultaneously represents the locus of social control, it is burdened by the dual processes of modernity and history, changing over time and across cultures.

So, crime is virtually impossible to define; of course we could use a dictionary for a literal outline or legal documents to formulate an epistemology, yet this is not how crime is understood or formulated in everyday life. Our familiarity with crime is largely constructed as both media spectre and spectacle. High on political agendas globally and locally, crime consequently exists amongst us as the praxis at which normality meets deviance and presents such a threat that it requires constant monitoring and, essentially, eradication.[7] Therefore, very much part of everyday life as news reportage and real-life crime reconstruction permeate digital and analogue media, crime is something we are aware of; we know it is a potential threat in which perpetrators create victims, and it is this ideological essence that perpetuates its invisible and menacing presence.[8] We live with it, but can't see or touch it; it is beyond our sensory experience, and we only recognise it as an end product, once the crime has been committed and the damage done.

So the way in which we primarily understand crime or what constitutes a criminal act is through its effects or evidence of crime and its effects. Perhaps acting as a deterrent to future acts of criminality, crying victims, blood-splattered pavements, broken windows and burning cars become part of the iconographic proof of the existence of criminality, emphasising its devastation to social harmony. Here crime is portrayed as the converse of normality, a rupture in the everyday, unexpected chaos in a world of calm. Yet such visualisation and sensory engagement experienced by the reader (the smell of burning petrol, the sharpness of splintered glass, the sound of sirens) acts as a medium for empathetic awareness, feeling for the victim and fear for one's own personal safety.[9] We become part of the crime scene as an emotional witness. Fear of crime is therefore perpetuated via a connectivity; between act and the potential for future acts, the locale before and after the event, and a cyclical connectivity develops between the victim and 'witness' as potential victim/s.[10]

Renata Salecl defines the contemporary world as an age of anxiety, a world in which traditional binaries of good/bad, right/wrong, truth/lies, male/female have been blurred to such an extent that to live in these times one is constantly unsure and afraid.[11] In an era of impersonal communication, potential threat from seemingly 'invisible' viral or chemical sources, a postmodern nightmare in which the fragmentary patterns of contemporary living create an environment of placelessness, isolation, fear and confusion permeate the everyday, seeping into language, popular perception and iconography. At the heart of this climate of anxiety is a suspicion of 'otherness' and an overwhelming concern for personal and collective safety, and indeed, for the security of private property. From this assumed starting point, this text focuses on an apparently silent group that impacts directly or indirectly on the lives of citizens globally, the criminal and the identification of said persons. (For the purposes of this book, criminality is defined as both actual and perceived; of actual 'law-breaking' but also as signs of deviance from social norms of propriety, and therefore questions the role of a collective morality rather than legality in determining norms of behaviour,[12] whereas the term 'criminal' is person-specific and describes an individual convicted of law-breaking.) Indeed, criminality and crime can be identified as a perception, an idea of law-breaking and the threat it potentially poses, a modern folk devil embodying a feeling of insecurity in contemporary times.

As crime is both apparent and absent, we see its effects, but cannot actually see 'it'; we don't know what 'crime' looks like, and, as the term encompasses so many forms of behaviour, it seems impossible to predict or recognise a potential occurrence. It is this invisibility that adds to the mystique of crime, and from this point one can start to assess criminality, crime and the criminal as a mythology. A mythology, as Barthes would suggest, is the sociocultural formulation of a belief system based on both actuality (in this case, crime or criminal behaviour) and imagined or perceived responses to that actuality (how we understand crime).[13] In order for this to occur and become established and perpetuated in a collective consciousness, the term 'crime' needs to be recognisable and therefore requires some kind of physical form. The more potent the form, the more credible the threat, and the more fearful we become.

There are many players invested in the development and continuation of public anxiety resulting from a mythology of crime. These can be obvious; for example, a fear of crime validates a large and well-funded police force, or fear of robbery, violence and vandalism may increase the sales of personal safety devices or alarms and locks. A fear of crime also fuels tabloid newspaper headlines, television drama,[14] works of fiction and real-life crime paperbacks.[15] Indeed, in the UK in 2010, two-thirds of all books borrowed from libraries were crime fiction, whilst the top three bestsellers were also in this genre, written by Stieg Larsson.[16]

The societal need to identify potential threat or to put a 'face' to the crime has a long and established history that can be traced from astrology through to the development of criminology in the nineteenth century. Studies in phrenology (the study of skull formations as an indicator of brain patterns), combined with the *science* of physiognomy[17] (methods of assessing behavioural characteristics from facial features), demonstrate a clear progression to the development of 'mugshots' as a means of considering potential perpetrators. Consequently, recent instances of mass criminal activity have been reported with specific reference to the dress of the perpetrator/s in an attempt to offer clues to the identification of future criminals. For example, the Columbine school shootings in the US, committed by students Eric Harris and Dylan Klebold in 1999, were described by the media as the 'Trench coat Mafia', whilst Tim Kretschmer, who murdered 10 schoolmates in southwest Germany in 2009, was described as a young man with a penchant for 'black, military-style clothing'. One might conclude that such description plays on the notion of the romantic outsider, the man in black, the loner who cannot conform to societal norms and distinguishes himself as such through his apparel.[18] Yet, military-style, black clothing and trench coats are everyday wear, particularly for discontented youths, and as such imply that dress indicators are less than reliable, confusing identification further. Similarly, one might argue that to adopt this form of dress may well be a sign of social discontent, and therefore these types of clothing become a self-fulfilling

Figure 0.1 Damage caused by rioters in Hackney, London, UK. Photo by Julio Etchart/ullstein bild via Getty Images.

prophesy, as exemplified by the dress of London rioters (2011), who deliberately wore 'hoodies' in order to participate in the mayhem (Figure 0.1).

This book, as the title indicates, addresses the relationship between fashion and crime. Clothing, and in particular, clothing deemed as 'fashionable', has an established communicative role as an indicator of identity, resulting from its inherent characteristic of simultaneously revealing and concealing the body. These concomitant aspects of body dressing assume social and moral models of 'respectability' or 'propriety' and any deviation from these unwritten sartorial codes define the wearer as an 'outsider' or 'other'. This is most notable in the dress of victims, particularly women in rape trials, which is constantly under scrutiny by the media and indeed defence lawyers in order to act as a moral barometer, suggesting that revealing clothing equates with sexual availability which seemingly (and wrongly) negates the crime of 'rape'. In other words, the 'victim' is perceived to be dressing in a way that is not respectable and by stepping outside of a moral boundary becomes almost 'acceptable' prey.

Like the relationship between clothing and the moral woman, the clothing of deviant behaviour is very much part of Western visual popular culture. The burglar in his striped jersey, eye mask and swag bag, the gangster in his wide-shouldered expensive handmade suit and his moll in a fur coat and stiletto heels are all stereotypical manifestations of those who appear to embrace lawlessness. Likewise and conversely, prison uniforms offer a clear demarcation between the

Figure 0.2 African American convicts at Reed Camp, South Carolina, working with axes and singing. Photo by Photo12/UIG via Getty Images.

criminal status of the wearer and everyday dress in normative society, sartorially reinforcing the value of stigmatisation and ostracism in relation to criminal activity and thus threat (Figure 0.2). Yet in everyday life, crime and its perpetrators are less easy to identify – indeed successful criminality is reliant on invisibility or non-detection – but there nonetheless remains a desire within popular consciousness to respond to visually stereotypical coding, fundamentally responding to the appearance of a suspected criminal. For example, M. Kimberly MacLin and Vivian Herrera's study of perceptions of criminality concluded:

> The top eight frequently provided characteristics for criminal hair were: short, black, dark, messy, bald, long, brown, dirty, comprising 77% of total responses. The top 14 most frequently provided responses for criminal clothing were: jeans, baggy clothes, black clothing, t-shirts, cap/hat, old clothing, jumpsuit/jail uniform, ski mask, sleeveless shirt, tennis shoes, white shirt, suits, boots, jacket, comprising 83% of the total responses to this question. The number one physical characteristic associated with criminals

was the presence of tattoos. The top three types of crimes associated with criminals were murder, robbery and rape.[19]

Appearance is one of the most significant forms of communication in our increasingly visual world. The way one 'appears' (looks and behaves, alone and with others) continues to dominate the contemporary media and consequently informs the ways in which we interact with and understand those around us. *Fashion Crimes* intends to focus on the ways in which dress communicates, represents and is associated with seemingly criminal behaviour, and how this sartorial coding becomes assumed popular knowledge, and is subsequently appropriated and manipulated by wearers, cultural commentators and the fashion industry. Can specific garments influence or mediate social behaviour, for example, 'hoodies' are both garments *and* a specific group of young people, and to what extent is clothing really a communicator of social disintegration, disarray and loose morality, as the media would like us to believe?

This book draws on contemporary attitudes to 'otherness' and dress, focusing on fitting in and standing out in relation to written legislation and perceived sartorial codes, highlighting the interaction between the individual, society and the state. With the election in the UK of Prime Minister David 'hug a hoodie' Cameron (2010–16), the relationship between the state and those deemed outside of it has never been so important. Indeed, as the labelling of antisocial youths as 'hoodies' – so called as a response to their penchant for hooded sweatshirts and concealment within – shows, the relationship between clothing, behaviour and marginality has somewhat deepened. Simultaneously, reportage in the popular press has commented on recent clothing and antisocial behaviour-related court cases, such as 18-year-old Ellis Drummond's assertion that his ASBO (Antisocial Behaviour Order) prohibiting him from wearing 'low slung trousers' was a breach of his civil rights.[20]

Using an interdisciplinary methodology, and drawing from primary and secondary sources, this book develops new approaches to the study of everyday dress, fashionability and the negotiation and navigation of the individual body in public space. It focuses on specific garments, innocuous objects that have been demonised socially and in the media, and the book therefore, aims to establish a dialogue between the object, the personal and the social or institutional, addressing and questioning the praxis where issues of morality as a form of social control meet criminality. *Fashion Crimes* is an interdisciplinary study that speaks directly about contemporary life and clothing, focusing on groups, garments and dress practices hitherto marginalised and ignored within more traditional fashion and dress studies. In this book, seemingly established sartorial codes such as 'fashionability', 'propriety and suitability', and terms such as 'glamour' and 'luxury' are upturned, inverted and renegotiated through everyday dress practices in response to notions of criminality and/or deviant behaviour. This book is indicative of new academic writing that questions existent methods of discourse surrounding dress, the body and society. It has an ethnographic focus and therefore embraces the new discipline of wardrobe studies. *Fashion Crimes* speaks dialogically, with contributors representative of a global community of scholars, each of whom focuses on shared models of dress and 'criminal' behaviour, whilst positioning discourse within disparate and specific cultural frameworks. Ultimately, this discussion of fashion and its relation to crime, in whatever form, aims to establish a new field that expands fashion studies.

Structure and organisation

This book is divided into chapters, each of which addresses specific approaches to dress, crime and its representation and experience. The first three chapters investigate the ways in which specific items of 'ordinary' clothing have become associated with criminal activity. Here, the suit (Jonathan Faiers), the hoodie (Joanne Turney) and low-slung trousers (Holly Price Alford) are interrogated as simultaneously ordinary and extraordinary, exemplifying the impossibility of clothing delineation as 'criminal'. Likewise, each chapter questions the validity of demonising both clothing and wearers and the means by which this becomes apparent.

These are followed by chapters concerned with representations of criminality in popular culture, with close studies interrogating the ways in which the iconography of crime is appropriated by the fashion industry. The relationship between fashion and death, a key discourse in the works of Walter Benjamin[21] and more contemporary theorists such as Caroline Evans,[22] considers the ephemerality of fashion and the quest for fashionability as an encounter with death, or that which has already moved on. The focus therefore relies on popular perceptions of criminality in relation to the dressed and gendered or 'ethnic' body, emphasising sociocultural norms of respectability and behaviour.

Referencing the iconography of criminology, Stephanie Sadre Orafi's discussion of the Polaroid photograph as the casting/modelling agency version of the mugshot questions the stripping bare of the model's face, thus offering the possibility for some kind of recognisable 'truth'. Here, the relationship between the image of the model, one largely seen as constructed and indicative of artifice, is unmasked, and, like the captured criminal, becomes a sign of mere identification.

Both Sharon Kinsella and Alex Franklin investigate the sexualisation of young women in opposing contemporary cultures. Kinsella considers the *kogyaru*, a subcultural form of dress and behaviour appropriated by young Japanese women that imitates white Western schoolgirl culture. She argues that such behaviour is both 'deviant' (the style requires expensive branded products and the ways in which money is obtained to purchase these goods implies criminal or immoral activities) and culturally normalised, outlining the overt and socially inappropriate sexiness of the clothing worn and the disrespectful attitude to racial type, whilst addressing issues of role-play and costuming in Japanese culture. For Franklin, revealing fashions and cultural and racial appropriation are also at the heart of the discussion, but here she addresses the ways in which Black hip-hop styling, and in particular the 'thong', have been disseminated into White mainstream clothing. For both authors, the significance of dressing like a prostitute when one is not a prostitute is criminally ambiguous and acts as a means of reinstating patriarchal norms of the 'good' woman.

From discussions of gendered norms of dress and behaviour pertaining to the representation and performativity of femininity, Turney's analysis of masculinity, dress and 'hardness' alludes to gendered constructions of the violent and aggressive male. Focusing on the dress of soccer hooligans in the 1980s, this chapter questions and charts the rise of the 'new' man in the context of the perceived gendered transition of the period.

Fundamentally the opening chapters respond to and reside within understandings of the dress of specific groups and how these are interpreted and compared with representations of criminality in the media. Therefore, the focus hitherto has been on sociocultural concerns relating to 'otherness' as a means of distinguishing behaviours and appearances that deviate from the norm. The chapters that follow move away from the media to more political concerns, and the emphasis shifts to the state, positioning the dressed individual in opposition to legislation and government policy. For example, the perception of criminality as a binary dependent on good/bad and one's perception of such distinction, the severity of state clothing restrictions in Communist Hungary during the post-war period and their negotiation by a fashion hungry public are explored by Kaitlin Medvedev. The chapter outlines the ways in which the necessity and desire for new and predominantly Western clothing fuelled ordinary people to commit criminal acts such as smuggling as a defiant response to state legislation. When the fashion system is reliant on desire and change, is it unreasonable for people to want new and appealing clothes?

The distinction of right/wrong or acceptable/not acceptable is case-studied in Philip Warkander's dress-centred ethnography of 'queer-bashing' in Stockholm. Although, of course, this is a crime, the notion of 'otherness' as constructed through dress and sexuality is deemed deviant and threatening by those committing the offences. The criminalisation of the victim through their dress is interrogated in Turney's 'Material Evidence', which considers the ways in which the dress of victims of sexual assault are used in court cases as a foil for the individual and personal body. Here, the focus is on what might be considered provocative dressing, in daily life and court, and how and why this might be merely an attempt to be 'fashionable'. Each section will consider the problems inherent in identifying and negotiating criminality, none more so than the final chapters, which draw together garments that 'deliberately' traverse and transgress normative boundaries. In Anne Cecil's discussion of the skull and crossbones motif, the division between the eighteenth century and the contemporary outsider is bridged, de-politicised and reinvented for a mass market of would-be deviants and fashionist as alike.

In a quieter, and perhaps more shocking blurring of boundaries, Ingun Grimstad Klepp's investigation into the re-appropriation of national costume, the Lustkoffe sweater, by defendants in major criminal court cases in Norway, questions the appropriation of seemingly 'innocent' clothing worn by the seemingly 'guilty'. Criminality here, is perceived, as in many of the chapters in this book, as a sign of 'otherness' and becomes entwined with notions of the non-Norwegian racial outsider and in turn levels of criminality.

Marilyn Cohen's discussion of the trench coat demonstrates the persistence of a marginal garment. The coat has a long history in representation as the chosen garb of the man on the margins, of both the detective and criminal. The ordinariness of the coat, along with its design, facilitates its appropriation by those wishing to fit in with the crowd and move seamlessly amongst it undetected. Famed for its association with sexual deviancy (the 'flasher-mac', the dirty raincoat) it is equally celebrated as the sign of the unkempt lawman (Columbo; Sam Spade) and consequently the trench coat is the ultimate disguise, negotiating and transcending boundaries of acceptability and social norms.

Finally, Joanne Turney's 'From *Revolt*ing to *Revolting*' offers an expose of the tracksuit as a garment for potential revolt. This chapter discusses the notion of 'revulsion' and 'revolution' as socially abject entities that use clothing as indicators or measures of and for specific behaviours. Although frequently vilified by the media as the dress of the 'yob', here, the tracksuit is posited as a sign of disaffected and infantilised masculinity, and an indicator of disenfranchisement and exclusion from traditional patriarchal norms.

Fashion Crimes is by no means the definitive guide to clothing criminality, but it does offer an introduction to an innovative approach to dress and behaviour. As with any introduction, it offers a snapshot (or mugshot) of the ways in which clothing has been and continues to be represented or appropriated as a sign of social deviancy and potential criminality. There is no doubt that clothing can and does mediate behaviour; whether we can still clearly delineate between the good and bad, criminal and non-criminal is less easy to assess, as these examples attest. Clothing and how and why it is worn, like concepts of 'criminal' or 'deviant behaviour', is fundamentally determined by unwritten social laws that are predominantly driven by the moral climate and notions of acceptability in a given culture at any specific time. Therefore, these concerns are fluid and are constantly under review. Nonetheless, the impossibility of absolutes regarding both dress and behaviour creates a confusing paradigm in which everyone who *appears* different from the norm is under suspicion of potential wrongdoing. The 'other' therefore can be considered as anyone who is not 'us', and as such uncover a whole host of prejudices, myths and perceptions that exist at the epicentre of contemporary society.

1

WHITE LIES AND THE TAILORING OF EVIL

Jonathan Faiers

This property of whiteness, to be everything and nothing, is the source of its representational power.[1]

The relationship between an excessive attention to stylish and conspicuous forms of dress and criminal activity and character has been a recurrent visual narrative 'shorthand' throughout cinematic history. Immaculate, and often exceedingly fashionable or flashy, tailoring has become the hallmark of the cinematic and literary gangster alike, providing the perfect vestimentary counterpoint to the destruction and bloodshed wrought by the wearer. It is as if the perfection of his tailoring provides, if not entirely effective camouflage, certainly a sartorial veneer for the villain, an immaculate and spotless disguise that cloaks a dysfunctional and chaotic disposition.

The desire for admiration and acceptance that accompanies good tailoring is so central to many of the earliest cinematic incarnations of the gangster, that it can almost become the raison d'être for their criminal activities and ascendancy. Paul Muni, playing the mobster Tony Camonte in *Scarface* (1932), directed by Howard Hawks and Richard Rosson, is a case in point; as we chart Tony's violent rise to criminal stardom we also witness him buying increasingly flashy and loud suits, jewellery, expensive handmade shirts and so on.[2] But of course no matter how showy or expensively dressed, Tony's psychopathic tendencies will surface, and his permanently scarred face acts as the true indicator of his equally disfigured psyche, transcending his silk ties and collar pins. Films such as *Scarface*, *The Public Enemy* (1931) and *Little Caesar* (1930) established a cinematic template that both reflected organised criminal activity during prohibition America and helped to construct the public image of what the typical gangster looked like and aspired to.[3] Indeed, it is rumoured that Al Capone himself liked *Scarface* so much that he had his own copy of the film.

The heightened, overly fashionable clothing of the classic cinematic gangster of 1930s Hollywood acts as a form of sartorial defence, tailored armour perhaps, that distinguishes the mobster as an extraordinary being, beyond the pale of bourgeois conventions of correct and acceptable dressing. The criminal's spectacular clothing, however, is simultaneously suggestive of a fundamental flaw, for throughout history the male who pays too much attention to personal appearance and clothing has always been depicted as 'other', deviant and unhealthily particular. The fastidious man who dresses to be noticed is represented as suspect, untrustworthy, often effeminate and homosexual. This equation between obsessive appearance, criminality and homosexuality in the classic Hollywood mob films from the 1930s, when such explicit reference to male sexuality was taboo, has been considered as a way of indicating the mobster's sexual preference without direct reference to it, a form of sartorial signposting, where 'inappropriate' dressing equals 'unacceptable' sexuality. The previously mentioned *Little Caesar*, directed in 1930 by Mervyn LeRoy, is one such example, where Edward G. Robinson playing Rico Bandello (obviously modelled on Al Capone) is depicted, once his criminal ascendancy has been charted, immaculately, if flashily tailored, complete with diamond studs and tie pins. Rico, a paranoid petty criminal with a superman complex who has risen through the criminal ranks, displays throughout the film a rampant misogyny and condescension towards romantic heterosexual love. Accompanying his cynicism is an equally strong, and at times thinly veiled, attraction to his long-time buddy Jo, whose love for Glenda (Jo's long-time girlfriend) is incomprehensible to Rico, and regarded as a sign of weakness.

Given the censure that has for so long surrounded the narcissistic male, it is perhaps ironic that such an overtly masculine construction as the cinematic gangster should be so often characterised as foppish and self-obsessed. However, it is precisely through this excessive attention to personal appearance that the criminal distinguishes and elevates himself from the crowd. He has the means, self-regard and arrogance to purposely defy convention and court the approbation of the law-abiding status quo in matters sartorial. Stella Bruzzi, in her *Undressing Cinema: Clothing and Identity in the Movies*, suggests,

> When considering the costumes of the screen gangster the spectator is struck by this ambivalence, that here are characters who have both cultivated an aggressively masculine image and are immensely vain, and whose sartorial flamboyance, far from intimating femininity or effeminacy, is the most important sign of their masculine social and material success.[4]

Bruzzi identifies a number of fundamental characteristics of the flashily dressed gangster, including the obvious function of noticeably fashionable or expensive clothes to signify economic superiority and success. The gangster demonstrates not only his ability to afford (or at least procure) expensive clothes, but in their very luxuriousness and impracticality suggests that the wearer either does not have to work for a living or at least is involved in a profession that does not entail manual labour or physical exertion and therefore the risk of soiling his clothes. As Thorstein Veblen notes in his *The Theory of the Leisure Class*, 'Our dress, therefore, in order to serve its purpose effectually, should not only be expensive, but it should also make plain to all observers that the wearer is not engaged in any productive labour.'[5]

Notwithstanding the lack of cultural capital that is so often understood as the natural accompaniment of a refined dress sense, many cinematic gangsters are not afraid to embark on an accelerated course of sartorial refinement. One of the first things Tony Camonte in *Scarface* does is to make a bulk purchase of luxury shirts, one of which he declares to his girlfriend Poppy he intends to wear each day. This scene immediately brings to mind another famous fictional character, of dubious antecedence – Jay Gatsby, the eponymous character from Scott Fitzgerald's seminal story *The Great Gatsby*. In the story much is made of the gossip and speculation surrounding the source of Gatsby's wealth, whether he was a bootlegger, his possible wartime criminal activity and so on. In his attempts to woo Daisy Buchanan he provides her with a tour of his mansion that includes the famous scene bought to the screen in the 1974 film version of the novel, where he shows off his collection of handmade English shirts, reducing Daisy to tears as she wallows in Gatsby's perfect linen.[6]

Whilst Gatsby's and Camonte's abundance of shirts is a cinematic indicator of their possible criminal proclivities, the archetypal garment that perfectly expresses this equation between tailoring and the sociopath; the basting together of cloth and cruelty is the white suit. Notwithstanding that when found in other forms of clothing – wedding dresses, clerical vestments, and baby clothes, for example – white is equated with purity, sanctity and innocence, when used for a man's suit the wearer is inevitably viewed with distrust and condescension. The aforementioned Jay Gatsby, for all of his wealth, is regarded as somehow never quite 'right' for Long Island society, due in no small part to his predilection for white suits, whilst Tony Manero's self-centred arrogance is indivisible from his love of the white suit in *Saturday Night Fever*.[7] The difficulty of keeping all-white clothing in pristine condition is another pitfall facing those who opt for this palette, witness the inappropriateness of Rico Rizzo's choice of white lounge jacket and off-white trousers for his first appearance in *Midnight Cowboy*.[8] For Rico, the terminally sick, crippled, small-time crook and would-be pimp, white seems the aspirational choice for a petty thief who wants to make the big time and yet is doomed to live out his fantasies of an all-white lifestyle in Miami whilst languishing in squalor in New York. Even Sidney Stratton's spotless character and lofty intentions of revolutionising post-war British textile manufacturing that comprises the central plot of *The Man in the White Suit* are transformed into a threat to the economic security of the worker once his cloth is perfected, and he dons his miraculous white suit.[9]

These relatively innocuous and unwitting examples of the inadvisability of donning white each deserve lengthier investigations of the correlation between wearing white and social unacceptability, white and egocentricity, white and disability and white and hubris, for example, but Jay Gatsby and his sartorial comrades mentioned above pale by comparison to the vestimentary sleight of hand adopted by another order of white-suit wearers hell-bent on cinematic destruction. These snowy psychopaths know only too well the saintly camouflage white can provide and use to deadly effect the outré distraction they generate. As Stella Bruzzi again proposes,

> The use of white or off-white ensembles to denote extreme brutality probably derives directly from Al Capone. Both the real and the fictionalised gangster, therefore, occupy a paradoxical position in relation to fashion: whilst they appropriate the styles of high fashion, they do not ultimately want to blend in or be lost in it, so they cultivate an identifiable school of stylishness that, far from operating as camouflage, ultimately functioned like warrior dress.[10]

Before studying three key examples of the cinematic white suit, a distinction needs to be made from the previously discussed love of the mobster for a tendency towards flashy modes of dressing and the specific case of the completely white wardrobe. As Bruzzi identifies, the use of off-white ensembles by the psychopathic mobster has its origins in Al Capone's predilection for pale tailoring, and in many cinematic demonstrations of this phenomenon from the 1930s onwards we see a variety of pale greys and off whites clothing the bodies of assorted mobsters and megalomaniacs from 'Hood' Stacey in *Each Dawn I Die* to *Dr No*.[11] Similarly, a number of the screen's most memorable crime bosses have favoured pure white in the form of a tuxedo for evening and formal occasions, such as Tony Camonte in the enormously influential Brian de Palma remake of *Scarface*,[12] but these examples are fair weather or special occasion white wearers; in the discussion of the films that follows, dazzling white is compulsory for these sartorial sadists throughout the majority of their on-screen appearances. For Frank Nitti, Al Capone's ruthless henchman in *The Untouchables*, the genocidal Nazi, Dr Josef Mengele in *The Boys from Brazil* and Adam Cramer, the hate-mongering racist in *The Intruder*, the white suit is *de rigueur* for their charted courses of annihilation; for them white is the non-colour that bleaches and atomises all those who come into contact with it.[13]

The viewer's first sight of Dr Josef Mengele, the Angel of Death (*Todesengel*) or White Angel (*weiße Engle*), in the 1978 film *The Boys from Brazil* is truly divine. We see Gregory Peck, playing Mengele, arriving by seaplane in Paraguay in the dead of night, and as he steps ashore lights from the waiting cars dispel the darkness

Figure 1.1 Josef Mengele's incandescent entrance. Still from *Boys from Brazil*. 1978 dir. Franklin J. Schaffner. Photo by ITV/REX/Shutterstock.

and illuminate Mengele, dazzling his expectant Nazi entourage (Figure 1.1). His brilliant appearance is compounded by his wearing a pure white suit and shirt, and whilst the costume designer Anthony Mendleson was obviously referencing the name he earned in the concentration camps, this bravura display of sartorial attention seeking can be seen as representative of a persistent multivalency that characterises the cinematic white suit. On the most fundamental level, dressing evil characters in white subverts the universally accepted cinematic convention of white signifying good and black bad, established ever since pioneering silent cinema directors used white and black cowboy hats to assist in the narrative progression of the early Western film. The contrast between these characters' dazzling outward appearance and their inner depravity is irresistible of course, and as Jean Baudrillard suggests, 'Everything is metamorphosed into its inverse in order to be perpetuated in its purged form. Every form of power, every situation speaks of itself by denial, in order to escape, by simulation of death, its real agony.'[14]

The paradox of Mengele's wearing white, the colour of purity, juxtaposed with the experiments in racial 'purification' we see him conducting later in the film is reinforced throughout *The Boys from Brazil*. Whether it be his choice of white lounge suit in which to outline his Aryan cloning plan, the all-white safari suit for experiments on Paraguayan children in his jungle laboratory, or his white tuxedo for the Nazi dinner and dance, white is 'the new black' for Mengele, but returning to his first radiant entrance, his white suit becomes more than merely another example of the criminal predilection for ostentatious tailoring; it exudes the quality of whiteness that ironically is historically associated with divine, ineffable sanctity. Mengele's white and that of the other examples discussed shortly signifies not just goodness, but inviolability, a whiteness beyond the understanding of mere mortals. John Gage traces this incomprehensible whiteness back to the concept of divine light as formulated by theologians in the early Middle Ages, '... we posit intangible and invisible darkness of that Light which is unapproachable because it so far exceeds the visible light.'[15] Mengele's manifestation is both visually unintelligible due to its blinding whiteness and incomprehensible in terms of what he is attempting to carry out – the cloning of 94 Hitlers.

Unlike Mengele's dazzling entrance in *The Boys from Brazil*, Frank Nitti's in *The Untouchables* is initially, at least so low key as to be almost overlooked (Figure 1.2). We first encounter Al Capone's most deadly assassin white-suited and accessorised in white, with matching gloves and hat, sitting against a backdrop of newly washed shirts in the laundry-cum-drugstore that he is planning to blow up if the owner refuses to pay the required protection money. As the owner serves the little neighbourhood girl who is running errands for her mother, we see him in the background rise silently from his bar stool and

Figure 1.2 Frank Nitti in white armour plating. Still from *The Untouchables*. 1987 dir. Brian de Palma. Photo by Paramount/Kobal/REX/Shutterstock.

leave the briefcase containing the bomb and walk out. Seeing this, the girl picks up the bag and starts to catch up with him to return it, at which moment the case explodes annihilating the drugstore and the little girl, as Nitti the White Angel of 1930s Chicago disappears from sight. Nitti as a character is even more inexplicable than Mengele, silent for most of the film, spectral, even supernatural in his apparent indestructibility and speed. For example, in the scene where he slaughters Jim Malone (played by Sean Connery) the honest cop and mentor to Eliot Ness, we first see him outside Malone's apartment; a street-lit pale phantom casing the joint, and then, after luring Malone outside, we see Nitti perched like some snowy bird of prey on the fire escape, from which vantage point he guns Malone down. In the time it takes Malone to crawl back inside, Nitti appears with supernatural speed as a phantom presence in Al Capone's box at the opera, a pallid angel of death reporting back to his master, his otherworldliness echoed on stage by the white-faced Pagliacci.

For the ultimate in dazzling whiteness as *invisible darkness* we need the sharp contrast of black and white film and the polarisation of colour not only in terms of the film's production but as an ideological polarisation also.[16] In Roger Corman's remarkable 1962 indictment of racial hatred *The Intruder* we return once again to notions of racial purity signified by the use of white clothing for the main protagonist Adam Cramer, played by William Shatner. In the shimmering heat of the small southern town of Caxton, Cramer arrives to incite racial hatred and unrest on the eve of the town's integration of Black and White school children. The opening titles present the tableaux of the white-suited Cramer, in dark glasses (to shield his eyes from his own radiance perhaps?) looking out from a train window at a group of cotton pickers, a visual distillation of the themes of racial segregation, intolerance and injustice that will be played out to masterly effect in the film. On Cramer's arrival in Caxton we see his progress through the town, a white-suited redeemer smiling beatifically, helping a little girl off the bus (both Nitti and Cramer are contrasted by the innocence of children, as indeed is Mengele, who ironically seems at his most human whilst experimenting on his Paraguayan infant subject), and in the shimmering heat of the town appears to all intents and purposes as a white knight in shining armour, or at least white seersucker. Cramer's triumphant progress through Caxton, charming all those he comes into contact with, is helped in no small degree by the dazzling whiteness of his suit, a vestimentary testament to his saintliness, but it is when he checks into the boarding house that we realise that his intentions are far from virtuous, and on being asked by the landlady what brings him to town he replies, 'You might say I'm a social worker. I've come to do what I can for the town. ... The integration problem.'[17] From this point onwards the film makes explicit Cramer's true identity as a megalomaniac consumed by racism, his ideological 'whiteness' radiating outwards, solarising the town and its inhabitants. 'White expresses a certain corporeality', Mark Wigley observed in his *White Walls Designer Dresses*, and due to the masterful cinematography of Taylor Byars, Cramer's whiteness throughout *The Intruder* is similarly positively tangible.[18] Cramer's whiteness is whiter than the midday sun in Caxton, whiter even than the robes of the Ku Klux Klan he rides with, and in the supremely supernatural moment where he appears almost as an apparition in Ella's bedroom (the underage daughter of the town journalist whom we have seen Cramer systematically seduce and manipulate to incite further racial hatred) he is transfigured by the light piercing the gloom of her small-town teenage environment. In this scene Cramer's brilliance is of the order that the Classical scholar Origen recorded: '… since there are even degrees among white things, his garments became as white as the brightest and purest of all white things, that is light.'[19] Cramer has *become* light, and it is perhaps fitting that this most iniquitous and mortal instance of reason blinded by light should be the most effective. For all of the Technicolor brilliance of de Palma's contrasting of Nitti's razor-sharp whiteness against the blood-red decor of Al Capone's hotel room and opera box, or the exotic whiteness of Mengele's Paraguayan medico-safari ensembles, it is the ubiquitous white suit of a small-town hate-mongerer that is ultimately the most chilling.

When discussing the modern-day suit, most commentators on men's fashion, liken it to a form of sartorial armour, an immaculately tailored carapace that renders those inside it impervious to insults, invulnerable to attack and ready for any occasion. With its provenance deriving partly from sporting and military dress, and developed and refined with the additions of subtle padding and shaping that transforms the male body into an idealised set of masculine physical proportions, the well-cut contemporary suit is to a certain degree metal made cloth. Its indestructible qualities in cinema have also been noted, most significantly by Ulrich Lehmann in his essay on Cary Grant's apparently 'eternal' suit worn throughout Alfred Hitchcock's *North by Northwest*.[20] Cramer's suit seems equally indestructible, remaining brilliantly pristine and resistant to fights, cross burnings, nights spent in jail and the ever-present heat of Caxton. His protective whiteness is most effectively displayed in the scene where he incites the 'good folks' of Caxton to racial violence by delivering a rabble-rousing night-time speech, illuminated on the court house steps. During his increasingly fanatical oratory Cramer becomes incandescent with both rage and successive displays of the layering of his whiteness, unbuttoning his jacket, exposing his white shirt, taking the jacket completely off, bundling it up and casting it aside then finally rolling up his shirt sleeves as he becomes more and more hysterical. He is in fact performing a form of ideological striptease, for no matter how much he takes off he remains outwardly white, demonstrating that he is white skinned as well as white thinking. This form of 'non-strip tease' has been discussed in sartorial terms by John Harvey, who notes that even though the male suit plays with notions of exposure – the turning back of a lapel, obsolete buttons that are never fastened and so on – the wearer remains unexposed.[21] So it is with Cramer, but ideologically as well as sartorially, for no matter how much he exposes of himself he remains a bigot to the core, cocooned in his protective white cotton armour, and it is worth noting that at the end of his speech one of his converts hastens to return his jacket to him, an action that is repeated in similar 'preaching' scenes throughout the film.

Having established that the white suits in *The Boys from Brazil*, *The Untouchables* and *The Intruder* are fundamental to the almost supernatural propensity for evil of the films' central criminal figures, these same garments must therefore also provide the means for their eventual destruction. Like all mythical beings, whether good or evil, an Achilles heel is as vital to their construction as is their apparent invincibility. From Samson's hair to Superman's costume (whether fashioned on Krypton itself or by Martha Kent out of the blanket he was found wrapped in as an infant) male style equates to male prowess. So it is only when Mengele abandons his love of the all-white outfit that he meets his demise. With his eugenic master plan in peril he decides to personally secure the safety of his remaining cloned Hitler, Bobby Wheelock (the last of the 'boys from Brazil') and murder his adopted father. It could be argued that Mengele's addiction to sartorial consumption is the cause of his ultimate downfall, as he chooses autumnal-shaded tweeds for his trip to Pennsylvania, blending in with the American landscape, where presumably he thought all white was somehow too outré even for his megalomaniac style. It is whilst dressed for the country in reserved green and brown that he meets his grisly and bloody end, savaged to death by Bobby's obedient pack of Dobermans.

Similarly, Frank Nitti meets his fate only after Eliot Ness puts a bullet through his immaculate white hat, knocking it off his head; he then proceeds to grab Nitti, pulling off his jacket in the process, a further stripping away of Nitti's tailored defences. This act leaves Nitti vulnerable, and as he walks away combing his hair in an attempt to restore sartorial order, and presumably immortality, Ness pushes him off the roof of the courthouse building that has been the scene of their struggle. With Nitti plummeting to earth, De Palma presents the audience with a typical cinematic tour de force as we see the flailing white body of Nitti crash through the roof of a car below. In the concluding shot of the scene the audience sees his body sprawled and bloodied across the car's seats, his immaculate snow-white tailoring now fatally ruined, along with Nitti himself, the fallen Angel of Death now fallen to earth for the final time.

Finally, what of Adam Cramer, simultaneously the least 'supernatural' of the white-suited psychopaths but also arguably the most effective and ultimately deadly 'white angel'? Not for him the stripping of his protective suit but rather another form of sartorial humiliation. At the scene of an abortive lynching he has attempted to engineer he is struck to the ground by his erstwhile supporter, the local 'big shot' Verne Shipman, and he remains on his hands and knees, his white suit now incongruously pristine in the cold light of morning flooding the school playground where the scene takes place. It is perhaps the final humiliation for Cramer and a testament to the necessity for a villain's Whites to remain in perfect order that he is advised to get up off the ground by Sam Carter, his nemesis and to a degree his conscience throughout the film, with the words: 'Boy, you gonna get grass stains all over those trousers if you don't get up', on one level an apparently and, one could argue, inappropriately flippant conclusion to the film,[22] but this comment on sartorial cleanliness can also be understood as a way of emphasising how fragile the construction of masculinity is, and that someone whose destructive tendencies are reliant on the spectacle of immaculate tailoring can all too easily be brought down by the slightest of imperfections, and as Guy Debord suggests,

> The spectacle presents itself as something enormously positive, indisputable and inaccessible. It says nothing more than 'that which appears is good, that which is good appears'. The attitude which it demands in principle is passive acceptance which in fact it already obtained by its manner of appearing without reply, by its monopoly of appearance.[23]

Once this monopoly of appearance is dispelled, whether by choosing another colour, having it stripped from the body or even stained, the spectacle of whiteness is destroyed and along with it the tailoring of evil.

2

THE HORROR OF THE HOODIE: CLOTHING THE CRIMINAL

Joanne Turney

The aim of this chapter is to assess what has become, in recent years, a media furore and by association a moral panic, stemming from a seemingly innocuous piece of clothing – the hoodie. In the wake of rioting in urban areas in the UK (2011) and in conjunction with attention to the clothing worn by the participants, the sweatshirt with a hood became the symbol of social disobedience. For a piece of mass manufactured clothing the hoodie's availability and ordinariness is significant in respect of its transcendence from wardrobe staple (potentially everyone can wear a hoodie) to a sign of criminality and criminal intent. By merely raising the hood, the wearer transforms from comfy dresser to something far more socially disturbing.

Following the 2005 ban on the wearing of 'hoodies' at the Bluewater Shopping Centre, Kent, UK, the hooded sweatshirt became firmly associated within the media and, by association, society at large, with criminality, antisocial behaviour and an out of control youth. Yet a 'hoodie' is just a sweatshirt, but it seemed, that once the hood was placed over the head, the garment took on transformative properties, changing it from casual wear to something much more problematic, and considered threatening to the status quo. Indeed, the garment's name became synonymous with its wearers, so both wearer and worn object became merged into the contemporary folk devil, the hoodie. By 2007, the hoodie had become 'faceless' as a garment and as a stereotype described by then shadow Home Secretary David Davis as part of a 'hooligan's tool kit'.[1] This investigation will draw from previous analyses of moral panics in an attempt to assess the significance of clothing as an indicator of behaviour, particularly antisocial behaviour, and as a means of identifying potential threat. Likewise, it is anticipated that this discussion will emphasise social concerns and attitudes to behaviours and peoples that extend way beyond the clothing they choose to wear, highlighting the *unheimlich* relationship between normative social propriety and that which is considered 'different' or deviant (Figure 2.1). Clothing under these circumstances is metaphoric; it sublimates deeper social anxieties, particularly those adjunct to personal safety, even mortality.

Feared, derided, misunderstood and still resolutely unhugged, the utilitarian, hugely popular sportswear garment, the hoodie, has staged a comeback against a backdrop of pyromania and rioting. Worn by millions every day, a generation's default wardrobe choice was transformed into an instant criminal cloak for London's looting youth.[2]

The focus on hooded garments as an indicator of a society that was well on its way to hell in a handcart emerged as a response to several related issues. Firstly, the then Labour government attempted to instigate a zero tolerance policy in relation to petty crimes and antisocial behaviour. It appeared that lack of discipline and social responsibility had created an environment in which antisocial

Figure 2.1 David Cameron visits a community enterprise project in Manchester, UK. Photo by Christopher Furlong/Getty Images.

behaviour flourished. Ranging from stone throwing and using abusive language, to full-blown GBH, even murder, antisocial behaviour was making life impossible for many UK citizens. Simultaneously, poor adult same-sex role models, an increase in teen pregnancy and lack of education and employment prospects had created an underclass of state-supported citizens, who had found a voice through the *Jeremy Kyle Show* (2005–to date, Granada TV). The combination of these issues was spiralling out of control, with neighbourhoods declared no-go zones for the emergency services as well as social workers, council officers and other social support workers/systems. This was the birth of the anti-social behaviour order (ASBO), – the award of which could result in subject-specific outcomes, including prison – and the subsequent tabloid outrage aimed at the perceived slip in moral and behavioural standards, of which juvenile crime was just one aspect, described Britain as an 'ASBO nation', seemingly blacklisting all teenagers and hoodie wearers:[3] 'The hooded top – the must-have fashion accessory for teenage boys – is being banned from shopping centres in the latest police crackdown on juvenile crime. Hats, including baseball caps, are also being prohibited.'[4]

Indeed, ASBOs were issued prohibiting (in certain cases) the wearing of said garments (and baggy trousers), which facilitated further legal and media wrangling, when those issued with clothing-related ASBOs took their cases to the court of human rights. And won; this was an infringement of their civil liberties, the court ruled.

Since its cultural inception in the early 1950s, youth culture has always been shrouded in an air of disbelief and misunderstanding – deliberately so – separating youth from everyone else.[5] Clothing has been central to this form of separation: a visual indicator of difference and a sign of rebelliousness. As an adjunct to the sartorial sign of the establishment, the business suit, the wearing of a hoodie, particularly one with a zip, when combined with loose fitting trousers (as in a tracksuit) offers an obvious opposition to conformity; it is both suit and leisurewear, and lacking the structure of tailoring it is both casual in appearance as well as in its approach to white collar work and the society it represents. Unlike earlier incarnations connoting the 'rebel', such as the leather jacket, the hoodie acknowledges contemporary surveillance culture, offering the wearer access to socially coded clothing at a low cost that facilitates ease of movement and personal concealment. Similarly, the hoodie does not have the subcultural kudos of previous youth clothing; from gangs to grannies, the hoodie is universal, enabling the wearer to seemingly merge invisibly within those around them. As Braddock states in an article in *The Guardian* in 2011,

For sure, a hoodie is a useful tool to avoid identification for a range of gang-related rituals. Yet for teenagers under intense peer pressure to conform to a collective identity, acceptance means adopting a prescribed outfit. For some,

there may be no choice but to wear one and shoulder its associations. …
David Cameron, in a rare outbreak of understanding, told the Centre for Social
Justice in 2006 that hoodies were 'a way to stay invisible in the street. In a
dangerous environment the best thing to do is keep your head down, blend
in, don't stand out.'[6]

The deliberate distancing of youth clothing from that of the mainstream is
significant not merely in its style but in its gestural potential and its performativity.
The clothing one wears is significant, but the ways in which clothes are worn
are more so. The hoodie itself is not a threatening garment, as outlined, but
when worn with an attitude of disaffected youth, when paraded on a languid
but aggressive gait and when worn with jeans or sweatpants with the crotch at
the knee, the hoodie becomes a sign of difference. The relationship between
clothing, youth and gesture is not new; all youth cultural clothing, particularly that
which is associated with violent groups who potentially threaten the status quo,
embodies a sense of threat, which is heightened and perpetuated through media
portrayal and commentary.

The fashion historian Aileen Ribeiro notes that morality aims to establish and
maintain a group understanding of what is right and wrong, and in relation to
clothing acts as a social signifier that acts as a means of belonging or, indeed,
isolation or alienation from the group.[7] Clothing therefore in itself is neither 'moral'
nor 'immoral', but subject to social mediation, which the art historian Quentin
Bell describes as a 'sartorial consciousness'[8] cultivated by social norms and
responses to changing sociocultural circumstances. The development of a
sartorial consciousness highlights the social impact of clothing, and more notably
fashion, as both an aspect of the avant-garde and everyday life, emphasising
a contradictory praxis that potentially challenges the norm. This distinction
between culture and society is immediately recognisable as an implication of
the modernist avant-garde – the quest to challenge and overthrow existing
boundaries of acceptability or an understanding of the importance of conformity.
In the case of the hoodie, there seems to be no real fashion-led impetus in
wearing the garment; it is not avant-garde and appears to be unchallenging,
primarily because it's so ordinary, but its social association, its class or the class
of its wearers is central to the garments' outlaw status. Both urban and urbane,
the garment and wearer have become representative of a British underclass and
a lifestyle alien to the moral majority, and it is these class associations, combined
with an inability to recognise and identify wearers amidst a crowd, that create and
fuel an everyday terror; the balance between *good* and *bad* is blurred. Professor
of Sociology at Glasgow University Greg Philo describes hoodies as part of

a long-term excluded class, simply not needed, who often take control of their
communities through aggression or running their alternative economy, based

on things like drug-dealing or protection rackets. If you go to these places, it's very grim; the culture of violence is real. But for the British media, it's simple – bad upbringing or just evil children. Their accounts of what happens are very partial and distorted, which pushes people towards much more rightwing positions. There's no proper social debate about what we can do about it. Obviously, not all young people in hoods are dangerous – most aren't – but the ones who are can be very dangerous, and writing about them sells papers because people are innately attracted to what's scary. That's how we survive as a species – our body and brain is attuned to focus on what is likely to kill us, because we're traditionally hunters and hunted.[9]

Of course, the media furore surrounding the intimidating presence of such garments gave them a new 'street credibility', popularising them further with a section of society seemingly isolated for wearing them in the first place. The hoodie and their wearers, it seemed, became a self-fulfilling prophecy. As India Knight suggests in an article in the *Sunday Times*, 'Everybody is scared of hoodies: other teenagers, men, women – and dogs probably. That's why hoodies sell. No teenager is so well adjusted that he can't do without a bit of anti-social backup from his clothing.'[10]

The hoodie therefore appears to represent a clear distinction between wearers and the moral majority; it becomes a sign of attitude and conformity to social stereotypes surrounding the problems of youth and class, but more importantly as a signifier of moral decline, ASBO culture and the manifestation of the 'Other'.

This 'Othering' cannot be seen within the very real antisocial, violent and downright dangerous context of the 2011 London riots as offering a solution to the disaffections of youth, even though, when in opposition, later-to-be prime minister David Cameron encouraged us all to 'hug a hoodie' as a means of understanding and addressing social problems. Yet hoodies remain unhugged. For example, following the looting in London and in an attempt to reinstate the status quo, Eric Pickles, the Communities Secretary warned rioting looters in London:

This is a city with a lot of surveillance cameras and it's all right putting your hoodie on now, but you are going to have to put your hoodie on for a long time to escape justice. That stuff you stole over the last few days is going to lead directly to your arrest.[11]

Hoodies are therefore understood as a sign of contemporary terror, yet this is not new. All of the great villains of myth wear hoods, from the grim reaper to mysterious hooded figures in Victorian novels through to the Hooded Claw in the Penelope Pitstop cartoons and the Klu Klux Klan, suggest that the covering of the face or head hides the wearers' true identity, personality and intent. We know they exist amongst us, but we don't know who they are.

Masking and fear in the contemporary environment can be aligned with the hoodie's similarity to the ski mask – which has become, since the 1970s, the literal face of the contemporary terrorist, photographed and displayed in both print and televisual media. The ski-mask covers the whole face, with cut out eye-holes, rendering the wearer seemingly invisible. Such a garment is emotively significant because it denotes terror on actual and metaphorical levels. Firstly, the presence of such imagery in the media and its association with actual acts of terrorism firmly places the ski-mask in the public consciousness as a sign of political dissidence and fear; secondly, the masking of the terrorist contributes to a sense of unease, in which that which is 'invisible' and potentially horrific could be lurking anywhere. In contemporary society, where the threat of terrorism pervades the social climate, such forms of dress become potent symbols of a collective fear, not merely of terror itself but of a difference of race, religion, politics and so on.

The mask has a long history and significance within dress and display. The mask is ambiguous; it conceals the wearer, yet it offers the exciting potential of revealing the secrets that lurk beneath. The mask then acts as a fracturing device; it hides like a shroud; it camouflages and conceals, rendering the wearer oblivious to the concerns of vanity, social norms and behaviours, which consequently is viewed suspiciously by non-mask wearers. One might assume that this form of dress as anonymity is mysterious to the extent that we are always awaiting the moment of 'reveal' – the removal of the mask – that will in some way restore harmony and connect individual bodies, and thus to amplify the function of clothing in general as both a boundary and a margin. We might see this as metaphorical; the hoodie marking a separation between the socially disadvantaged and the moral majority.

The ski-mask, however, is worn as an item of deliberate concealment; there is no potential 'reveal', which heightens its potency as a garment of threat. The mask conceals the face but not the body; the body is present but the face disappears, and this is the site of terror; the physical presence is amongst us, but we don't know from whom we could be under attack.

Hoodies, unlike ski masks, are not merely garments that cover the head rendering the wearer 'faceless'. They are also notoriously baggy, concealing the body of the wearer to the extent that they become gender neutral. Essentially the garment conceals, but it also conceals to such an extent that it disembodies. The hoodie can be described as demonstrating a surface of the abject, a breaking free from the boundaries of the body into a state of amorphousness. The body becomes ambiguous; it is neither man nor beast, inside or outside, veiled in a shapeless mass like a monster emerging from the quagmire. This can be seen as a move from the symbolic world of form, language and meaning into a realm of confusion, distortion and shapelessness: a realm beyond comprehension.

Such an analysis is appropriate for the discussion of both youth clothing and clothing representative of criminal intent. The abject represents a move from the awareness of the womb (which we could see as 'society') into a state of differentiation (lawlessness) which parallels the ambiguous and transitional stage between childhood and adulthood; the lack of form implies a stage of transition, a praxis, from which one will either emerge into the symbolic realm or return to the quagmire from which it originated. Similarly, a state of abjection can be marked as a foray into nothingness (or anarchy), a means of displaying no form of identity (invisibility from the glare of CCTV cameras), whilst simultaneously creating a primal oneness (a hooded mob), as demonstrated in the creation of an unstable unity of perceived disaffection in hoodie wearing and/or looters. Indeed, hoodies, when the hood is worn, offer a form of comfort; they shield the wearer from the gaze, not necessarily from CCTV cameras but from the world outside. The wearer literally distances themselves from their surroundings by covering the head and conceals identity and social engagement. This can be seen as a form of hiding, of fading into the background like an ostrich with its head in the sand, unable or not wanting to form a solid identity, or be absorbed by the norms of social conformity.

The hoodie allows the body to disappear. It allows the wearer to move away from form which is both natural and bodily, as well as that which is socially normative rendering it repellent, whilst creating attraction towards it in the same measure as indicated by media coverage of rioting, looting and the voyeurism of onlookers and television viewers. In *The Powers of Horror*, Kristeva acknowledges that 'unflaggingly, like an inescapable boomerang, a vortex of summons and repulsion places the one haunted by it literally beside himself'.[12]

Although for Kristeva the abject is the inability to objectify the object, the similarities between the potential for hoodies to be perceived as abject can be illustrated through this concurrent juxtaposition of attract/repel; hoodies hide the wearer, conceal and disembody the body, moving it from shape to shapelessness, whilst at the same time drawing attention to its alien mass. The hoodie wearer is therefore amorphous and able to move almost unseen, whilst simultaneously drawing attention to the horror that lurks within. Clothing here is of the mass, the physical body and the mass of the crowd.

Similarly, the shapelessness of the hoodie conceals an unformed identity and appears to exist outside of the realms of comprehension; like the wearer, identity has no form and appears alien, both hidden and visible, repellent and interesting, simultaneously. As Jennifer Craik acknowledges, 'The "life" of the body is played out through the technical arrangement of clothes, adornment and gesture',[13] and if the body seemingly disappears, the onlooker is confused and fascinated.

The hoodie therefore represents the removal of the significance of clothing as a means of expressing identity. Here identity is obliterated on two levels: a) the body and face are concealed by the garments and b) the garment is so commonplace that the wearer fits in with rather than stands out from the crowd. As a subcultural oxymoron, the garment does not distinguish its wearer from the society they may or may not be rebelling against, consequently adding to the potential and continual fear and ever-presence of both garment and wearer.

Hoodies do make us look both inwards and outwards: they demonstrate that our society is not as progressive as we care to believe. When we confront hoodies, we are confronting a society that is inherently racist, conservative and unforgiving, afraid of difference or the 'other', yet one that is attracted to the anarchy and the mythology that literally shrouds them. They also make us confront our innermost fears, the horrors that lurk within us all. So when we look into the dark recesses of a hooded head, we are addressing issues in both micro- and macrocosm; we are staring into the face not only of our collective and personal fears but also of our dreams and desires. We could say that the hoodie therefore acts as a social shroud; it conceals the elements of social and personal prejudice we would like to hide, pretend were not there. So our most potent image of social evil, our social evil, is a teenage boy with a penchant for flammable casual wear.[14]

Clothing alone cannot be immoral or horrific, but it can, and frequently does, encapsulate a mood of the times. Scapegoating a piece of clothing and marking it as an indicator of the antisocial highlights the garment as 'edgy', imbuing it with an 'attitude' of youth and rebellion. It can therefore be seen as the perfect fashion object; rock and roll, grungy, challenging and on the edge, yet simultaneously it remains ubiquitous and available to everyone. In the 2011 UK riots, where the hoodie was the garment *du jour* for rioters and spectators alike; a garment already vilified and cloaked in fear transgressed, capitulated and became a self-fulfilling prophecy, but here the 'youth' uniform was adopted by all ages, social classes and races, and one can assume that it was its accessibility and ordinariness that cloaked not merely the young but everyone who wanted to join in and remain unidentified. The hoodie is truly universal, a global garment, representing global concerns. Reuters reported from Hackney, east London,

At a nearby housing estate, heavily tattooed Jackie, 39, resented what she saw as the media's portrayal of the riots as mindless youth violence. 'This was not kids. This was youths and adults coming together against the crap that's been going on since the coalition', she said, referring to Britain's conservative-led government, which has made deep austerity cuts since coming into power last year to tackle a big budget deficit. 'They're saying it's all young hoodies. Look at me, now I'm a hoodie,' she said, putting her hood up, and with her small slender build instantly looking like the lithe teenage rioters shown in television footage. 'I was out in the riots. My 16-year-old daughter was calling me asking where I was,' she said, chuckling.[15]

But the hoodie is also a victim of its own success; it is a universal garment, so stigmatised, that it demonstrates the potential for appropriation, as a sartorial sign of disaffection and lawlessness. The 2011 riots clearly articulated this shift from everyday wear to costume of the criminal, facilitating its use as a guise during looting and acts of social disobedience. It is not without irony that a garment initially identified as a means to stigmatise disaffected youth, came to embody a much wider social disaffection and the potential for a whole population to behave criminally. The hoodie thus has become the garment of 'Broken Britain' worn as a sign of affiliation to the hidden masses, who are, ironically, hidden under masses of knitted sportswear.

3

THE CRIMINALISATION OF THE SAGGY PANTS

Holly Price Alford

The hip-hop movement began in the mid-1970s in the Bronx of New York City. As hip-hop music escalated into urban areas around the country, it became a cultural movement that included music, art and dress. Due to its popularity, hip hop infiltrated suburbia and the farm areas of the US, and eventually developed a global following. Although a culture in its own right, it is the hip-hop style that has captured the mainstream market with its universal appeal to young men and women. Worn by famous rap artists, movie stars and celebrities, hip-hop style has been communicated through the media, which has helped to escalate its popularity. It has also helped to escalate a new genre in clothing, urban fashion. Many of these hip-hop inspired trends are incorporated into the culture's iconography, i.e. the colourful graffiti, sweats, armbands, sneakers and the high society look of success incorporating luxury brands like Louis Vuitton, Prada and Gucci. Hip-hop fashion has truly evolved and revolved through the decades, but there are some historians who believe that many of the hip-hop fashion trends began in the streets of the urban ghettos. The gangster life, the pimp, the prostitute and prison life are sometimes glorified through not only the music but the clothing style as well. One of the most controversial aspects of hip-hop fashion is the saggy pants; these pants are so large that they fall down, exposing the wearer's underwear. Emerging in the 1980s, this style has grown into a phenomenon amongst young and old lovers of the hip-hop culture, but it is ostensibly worn by hip-hop lovers from varied backgrounds, by all races and in practically all countries, regardless of its origins. Seen as a style that is comfortable to wear, the saggy pants have gained popularity and have been legitimatised by its adoption by popular culture icons. Protesters of the look say it is a trend that is embarrassing, an imitation of the gang and street culture, and that it was influenced by the prison system. Some have even claimed that the trend stems from a homosexual gesture picked up from the prison system.[1]

Regardless of where the trend originated, there are many homes throughout the world where parents find themselves asking their kids before they go to school or go out, 'Are you wearing a belt?' and 'Please pull up your pants!'[2] Today, parents are used to seeing their children's pants sag, at least a little, but usually hidden under an oversized T-shirt. Saggin' has gained so much popularity that by the end of the 1990s pants sagged at an all-time low, placing the pants below the 'butt' and fully exposing the wearer's underwear. The aforementioned concerns and issues related to the saggy pants have caused social, legislative and court action. This has been in the form of policies implemented in the US in the public schools, legislation in some states – and alleged profiling by police. By 2010, many areas in the UK as well as states and provinces in the US pushed for legislation to have the saggy pants banned in their district. This created an opposition, arguing that a ban on any type of clothing impedes one's freedom of speech and dress, and because of the perceptions about the originators of the trend, racial profiling became an issue. Furthermore, the association between the garment and criminal activity has led to profiling in general, thus leading to conflict between police and urban youth and adults.

Saggin' has been around since the 1980s, first worn by large urban men, who were uncomfortable with the tight-fitting pants (US)/trousers (UK) of the 1980s.[3] They would purchase their trousers two sizes too big. In 1989, Designer Karl Kani (Carl Williams) created a brand of trousers to help accommodate these wearers of this street look, by increasing the size of the trousers. 'Black men do not like tight fitting jeans', Williams stated in an interview.[4] If you had a size 34 waist, boys would buy trousers that fitted a 36 or 38 waist.[5] By increasing the waist and hip sizes of his Kani brand trousers, his brand helped to increase the urban look of the time, i.e. one associated with the hip-hop culture (Figure 3.1).

Unfortunately, by the time Karl Kani's street wear became embedded into urban wear fashion, the trend was labelled as part of the prison/jail culture. The prison/jail look is one of the most common and controversial beliefs as to the origins of saggin'. The belief is that urban kids learned to sag in jail. Although many prison systems use orange jumpers, especially in federal penitentiaries, some jails and prisons use basic solid colour or striped two-piece tops and trousers as uniforms.[6] Those systems that have two-piece uniforms do not allow prisoners to have access to belts and shoe laces because they can be used as weapons as well as devices used to harm themselves and others. For example, many prisoners use belts and shoelaces to hang themselves. The mythology states that when the belts are taken away, the trousers naturally sag because, being a 'one size fits all' sort of system, they are sometimes ill fitting. When the prisoner was released from prison, he would forget to wear a belt, causing his pants to sag, or the ex-prisoner sagged to show he served time in prison. This associated saggin' with criminal activity.

Figure 3.1 Group of young men sagging in Dorchester Massachusetts. Photo by Yoon S. Byun/The Boston Globe via Getty Images.

Associating crime with fashion is not new in society. It can be observed during the French Revolution, and we observed it during World War II, with the zoot suit. The zoot suit, which required a baggy trouser that had a high waist, and was full at the hip, but then tapered towards the knee and ankle, was a suit worn primarily by African Americans and Latino Americans as a form of resistance against prejudice, war and a society that tended to ignore them.[7] Many feel that African Americans wear the saggy pants for the same reasons as the zoot suit; as a form of resistance, or an outrageous look to bring attention to the wearer, who is screaming for attention. But the zoot suit, a suit primarily used for show or for dancing, became criminalised as the suit worn by gangsters and ex-criminals.[8] Like the saggy pants, the look of the suit became associated with the thug life, and therefore the wearers of the suit were associated with having bad behaviour. The zoot suit had an exaggerated look. The saggy trousers recalled men in jail whose trousers sagged. Many boys who came out of jail would joke that kids in urban cities like Los Angeles and New York who were saggin' looked like they were 'jailin.'[9] The look became popular with ex-convicts and gangs and became a badge of honour because it showed they served time in prison.[10] Some say that they exposed their underwear as a way of telling the cops to 'kiss their ass'.[11] For some youths, especially those in gangs, it represents the idea of having a uniform, a self-identifying look, a sense of belonging. Others believe gangsters like wearing their trousers saggy in order to hide weapons and drugs.[12] It was a way to conceal their criminality or to make people think they were concealing or hiding something illegal or to look cool among their peers, thus creating a belief that anything associated with criminality was 'cool'.[13]

No matter why the ex-convicts and gangs liked the look, they popularised the look in urban areas, regardless of origins, and made the trend a staple of street culture. All of the activity related to the saggy pants during the mid-1990s created a pool of individuals, mostly youths and adults, who were identified by the garment they wore, thus putting them in an unfavourable light. For example, if a person commits a crime and is wearing saggy pants, some authorities make an assumption that the entire pool or most of them are connected to criminal activity or will commit a criminal act. If a student misbehaves in the classroom and is wearing saggy pants, some authorities assume that all students wearing saggy pants are troublemakers, and that they need to be monitored at all times. Of course the fad did not bother law enforcement officials, because there have been several cases in which the culprits have been caught because they were running and their saggy pants would not allow them to run, making it easier for police to catch criminals who sagg'.[14]

By the early to mid-1990s a new generation began to aspire to the look, particularly the rap stars; many were ex-members of gangs and had been in trouble in the past. Research, however, tells us that many youths tend to emulate the attire of those persons they respect. Youth looks up to parents, friends and family members. In cities some of those family members they looked up to belonged to gangs or had been in prison. As hip hop became a dominate force and inspiration for youth, many looked up to rap artists, many of whom had grown up in these areas, and wanted to emulate their style.[15] Rap artists such as Naughty by Nature and the duo group, Kriss Kross, young boys who wore their trousers backwards, sagged. In 1994, the brand Kani became so popular with rap artists that rappers such as Dr Dre, Snoop Dogg, Sean 'Puffy' Combs, Tupac, Redman and Baby from Cash Money Records helped to escalate the company image by doing advertisements for the Kani brand. Rappers like Tupac, Biggie Smalls, Eminem and MC Lyte wrote about the Kani brand in the lyrics of their songs, such as 'Karl Kani saggin', Timbos draggin".[16] Many urban youths were wearing the popular trend and some workwear companies were seeing their trousers worn bigger. Companies such as Dickies and especially Ben Davis found their workwear clothing popular among lovers of the hip-hop style. Ben Davis, a popular workwear company founded by Jacob Davis, one of the creators of the Levi's jeans, became a staple among LA rap artists.[17] They referenced the brand in their songs and wore the brand in their videos. The reason for this is because the tough workwear brand became popular with the Mexican/Chicano culture as well as the gang culture.[18] However, the wearers of these brands would sagg' their trousers, giving the brand names a reputation for being gang and hoodlum clothing.

As rappers promoted the urban look, designers helped to escalate the trend nationally. In 1992, a new series of advertisements appeared on billboards all over the country featuring the new Calvin Klein underwear model, Mark 'Marky Mark' Walberg, a celebrated White rap artist. Some of them featured Mark with a bare chest in his 'tighty whities'.[19] Others featured him in his Calvin Klein jeans, which sagged' to expose the Calvin Klein logo sewn on his boxer briefs. Those advertisements helped to bring the ailing Calvin Klein brand back to life and set the stage for other designers, like Giorgio Armani, to make money from their underwear.[20] Advertisements like Calvin Klein's, the popularity of boxer shorts and the birth of the boxer brief, helped to accelerate the popularity of saggin' as well. As the trend's popularity became more universal, denim and trouser companies, particularly in the new millennium, began experimenting with how low they could make their trousers. Hip-hugger trousers, which traditionally are only about two inches below the waist, were getting lower and lower, and now girls found it difficult not to expose their underwear. This was exacerbated when the underwear industry began selling more thong underwear, as well as thongs with 3D applications on the upper back of the thong for display with the lower-riding trouser.

Even the skateboard culture, mainly a White culture, picked up the trend. Many skateboarders adopted the trend because they skated better with more freedom of movement.[21] Not only skateboarders but snowboarders took up the style as well, which helped to integrate the popularity of the trend. A trend worn by a majority of Black youth was now seen on a lot of White youth, but it is important to remember that the reputation of the skateboarder was one of a rebel and delinquent. The skateboard culture was first associated with the punk culture and subsequently with the hip-hop and reggae movements.[22] The wearing of the trend has not helped dispel the myths of the culture, which some believe are associated with theft and gang culture.

No matter the criminality of the trend or where people think it comes from, historians and anthropologists who have studied youths who sagg' state that for many, wearing the trend gives the wearer a voice in his/her community and a sense of belonging. Lee Baker, an anthropologist, writes,

> Wearing baggy pants or saggin' … is a fashion statement that has emerged by articulating a consistent pattern of creative adaptation that involves inverting and transmitting the monikers and symbols of racism, disrespect and humiliation into symbols of power, pride and respect.[23]

There are many, especially in the African American community, who sagg' as a form of pride. The baggin' or saggin' trend escalated in the predominantly

Black urban neighbourhoods because many felt a sense of pride in wearing something that was considered trendy and worn by just as many White and Asian youths. Historians like Professor Mike Dyson indicated the wearing of extra-large trousers may

> represent, consciously or not, [young Black men's] restricted mobility in the culture. Baggy pants and oversized clothing in general may cover black bodies subject to unhealthy surveillance. Maybe black youth who can't hide in their skin are forced to hide in their clothes.[24]

No matter the reason, when you ask the majority of youth why they sagg', the most common reason given, after interviewing 10 boys and young men of different races who sagg', was the comfort factor. 'Who wants your jeans that tight around your waist and your private area?' was the comment made by Pierre Wright, a student at Virginia Commonwealth University. 'I like for my jeans to bunch at the knees, not only for comfort, but I look better in the pant.'[25] Pierre doesn't wear his trousers below the butt; he believes that is disrespectful; however, he does admit that wearing them down has always been more of a comfort issue. 'How could you walk if they were past the butt in the first place?' Like so many boys who like to sagg', Pierre admits that he wears a belt simply to keep the trousers in the right place. One such sagger found at a local supermarket stated that comfort was an issue as well. A local high-school student was found bagging groceries at a Food Lion in Chesterfield, Virginia. His shirt was tucked into his belted trousers; however, the trousers came three quarters of the way down his behind.[26] In an interview conducted in 2002 at North Carolina Agricultural and Technical State University, Jarmen Wesley, a sophomore, who wore his trousers baggy but in moderation, said, 'Some males wear their pants baggy to hide their normal size, especially if they are extremely thin.'[27] There are people who wear the fashion because it is cool and trendy. These are the youths who usually expose the underwear or wear the trouser below the butt, sometimes belted to keep them from falling down, and sometimes with no belt. On a website entitled Saggerboys.com, saggers' discuss what underwear they are showing off and wearing for the day, as well as how far they will go to sagg'. They also discuss the logos on their trousers. It seems that when you sagg', one can tell which brand of trouser or jeans you are wearing. When trousers are pulled up, you cannot see the logo.[28] No one mentions that they sagg' to emulate the prison system. To the new generation of saggers, saggin' is now a fashion comfort fad, but to the older generation, perceptions are damaging.

Although saggin' may be popular among youth, and for whatever reason they choose to sagg', the older generation hates it. At the 2010 Winter Olympics, Japanese snowboarding champion Kazuhiro Kokubo deplaned wearing dreadlocks, a loose tie and his trousers saggin'. Many commented that he looked like the typical young skateboarder/snowboarder, but the Japanese elders were not pleased. They banned him from the opening ceremonies, along with his coaches, who should have checked his attire before he landed.[29] This brought to light how influential saggin' is, as well as the protest against the fashion trend. Many believe the opposition to the trend comes from the possible influences of saggin', i.e. gangs and the prison system. There are also many who state the opposition to saggin' is purely racial, demoralising and stereotyping anything that is perceived to have come from the African American culture as bad and immoral. However, most of the opposition has come from an older generation of African Americans.

Many African Americans see the trend as humiliating and disrespectful, which is ironic as most people who are opposed to anti-saggin' legislation say that it is racially motivated. Bill Cosby, an opponent of saggin', said in a speech given at the National Association for the Advancement of Coloured People (NAACP), 'With their hats on backwards, pants around their cracks. Isn't that a sign of something, or are you waiting for Jesus to pull his pants up.'[30] In 2008, during an interview with MTV, then-Senator Barack Obama, who at first stated that anti-saggin' legislation was a waste of time, stated,

Having said that, brothers should pull up their pants. You are walking by your mother, your grandmother, your underwear is showing. What's wrong with that? Come on. Some people might not want to see your underwear. I'm one of them.[31]

Others have written about it. *The 21st Century Hip-Hop Minstrel Show* tackles the negative aspects of hip hop. Author Raphael Heaggans concludes that one of the negative acts of hip hop, which includes that of the saggy/baggy pants, is how it psychologically affects youths' perceptions about Black life, and therefore wearing such a trend perpetuates the legacy of slavery.[32] This observation was made on the grounds that young slaves' trousers sagged because slave masters would take away belts and cords as a form of punishment. There are even African Americans trying to make unique statements about their views of saggin'. In May 2010, African American State Senate President Malcolm Smith purchased a billboard, using $2,200 of his campaign money, to urge his constituents in Queens, New York, to 'Stop the Sagg",[33] and urged his constituents to pull up their pants. In 2010, a couple in Winston-Salem, North Carolina, handed out 'coupons for free haircuts, meals or even cash' to young men who wore their trousers at the waist.[34]

Why do these African Americans feel this way? Many who struggled during the civil rights movement see 'sagging pants as a sign of a youthful disconnect with history'.[35] Author and Professor of Sociology at Georgetown University Dr Mike Dyson has written about these feelings from the older generation.

He states that the baggy/saggy pants 'reveals the anxiety over a younger generation's adoption of their own style of expression, a generation who feels less pressure to conform to time-worn standards of behaviour'.[36] Also, a study conducted at Northwestern University found that White male felons had an easier time getting hired in the Milwaukee job market than Black felons did. Many African Americans feel that Black males are already at a disadvantage socially, and by wearing the saggy pants, they are automatically perceived in the gangster or ex-prison category.

Many African Americans may disagree with saggin', but equally, many do not agree with legislation to stop kids from saggin'. In 2007, the town board of Delcambre, Louisiana, voted unanimously to add 'exposure of … undergarments' to the local indecent exposure ordinance, making it one of the first jurisdictions to criminalise saggin'.[37] Since then, there have been several states that have proposed anti-saggin' legislation, as well as several districts in other countries. The British Crown Prosecution Service (CPS) has been trying to pass legislation to prevent saggin' or what the British youth call 'low batty',[38] but so far it has been difficult to implement. The popularity of the trend has been seen in Hollywood and therefore spilled over into Europe. The Brits have even seen a photo of Prince Harry wearing his trousers low during army training.[39] In the US, however, there are billboards as well as politicians running for office who have promised to pass anti-saggin' legislation within the states. Pro-rights groups have stated that passing legislation for anti-saggin' is not only unconstitutional but discriminatory. Many believe anti-saggin' legislation is just opposition to a youth movement. Ben Chavis, former director of the NAACP, stated that 'to criminalize how a person wears their clothing is more offensive than what the remedy is trying to do'. He further stated that 'we should spend time on the social conditions of these youth instead of their clothing'.[40] This is nothing new. As Marc Lamont Hill wrote, 'From the Zoot Suit to the Senate hearings of gangster rap, every generation of adults has expressed deep anxiety about the cultural practices of its children.'[41] However, it seems strange to some legislators that people always seem to have a problem and want to form legislation around trends founded within the Black community. Reggie Moore, director and co-founder of the Urban Underground, stated that 'a lot of young people dress in a way that is acceptable to their peers but it doesn't need to be criminalised. We are not going after white youth with purple hair.'[42] There are many lawyers and organizations, such as the American Civil Liberties Union, that argue that these bans are racially motivated.[43] The trend has come out of the Black urban areas of the country and is seen as a Black trend; therefore, when trying to get anti-saggin' laws passed, Black youth are targeted. There are also many bloggers who have pointed out that the word 'saggin'' spelled backwards has a derogatory meaning for Blacks. Those people believe the term came from the White community.

The opposition has also tried to ban this look in public school systems and private venues, which has led to the argument of first amendment rights. Many lawyers argue that 'limiting the way people wear their pants in public would enter into territory "having no discernible or defensible boundaries"'.[44] The problem is that some legislators are using some of the myths associated with the origin to make their cases. One such myth is the fact that it is a way one man is signalling to another in prison that he is available. The prisoner wears his trousers below his butt for what some call 'easy access'.[45] This lets another prisoner know that he is available. After blogging with some prisoners, many state that this is absurd. Yes, there are gay prisoners, and yes, there may be a way to get another interested, but to wear your trousers low is asking for trouble, and you could get more than what you bargained for.[46] There are several historians who feel that this is a way of convincing society to pull up their trousers, and that by saying it comes from the gay community, the opposition is playing on its homophobic fears, adding to the homophobic nature of some people in society. Mark Lamont Hill suggests that 'by connecting it (sagging) to homosexuality, they are able to play on the homophobic myth that being gay is a social contagion that can be avoided through the use of a sturdy belt'.[47] In Dallas, Texas, a deputy mayor hired a religious rapper to rap about the concerns raised about the fact that saggin' is equated with gay sex. In his opinion the song worked in helping to get many youths to think about the trend and not 'sag/bag' for fear of being teased in school. This raised concerns among the gay community, which stated there was no proof that the trend began that way, and that it was 'highly offensive and unnecessary'.[48] The deputy mayor stated that the song was effective and that the youths kept their trousers up; therefore, he was standing by the song.

It is amazing that many protesters of the saggin' trend are trying to convince youth to pull up their trousers, especially considering many of them sagged themselves. We must understand that each generation uses fashion in its own way to deal with the ills of society. Sometimes that fashion is associated with bad behaviour, which may lead to crime, but history has demonstrated that as society continues to change, a new generation will give us new art, music and fashion that some segments of our society will oppose, thus creating conflict between our criminal justice system and those persons who desire to wear the fashion. In every generation, we have had people identified as being criminal as a result of their fashion. This has resulted in the profiling of some youths/adults. The problem with this is that we as a society know that we are making a judgement based on association. Each person must be judged on his or her behaviour and actions, and not by saggin' trousers. However, parents who sagged when they were young have expected the fad to go away after time. The fad has continued through a new generation of rappers and young adults, but so has hip hop. Hip hop is 40 years old and is still being reinvented and reworked, and there are no signs of it ending anytime soon.

Even though the origins of saggin' may be incorrect, the reality is that the perceptions of the trend are not one parents want to be associated with their child.[49] Regardless of the history and laws related to the trend, this will not stop boys and now girls from saggin'. As stated before, many youths wear a long shirt to cover their underwear, even those who wear their trousers below their butt, and many do not see the relationship of the gang and prison culture associated with the look. In an article, Eric Montgomery stated,

> The glorification of the Gangsta seems to have lost much of its appeal and is looked upon as juvenile. It is not cool to be in a gang anymore. The people who seem to be holding on to the gang culture are seemingly lost in a time vacuum and have yet to realise that the era of the gang has long ended.[50]

So, for the new generation, the look is just 'cool' (Figure 3.2). 'I will eventually stop … when I get older', was a comment made by a young middle school student at the local cinema in Virginia. He was wearing his trousers past his butt,

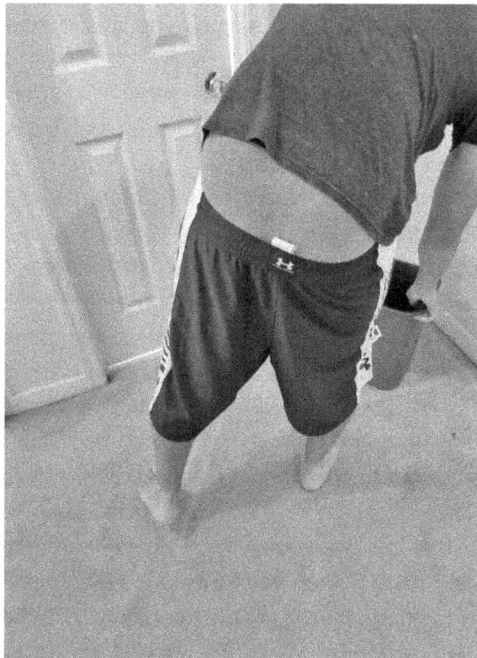

Figure 3.2 Author's son sagging. Author's own photograph.

belted. 'I know I can't dress this way for work.'[51] Maybe he will pull his trousers up. Look at Sean 'Puffy' Combs or Jay Z, two rappers who helped to promote the saggy look. They have opted for a suit and tie and have started to pull their trousers up. However, they are also older with more responsibilities. Maybe when these youths get older, they will look back with pride and talk about the crazy way they wore their trousers, or maybe they too will be yelling at their sons and daughters to pull their trousers up.

4

MUGSHOT/HEAD SHOT: DANGER, BEAUTY, AND THE TEMPORAL POLITICS OF BOOKING PHOTOGRAPHY

Stephanie Sadre-Orafai

Arresting images

Joined together in a single document, the stark profile, head shot and full body images of Charles Allen Reed tell an incomplete story. Hash marks painted on the wall behind him record his height (6 ft), the small board in front of his chest, the date and location (Friday, 24 June 1960, Cincinnati Police Department) and the clock mounted to his right, the time (3:47 p.m.). While a number (77373) stands in for his name, there is neither record of the charges brought against him, the resulting legal action, nor his guilt or innocence (Figure 4.1). Rather, the images are charged with possibility and potential. The mind wanders to likely scenarios that led to this photographic encounter and its aftermath. We read into the small details: the style of his hair and clothes, his posture and facial expression. Yet at the same time the image is already over-determined, instantly recognisable as a mugshot, tinged with deviance and danger.

Reed's photographs are one set of hundreds of found images and documents collected, exhibited and reproduced by Mark Michaelson and Steven Kasher in *Least Wanted: A Century of American Mug Shots* (2006).[1] Thumbing through these records, I was struck by how easily many subjects in the book – Reed among them, with his popped collar, carefully coiffed hair and seemingly relaxed stare – could be imaged in nearly identical ways 50 years later in the radically different context of the fashion industry. With similar lighting, poses, branding (the casting agency here replacing the police department name) and meticulous

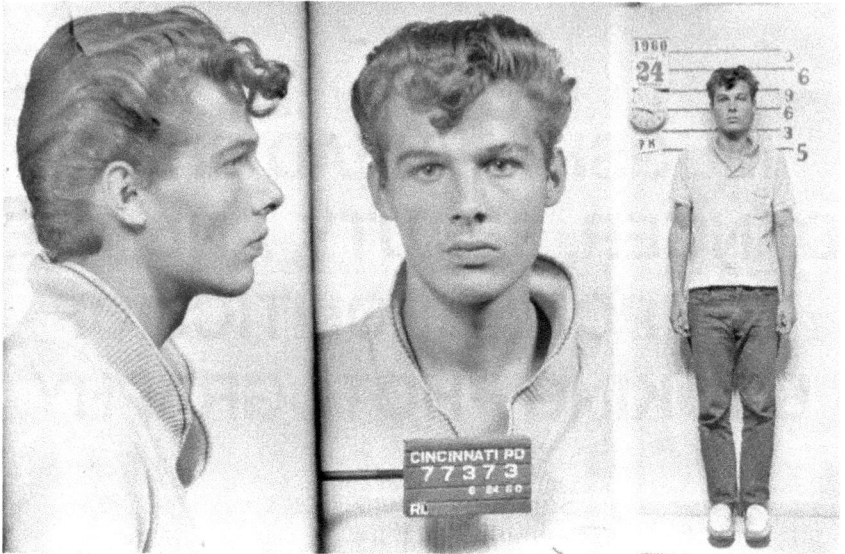

Figure 4.1 Mugshot Chas. Photo by Allen Reed, 1960. Courtesy of Steven Kasher Gallery, New York.

record of corporal measurements and photographic sitting dates, casting images share much in common with criminal mugshots – not only their formal aesthetic features but also their epistemological premises. Iconic and instantly readable, both are documentary portraits used to fix identities motivated by the spectre or promise of transformation: in the case of the casting image, the glamour of the fashion photograph; for the mugshot, the future recidivist in disguise. Both are images of potential overwhelmingly charged by association.

In this chapter I propose a comparative analysis of booking photographs, or documentary intake images, in criminal and fashion contexts. Reading casting images against the development of police mugshots, my goal is to rethink casting and its attendant photographic practices as more than just a preliminary step in the production of published fashion images. Instead, I ask how the creation of casting files intersects with other forms of expertise that similarly join empiricism, photography and classification. To do this I draw on 11 months of ethnographic fieldwork at LVX, a leading fashion casting agency in New York City, where I observed and participated in casting practices ranging from the selection of models for high-fashion jobs to the recruitment of 'real people', or non-professional models, for commercial and editorial work.[2]

I am particularly interested in the temporal dimensions and mobilisations of booking photographs: how agents use these images to both fix an objective and identifiable document of an individual and deploy them to construct shifting typologies. I argue that these schemas are geared towards retroactively predicting and explaining external signs of exceptional differences, whether keyed in terms of danger and deviance or desirability and beauty, and are explicit sites where the connections between appearances and cultural categories of morality, justice and inequality are negotiated and produced as expert knowledge.[3]

I begin with an overview of literature on photography, identification and classification, focusing specifically on its institutional uses. I note that despite current movements towards biometric security technologies that fracture the body into data, the face remains significant both within and beyond these domains.[4] I move then to consider the same themes of identification, classification and 'face' in fashion casting. I explore casting's contours as a professional vision and how agents populate their files. Through a series of ethnographic vignettes, I unpack some of their assumptions about the visibility, quantity and aesthetic quality of social types and how they interpret, imagine and image these for their clients. I conclude by showing how points of intersection between professional visions like criminal and fashion booking photography help us to think more expansively and synthetically about contemporary transformations in how we see, experience and make sense of signs of social difference.

Photography, identification and classification: The face in criminal and commercial contexts

As Paul Frosh notes, 'Whether on behalf of the state (passport and identity card photographs, prison mugshots, police files, medical records), the academy (the natural sciences, anthropology), or the corporation (catalogues, advertisements, product brochures)', photographs are both objects and agents of classification.[5] That the evidentiary status of these images should seem so over-determined is not a function of the medium of photography itself, but rather 'a complex historical outcome [that] is exercised by photographs only within certain institutional practices and within particular historical relations'.[6] Charles Goodwin describes these institutional and socio-historical ways of seeing as professional visions.[7] Serving as boundary markers and insignia of professional communities, professional visions are 'perspectival, lodged within specific social entities, and unevenly allocated'.[8] As such, their legitimacy and consequences of their performance vary across social contexts. Professional visions involve not only visual but also material and discursive practices. Goodwin's work dovetails with the large body of anthropological, historical and communication and cultural studies literature on photography, identification and classification that draws on Foucaultian theories of power, surveillance and discipline to argue that ways of seeing and classifying individuals are also ways of disciplining subjects; that is, they are forms of power. This power works in two directions, both honorifically and repressively, integrating all photographs into what Alan Sekula calls photography's archival paradigm, which, since its emergence in the nineteenth century, vertically integrates all portraits into 'a social and moral hierarchy'.[9]

Examining the development of mugshots in particular, Sekula notes that

> contrary to the commonplace understanding of the 'mug shot' as the very exemplar of a powerful, artless, and wholly denotative visual empiricism, these early instrumental uses of photographic realism were systematised on the basis of an acute recognition of the *inadequacies* and limitations of ordinary visual empiricism.[10]

Jonathan Finn argues that in examining images and technologies used in criminal identification we must see them not only as representations but also as inscriptions. Writing about Francis Galton, Cesare Lambroso and Alphonse Bertillion in the late nineteenth century, Finn notes that while their use of photographs was 'meant to document what they believed to be the signs of criminality, it in fact helped produce the very subject of study':[11] the temporal and causal flux was a function of their professional vision. While Finn shows how contemporary law enforcement imaging practices have shifted from inscribing known criminals to collecting and enrolling wider populations as potential criminals into databases that deconstruct the body into latent images of fingerprints, DNA and biometric signatures, attention to the ways in which inscriptions work in these contexts even when a 'criminal look' is not produced is vital. Recent work in both anthropology[12] and communication studies[13] has similarly sought to highlight the social construction and contingency of photography's uses in institutional contexts as a strategy for critique.

Yet this critical distance can be difficult to achieve, especially when professional visions and their iconic image types – the casting photograph and mugshot among them – are so deeply entrenched. Indeed, when speaking to an assistant police chief about my project, he quickly dismissed my interest in contemporary mugshot imaging practices, saying that the process is largely mechanised and lacks reflection. 'It's as close to a photocopy of a human being as you can get', he said, suggesting instead that I look into traffic, crime scene or surveillance photography, where 'real' and 'interesting' police photography was happening. Casting agents I worked with similarly downplayed the significance of casting photographs, insisting their purpose was simply to 'show what the person really looks like'.

However, these seemingly neutral imaging techniques not only create representations of individuals but, as Finn notes, given their framing in criminal and fashion contexts, charge them with moral categories like beauty, desirability, danger and deviance. This is strongly connected to their focus on 'face', which

Greg Noble argues 'conjoins questions of morality, affect, cultural difference and humanity'.[14] Writing on the vilification of the Arab Other in contemporary Australian society, he argues,

> To give a face to evil paradoxically produces it as concrete and abstract, knowable but elusive. … [It is] the suturing together of disparate events and is ultimately an act of defacement. It involves reduction, displacement and intensification. It decontexualizes social acts yet renders them more amenable to 'explanation' drawing on cultural pathologies.[15]

He continues that, rather than allaying anxieties, these processes of 'reduction, displacement and identification' provide a 'virtuous paranoia' wherein 'we remain insecure about what we are but we have a kind of working explanation that at least reassures us of an overriding moral unity'.[16] While images of deviance and danger work to deface populations, how do images of beauty impact them? 'Beauty', Susan Sontag writes, 'is a quasi-moral project'.[17] Like race, beauty is perceived through a process of 'selfing' and 'othering', or what Anne Cheng describes as 'a vertiginous experience, launched by and launching crises of identification in the eyes of the beholder'.[18] In arguing that beauty 'is such a likely conduit for racial – not just racist – imaginings',[19] Cheng demonstrates that race and beauty not only intersect similar moral projects but also are intimately constructed through one another. Compounding this, the commodification of race and beauty is instrumental in the production and differentiation of both commodities and consumers. As Claire Dwyer and Philip Crang argue, 'Commodification is not something done to pre-existing ethnicities and ethnic subjects, but is a process through which ethnicities are reproduced and in which ethicised subjects actively engage with broader discourses and institutions.'[20] In this way, the 'face of beauty' in fashion has similar discursive and social power as the 'face of evil' Noble describes. To adequately address how the 'face of beauty' is inscribed in fashion, one must first understand how casting itself is organised as a professional vision and then the ways in which agents populate and animate these archives.

Casting as professional vision: Populating and animating the archive

To analyse casting as a professional vision, we must first ask what kind of practice casting is. While in the service of aesthetic judgement, casting must distance itself from other aesthetic imaging practices.[21] It is not only empirical and documentary, producing and recording bodily knowledge about a model, but also diagnostic and predictive, used to determine a model's suitability for another photographic or performance-based context. It is largely about placing models, or locating them in social and geographic space, in order to replace them in commercial contexts. As such it requires knowledge about populations and types – the ability to imagine what they look like and where one might find them – and thus is speculative with both temporal and spatial dimensions.

If we move then to consider casting in terms of prediction, recognition and the management of information, more along the lines of recent work on biosecurity, what does this reveal? For one, it highlights the constant vigilance expected of casting agents that extends beyond their time at work. As Hank, a casting assistant at LVX, described it,

> Day in, day out, largely we are meant to be aware of everybody that's out there … just to know who people around town are, and what's going on, and who's around, and what people look like and how they're styled and that sort of thing.

Indeed, the agency owner, Claudia, often admonished her staff for meeting interesting people and not having them come by the agency to be 'put on file'. 'You are my eyes', she would say. 'That is what I pay you for.'

This type of surveillance, while recorded in the agency files, was more an embodied than externalised expertise. Unlike the logic of biometric databases to enrol as many individuals as possible to increase the likelihood of getting a match, the work of casting is more low-tech and based instead on aesthetic and affective memories of individual appearances and personalities. Agents were judicious in who they added to the files. Only those likely to book fashion jobs were included. Still, the majority of individuals represented in the files had yet to book jobs through the agency. Thus their inclusion, while signifying potential, like the mugshot, did not confer commercial visibility.

Agents populate this archive through their social and professional networks as well as cultural geographies, or mental maps, they construct to identify and place individuals as types. Exploiting and reinforcing 'public images' of the city, including known travelled routes and inhabited spaces, they rely on these maps as expert shorthand or pragmatic tools that mitigate the cost and time investment of street scouting.[22] Scouting requires not only calculating the geographic distribution of types across public spaces but also the probability of finding large numbers of people. Thus they look for both targeted homogeneous places, like ethnic enclaves, and large heterogeneous spaces where a variety of different kinds of people can be found and where they themselves can blend in. Indeed, scouting is as much about placing people as it is being placed. For these reasons, public parks, universities and shopping centres are popular sites. Scouts and casting agents collaboratively produce these geographies, which can be seen as both a logistical and interpretive practice, a kind of expert knowledge that they cultivate.

For example, while working on a hair trends brochure for Saeta, a hair product company with an international network of salons and cosmetology schools, scouts had trouble finding one of the casting categories: 'Asian Female, Any Age, 50% Grey Hair'. After several unsuccessful attempts in Chinatown, Hannah, one of the agency scouts, met with Liz, the lead casting associate, to discuss their options. She began the conversation by saying that scouting in Chinatown was difficult for outsiders because of the language and the insular feel of the community.

'Nobody wants to talk to me,' she said. Liz, too, was exasperated, having gone so far as to place Craigslist ads and look into low-level agencies for suitable candidates.

'Maybe it's just that their hair doesn't go grey,' Liz said.

'Or maybe they colour it,' a freelancer quickly rebutted.

'What about libraries?' Liz joked.

'Seriously, though', Hannah said, 'what about museums? There are really classically beautiful women there and they tend to be more natural and let their hair go grey and not wear much makeup.'

Liz agreed, 'Try that, and maybe some Japanese salons, you could ask to post the job details there.'

Liz and Hannah's frustration at not being able to locate or access the spaces that Asian women with 50 per cent grey hair inhabited demonstrates how much 'real people' casting depends on scouts' ability to physically access these places, as well as, more importantly, to *imagine* them. These frustrations reveal how cultural geographies and social networks converge in the casting process, which has implications for the kinds of images of 'difference' that can potentially be produced through 'real people' casting. Comments like, 'It's just that their hair doesn't go grey' or 'There're just not that many of them', reveal casting professionals' ideas about both the quantity and quality of particular types that are shaped by their exposure to, familiarity with and imaginations of certain groups.

For example, Hank, who in addition to his casting assistant duties sometimes worked as a scout, told me about his difficulties finding 'Indian middle-aged women' for a bank advertisement versus 'young white girls' and 'young white boys' for a fashion casting:

So, because it was such a particular thing that is not really that abundant, I came back with not a ton – some people who weren't just right, but I wanted to have some numbers for, to come back with, for my first scouting thing. And um, then, when I was booked out for this one and I'm looking for young white girls, young white boys, I was like a lot more pumped and like it's going to be kinda easier just because they're everywhere. … It's just a different approach 'cause when I was doing [the bank job] I was just looking for anybody that qualified. I was like, 'Where are you? Where are you? Where are you?' That's why some of them were big and some of them were like not pretty and some of them – but I wanted the numbers. [Hannah] was having the same problem. She came back and said, 'It's hard to find Indian women.'

When I asked Hank if he thought it really was a 'numbers thing' or if it had something to do with either his 'eye' or social network, he responded,

I think first and foremost there – it's just numbers. Like ['young white girls, young white boys'] are everywhere and there is just a larger selection. Within that, yeah, it's because of what I've been exposed to, like that it's like easier to recognize and for me feels more innate … but approaching Asian females is different for me than like approaching all the white girls and the white boys. 'Cause I judge and value the Asian girls differently because I know them in a different way [having grown up Korean-American]. Where like if I like a certain Asian girl and I know that she's like this kind of like Korean girl, like she's a Tory Burch equivalent of a Korean girl, a pretty girl, wears pretty dresses, that's just like a Korean brat. I'm really hesitant to go up to her because I feel like it's validating that in a certain way whereas if it's just some stupid white girl I'll go up to her anyway.

As Hank's quote illustrates, scouts' social networks and cultural geographies are inextricably linked in their placing practices. More than just the people and places they know, scouts draw on the ability to broadly typify and place people. These practices are strongly shaped by past experiences and recurring social interactions. While somewhat esoteric, these forms of cultural knowledge production are also profoundly mundane, connecting to broader types of social stereotyping and moralised geographies.

Once they collected, imaged and assembled individuals into the agency archive, agents animated them in multiple ways. They spent a great deal of time talking about their impressions and assessments of models, often as soon as the model had left. These conversations were initiated either by the person who had met with the model reporting some detail or by witnesses who asked questions like 'What was she like?' While casting agents usually privileged the opinion of those who had interacted with the model, others would sometimes challenge these evaluations based on their own past experiences or stories they had heard about the model second hand. Their judgements were not restricted to the model's appearance and often included several types of assessments of the model's personality and 'story', or the biographical and anecdotal details shared during the casting and the potential ways in which a model could be framed.

For example, after missing Yasmin, a 'street' model who had come to update her file, Claudia asked Liz, who had taken her photos, how she had looked. This exchange followed:

1   L: *She looked good*, she had on like this amazing outfit

2   all these layers, and this incredible eyeliner.

3   C: We should submit her for NZ. [a denim company]

4   L: But they're looking for <u>model-types</u>, you know, <u>pretty girls</u>.

5   C: *She's amazing.*

6   L: You know what I mean.

7   C: But NZ loves that kind of girl, you know, <u>ethnically ambiguous.</u>

8   H: <u>Ethnically ambiguous</u>?

9   C: You know, *you can't tell what she is.*

10 H: Really? I thought she was <u>Egyptian.</u>

11 C: No. *You really can't tell*. She's <u>ambiguous.</u>

12   Plus, they like when I can give them something different.

13   They'll like her, she just needs to come in a white T-shirt and jeans.

14 L: Yeah, pared down and they'll get her.

As you can see from the transcript, these conversations move from aesthetic evaluations, shown here italicised in lines 1, 5, 9 and 11, to categorising talk, underlined here in lines 4, 7, 8, 10 and 11, to hypothetical attributions about what a model could look like, in lines 13 and 14. Agents draw on different forms of evidence, from remembered affective impressions of models during casting interactions to knowledge about clients' tastes and preferences, to construct particular ways of seeing or framing a model's features. In this example, while Liz had seen Yasmin most recently, Claudia used her memory of Yasmin as 'ambiguous' and 'amazing' to frame her potential as a good model for NZ. While Hank attempted to challenge Claudia's assessment saying that Yasmin was actually Egyptian in line 10, Claudia countered that it wasn't really apparent that she was Egyptian and would be more marketable as 'ethnically ambiguous', a category she knew was recognisable and desirable to NZ. Finally, Claudia and Liz collaborated to find a way to highlight Claudia's positioning of Yasmin. By having her come back in a white t-shirt and jeans, they can heighten her ethnic ambiguity, stripping away any styling cues or signifiers that might contradict this framing. This example shows how, despite casting agents' reliance on 'objective' images, (1) these images are sometimes literally re-cast to achieve what seems to be discursively impossible, as in this example, an unambiguous reading of Yasmin as ethnically ambiguous, but somewhat contradictorily, (2) that ultimately these images are never secure enough to convey one specific message or way of reading, and nevertheless still require narration.

These conversations that casting agents have amongst themselves are also largely about placing models in both geographic and social space. Both constituting and reinforcing contingent social relationships and exclusions, placing simultaneously prescribes and describes the organisation and distribution of social 'differences'.[23] As anthropologist Katie Stewart writes,

> People who meet must *place* each other, sifting through signs of identity that drift off into drama and mysterious connection in the narrative logic of contingency, engagement, encounter, and revelation. Social place becomes a sign not of a fixed social order but of the social imaginary immanent in *ways*.[24]

In casting conversations, these placings are always relational, drawing comparisons between other models, either absent or present, and are frequently anchored in racial, ethnic and national identifications, alongside occupational and class-based categories. They are also always about re-placings, or entextualisation, seeking first to identify the objective place of a model, and then selectively framing these details for new contexts. These subjunctive re-imaginings required seeing past certain features while highlighting others. Explaining this process, Hank said:

> [A model] may come in wearing a hyper colour t-shirt and bike it at face value, like hyper colour t-shirt and bike shorts? They're '80s and we're not doing an '80s show. And it's our job to see past that, and be like, the body's great, the face is really interesting, long neck, beautiful, regal, you *could* really do something and force them to meet them and see that for them. … That's how we help them avoid just booking all the girls who are going to come into a casting wearing pearls cause they're looking for rich-looking people.

In addition to doing this kind of discursive framing, agents also drew on self-reported identity information they collected on casting information sheets to narrate models; however, they did so in inconsistent ways. As seen in the example of Yasmin, agents could overrule self-ascribed categories like 'Egyptian', preferring instead more marketable terms like 'ethnically ambiguous'. They used this kind of information as a flexible resource to create types but never in a definitive way that became part of the person's permanent file. Instead, it was always done verbally and in relation to specific projects and potentials. In this way, casting agents linked both their 'objective' imaging practices and creative discursive framings as mutually dependent tools of their professional vision. Ultimately, their goal was not to create fixed representations, but instead to construct contingent visual and verbal arguments that relied on generating affective resonances for their clients. There were frequent slippages, however, between explanations and appearances, which often served to reinforce and reify certain kinds of 'difference', as authentic or objective, while others depended more on a model of sincerity, or believability.

This can be seen in an exchange during an early editing interaction between Hank and Liz for a television commercial. The advertisement was for a new line of cocoa butter skin care products that would air in US, UK and South American markets. The client had explicitly requested a range of Black women to appeal to these markets and described the tone of the spot as 'sensuous in a way that is empowering and celebratory … [that] presents [black women's skin] in an original and emotionally genuine way'. In the casting brief she sent to model agencies, Liz requested the following:

> Women of different shades of brown skin, ages 20s–30s, (i.e. African American, South African, Brazilian, African, Caribbean, etc.) must have gorgeous, strong, fit bodies with clear and inspiring skin. Be comfortable with body movement and almost nudity. … Looking for not only different skin tones but distinct looks (from different countries). All body types, thin, muscular (not overweight). Girls will be auditioned in bikinis.

To supplement the agency suggestions, Liz had gone through the agency's ethnic female 'street' binders to find other models who could be considered. After pulling about 20, she asked Hank to help her edit. In their interaction you can see the ways in which they use different forms of evidence to place and replace models:

1 L: She's super cool, she's like different looking.

2   I don't know, I mean she put dancing on there,

3   but everything else is like <u>American Apparel.</u>

4 H: But she looks like she has a decent body, a little curvy

5 L: And what about her face?

6 H: I think her face is beautiful, she just looks weird there.

7 L: She's gorg – Like <u>what's her ethnicity</u>?

8 H: I don't know, I mean I don't even know what the body looks like.

9 L: Her lips? I just went there because of her different

10   like her body looks ripped actually.

11 H: Yeah, she was, I remember.

12 L: And she's French so she's got that like French.

13 H: And she's a jogger, so maybe she looks athletic.

14 L: Yeah, but you know like the French …

15   like a lot of African and French-type black people.

In this excerpt, Liz talks about the model's appearance, but searches for reasons for it. She asks placing questions like 'what's her ethnicity?' Hank, meanwhile, is focused on finding evidence for the condition of the model's body to meet the specific job requirements, saying in line 13 'she's a jogger, so maybe she looks athletic', including his own memory of her body being ripped in line 11. Ultimately, however, Liz summarises the model's most marketable look as being directly related to her self-reported French heritage, which she concludes signals 'like a lot of African and French-type black people'.

Again, this example illustrates the insufficiency of images and the need for casting agents to draw on both non-visual evidence and remembered affective and aesthetic judgements to frame and position models as suitable options for client presentations. Attending to the client's request for both 'gorgeous, strong fit bodies' and 'not only different skin tones but distinct looks (from different countries)', Liz must modify and describe the model's blackness, drawing on national and regional labels. Unsatisfied with the self-reported French identification, Liz collapses it to include 'a lot of African and French-type black people'.

In these conversations, casting agents rehearse arguments and framings for client presentations. As such, these informal exchanges are critical sites to explore how agents make sense of appearances, connect them to social differences, and how this is shaped by their material, discursive and visual practices. These, in turn, limit the range of possible representations that can be produced within the fashion industry.

Towards a comparative cultural analysis of booking photographs

A comparative reading of booking photographs must go beyond the images themselves and, more importantly, beyond the images of convicted criminals or valorised beauties that circulate outside of these professional communities.

What is needed is to think not only how fashion or law enforcement inaugurates, celebrates and denigrates types but also the ways in which these pools of potential images are created in the first place. As I have shown, a central part of addressing this lies in understanding the professional communities that inscribe and animate these images. Given the overlaps between these two domains and the increasing mediation of their practices in popular culture, critical readings of them together may help through juxtaposition to challenge the self-evident nature of these evidentiary forms and practices.

5

KOGYARU AND DRESSING UP AS A 'SCHOOLGIRL DELINQUENT' (*FŪRYO SHŌJO*)

Sharon Kinsella

Slumming it was at the heart of the joy of schoolgirl street culture in Tokyo in the 1990s. *Kogyaru* was a new term coined by journalists in the mid-1990s, traceable to a *Spa!* magazine article, 'The lure of the *Kogyaru*', published in 1993 and promoting a new generation set to replace the nightclubbing 'body-conscious girls' (*bodeikon gyaru*) of the late 1980s and early 1990s.[1] The first publicly broadcast depiction of a *kogyaru* was in a session titled 'La kogyaru night' (*Za kogyaru naito*) produced for Asahi television's late-night live show *M10* (*Magnitude*), aired 10 August 1993. *Za kogyaru naito* presented live examples of prototype *kogyaru* seated alongside specimens of older *gyaru* in their 20s and a third group framed as the natural *kogyaru* enemies. *Kogyaru*, or the *ikeike gyaru* (lively girls), were presented as the latest precociously confident versions of the apparently fearsome and materialistic *gyaru* office ladies and college students (*joshi daisei*) that occupied urban folklore of the 1980s.[2] The all-male specialist panel – labelled the *Kogyaru rinri iinkai*[3] – identified *kogyaru* by their flared miniskirts, blue mascara, pink rouge, tendency to carry *pokeberu* (pocket bell) pagers and a preference for *Fine* magazine and club nights at Gold and Eros.

Somewhat later, in 1996, a connection began to be made in journalistic material, between the emerging sassy *kogyaru* style or 'long hair, brown contact lenses and narrow eyebrows',[4] and shocking news stories about high-school girls reportedly taking part in a new style of amateur prostitution that they called 'compensated dating'. The sexy *kogyaru* street style, with its tell-tale signs of plucked brows and acting like an adult, converged with loose white socks and school skirts rolled up into miniskirts, worn with mustard coloured Burberry scarves.[5] This composite of luxury brand and school uniform became the outfit of deviance imprinted on the public imagination over the remaining years of the twentieth century. It was made ubiquitous to public space and communication through an extraordinary production cycle of photojournalism, television broadcasting, film-making, art, comics and animation, which focused on the breath-taking immorality and audacity of ostensibly wayward schoolgirls.

Teenage women in the *kogyaru* style hanging around in Ikebukuro and Shibuya didn't use the word *kogyaru*, however: they used the rather cooler names, *ko* (kids), *gyaru* (girls) or *gyaruko* (sister/babe), to talk to each other. Despite its socially constructed origin I shall propose that *kogyaru* fashion and posing became a powerful street fashion that thrived on media stereotypes of *lumpen* prostitute schoolgirls and the opportunities offered by capturing the attention of media, academic and government bodies. Within a few years, girls ran away with the baton, particularly visibly in the shift to the *ganguro* style in 1999, which was ignored or excoriated in editorials previously riveted in place by salacious *kogyaru* 'news'.

Kogyaru[6] style bore continuities with the iconoclastic and pragmatic posture of urban female subcultures and their attendant journalistic records and cultural parodies, stretching from those of indentured factory girls and *komori* nurses sweetening their hard labour with ribald songs and jokes in the provinces in the nineteenth century, to pre-war café waitresses available for after-work appointments and the would-be promiscuous modern girls of the 1920s, to the *pan pan* prostitutes of the occupation period, who correspond to liberated and burlesque immediate post-war *kasutori* culture. The *kogyaru* pose and its journalistic interpretations were rooted in a chain of subcultural styles based in the experience and imagination of lower-class Japanese and East Asian women, whose livelihoods or public personae were often loosely sexualised, and, in many cases, explicitly linked to hostessing and the sex services industry.

Changing clothes (*kigaeri*)

In a pattern that recurs at intervals through girls' subcultures in Japan, *kogyaru* style had two quite distinct but interchangeable sets of apparel. In common with *bodeikon* ('body conscious') office women and platform dancers in the 1980s, cosplay posers of the 1990s and Lolitas and Goths of the 2000s, the moment of switching appearances has often constituted a pleasurable and conspicuous performance.[7] *Kogyaru* school uniforms (*seifuku*) were worn in a customised style. School skirts were turned into ad hoc miniskirts by rolling up the waistband to hoick up the skirt hem. Instead of smooth and tight knee-high school socks, *kogyaru* calves wore baggy oversize white socks reminiscent of 1980s-style aerobic legwarmers, which crumpled around their ankles. Loose socks (produced by Solid Harmony from 1994) were worn with black regulation school loafers. *Gyaru-ko* (girls) also wore baggy school-style jumpers, sometimes so large that the jumper fell to the hemline of their improvised miniskirts. In spring 1996, the streetwise Okinawan pop singer, Amuro Namie touched on and helped to glamorise the *kogyaru* street style in a Morinaga ice cream advert in which she dawdled in school uniform and loose socks. In winter 1996 and 1997, doughty *kogyaru* wore mainly Fendi or Burberry scarves – the latter usually in the trademark mustard check colour, tucked into their school blazers. At this time some sported Ralph Lauren vests under their shirts too.

Accessories that played games with teenage sensitivity to the public ranking of each middle and high school came in and out of vogue, leading to an anti-authoritarian mix and match approach to official school uniforms, which incorporated some of the signature items of better high schools. In 1997, for example, Showa Daiichi Kōkō school satchels became a sought-after item for girls from all high schools. Schools in the Tokyo region found it increasingly difficult to insist that students adhered to school uniform regulations (*fukusō shidō*), if they had them.[8] The *kogyaru* penchant for wearing school uniforms involved a complex subterfuge in which rule breaking was disguised as conformity, making it especially difficult for teachers and parents to detect and discipline offenders. High-school students sometimes acquired used items bought second hand from 'bloomer-sailorshops' (*buru seera ten*), otherwise selling pre-worn items to male uniform fetishists, or swapping them with friends, to bolster their own uniform-like uniforms with sought-after school insignia. By the 2000s the high-school uniform had become not just mixed-up but in some cases entirely 'fake' (*nanchatte*), and a subset of fashion apparel serviced by labels such as East Boy and Elle emerged, which specialised in mock school uniforms. While Tokyo Metropolitan high schools (*tōritsu kōkō*), not generally high in the rankings, had no official uniform in the 1990s and lower ranked private high schools had introduced relatively relaxed rules regarding clothing in the capital, the majority of girls attending these schools nevertheless did wear a full school uniform that they assembled themselves from a range of fake school neckties, tartan skirts, blouses, jumpers and blazers.[9]

Uniform mixing impacted on adult fashion too – trend-conscious older men and women could be seen sporting *kogyaru* style Burberry checks and check-pattern skirts. The customised school uniform flowed into art and design: in April 2003 the sophisticated style magazine *H*, targeted at an older readership, placing a young idol dressed in a weather-worn designer version of the sailor suit uniform in a photo shoot, also featured on the cover accompanied with the cover banner 'Our alternative way'.[10] Overseas, the impact of trend-setting *kogyaru* 'Japanistas' was evidenced in the spread of Burberry check patterns, and documented in American fashion magazine *Harpers Bazaar*.[11]

In the summer of 1998 I had the opportunity to spend some evenings with a group of *kogyaru* who had taken to gathering on a pedestrianised street in front of a shopping mall in Kichijoji, West Tokyo. These stylish girls were in the habit of carrying an alternative outfit in their school satchels. Intermittently, girls in *kogyaru* style blouses, miniskirts and loose socks excused themselves from the group, to trot off and get changed in the public restrooms in the mall, whence they reappeared with some aplomb a short spell later, dressed in tight one-piece dresses akin to cocktail dresses – an 'adult look' in favour at that moment, bangles, faux tropical accessories and sometimes, platform sandals (*atsuzoku sandaru*) and dramatic false eyelashes. Adapting school uniforms, applying face stickers, face glitter and make-up and changing into casual wear were all pseudo-clandestine activities with high visibility (Figure 5.1).

Girls were witnessed rolling up their school skirts, applying make-up and making other transformations while in transit – in the narrow space between the doors of coupled train carriages, in department store stairwells and toilets and train station restrooms. Along with an often caricatured impression of blunt *kogyaru* mobile phone conversations beginning with a gruff (Where ah' ye' now? [*Ima doko?*]), their public changes of outfit (*kigaeri*) became the stuff of scandal and urban myth.

Figure 5.1 *Kogyaru* in Kichijoji putting on her make-up while squatting in a pedestrianised zone. Photo by Maggie Lambert, 1998.

The 'adult look'

The alternate apparel of *kogyaru* who had shed their uniform was mature, semi-classical and showy. It gave the girls the overall appearance of glamorous models ready for nights out in a casino or a filmed night-scene. This *gyaru* style was sometimes described as showy (*o share*) or lingerie style (*shitagi-kei*), *otona-fu* (adult style) or *one-san-kei* (big sister style). *Kogyaru* wore slender 1970s-esque full-length coats with fur collars, over miniskirts and slinky dresses, leather micro-shorts and tights or tight-fitting women's trouser suits. The chief editor of *Cawaii!* magazine explained its mood in the following terms: 'They've wanted a grown-up culture for a few years, but until now there were no magazines for them. They are into having love affairs, playing, drinking, going out on the town at night time, and buying expensive things.'[12] In summer 1997 and 1998, the *kogyaru* look bared more skin and incorporated retro-style platform sandals, flower prints, flared trousers and cropped sling back tops. In winter 1998, the *kogyaru* outfit lingered on in calf hugging, knee high, platform boots worn with bare tan legs or tan tights and knee length pastel-coloured duffel coats. At its height the *kogyaru* look was that of girls dressing up as sophisticated women out on the town for the evening. The chief editor of *Cutie* magazine disparagingly identified a desire to solicit the male gaze as the defining principle of the *kogyaru* look: 'They want to look cute to men and adults.'[13]

Kogyaru styles created the impression of inappropriately sexualised young girls. Their look, in combination with their loitering at night, body gestures and fashionably coarse chatter, even suggested that they were actively soliciting customers. It was a highly provocative style that fed on external attention and flourished precisely at the interface between schoolgirls and the news media or institutional professionals on the search for stories about compensated dating. This was a particular type of attention that *kogyaru* learned to cultivate. 'Loose socks' and 'mini skirts' barely hiding a girl's underwear bore all the essential attributes of the sexualised waifs otherwise visible principally in men's pornography and Lolita-complex animation. *Kogyaru* in customised uniforms absorbed and mimicked aspects of the looks of desirable little schoolgirl teasers created for a male-oriented visual culture. A similar type of mimicry of the mimic pertained in nineteenth-century America, where apparently 'it was possible for a black man in blackface, without a great deal of effort, to offer credible imitations of white men imitating him'.[14] Charmingly fallen proto 'loose socks' appear on the nubile character of Miya Chan in the early male-oriented Lolita-complex comic *Scrap Gakuen* (Azuma Hideo) in 1986.

Rather like the *bōsōzoku* bike gangs of the 1980s who boisterously pressed journalists for appointments in which their deviant performances would be observed, photographed and reported, being a *kogyaru* was a pastime that played blatantly with the media narrative about underage prostitution and compensated dating.[15] The fun *kogyaru* had with their dressing up and improvised tarty performances is reminiscent of the emphasis that anthropologist Ikuya Satō placed on the generally overlooked pleasures of deviance and its 'playlike' rhythm and quality.[16] While professionals representing various academic and institutional bodies seemed unable or disinclined to recognise this subcultural game, sociologist Fukutomi Mamoru noted that one of the complications in carrying out the large-scale survey on compensated dating that he supervised in summer 1997 was that '*Enjo kōsai* has become an arena in which to play a "stylish" and contemporary role.'[17] There was a fine line between looking sexy and mischievous and looking simply like a teenager prostituting herself. As the chief editor of *Cawaii!* pointed out, 'No one wants to look literally like "a girl who does compensated dating", they want to look just sexy enough to get adult attention.'[18] *Kogyaru* style became synonymous with compensated dating and wilfully misread not as having risky fun but as literal and highly visible evidence of sexual deviance.

Flash and cheap clothes

Several other elements in the flow of *kogyaru* looks and behaviour – scruffiness, lewdness, the flaunting of money and brand-name products – compounded the impression of uneducated young working women, with frankly prostitute-like garish tastes and social habits. *Kogyaru* style at times involved the pursuit and conspicuous display of real and fake brand-name items and a mock nouveau riche (*narikin*) aesthetic. The interest in brand-name handbags, more prominent early in the evolution of *kogyaru* style, is showcased in a *Cawaii!* article identifying Prada, Gucci, Louis Vuitton, Chanel, Versace and Fendi, as the top six names to own in the cult of 'Cheeky Pride in Foreign Brands' (Figure 5.2).[19]

The materials used in *kogyaru* clothes and accessories were generally cheap imitations of expensive materials, including fur, leather, metallic lamé or silky acrylic shirts in prints reminiscent of Hermes silk scarf designs. The original Hermes designs already involved conspicuous symbols of wealth and status such as tromp l'oeil shining gold chains, pendants, anchors and heraldic and military equipment. The gaudy look was accessorised with tanned skin, elaborate and multicoloured 'nail art' manicures, temporary tattoos and hair tinted brown (*chapatsu*).

Subsets of *kogyaru* style known as *saafu* (surf) *rook*, ('Hawaiian local') and tropical prints and accessories conjured up a hazy impression of luxury tourism in the South Seas, yachts and penthouses. Stylistic self-aggrandisement was connected to current ideas like 'respect', 'pride' and 'getting' what you want (*geto suru*). By coupling themselves with the signs and symbols of a classy

Figure 5.2 See 'cheeky' girls holding up their grown-up looking handbags in *Heart Candy* magazine (15 October 1997 issue).

lifestyle, the materialism embedded in girls' style provocatively asserted a sense of entitlement. In this way the uppity *kogyaru* mode was on a parallel with materialist ambitions inscribed in rap culture from the US, so it was hardly surprising that Lil' Kim and her survivalist fighting lyrics were easily exported to Tokyo in this period. While the 'moneyed' theme in schoolgirl subculture was interpreted as visible evidence that girls were acquiring funds through compensated dating and were afflicted with a regressive and tasteless adoration of consumption, evidence suggests that the luxury displayed was more symbolic than real. *Kogyaru* play with material ambition in fact brought back into the limelight the imitative nature and play with the class stereotypes that take forms in street fashion.

The type of 'fancy' outfit assembled in *kogyaru* style was closely allied to the wishful 'love of finery' researchers have detected in Victorian servant-class subculture.[20] *Kogyaru* style also bore more than a superficial similarity to the passion for 'doing it in style' with shiny, bright and grandiose ornamentation that was favoured by the English working class until at least the 1950s, according to early cultural studies writer Richard Hoggart. Hoggart goes on to explain that the aspirations that imbued English working-class style were based not so much on any actual encounter with wealth but a lifestyle in which 'posh folk are hazily assumed to pass their every day'.[21] In Japan, the class economics underlying styles of female consumption became highly visible from the late nineteenth century as both a new youthful and female industrial working-class and the middle-class urban consumer economy expanded. As historian Hirota Masaki reports,

> Young women of the 'barbarous' classes fantasised about and aspired to the lifestyles of the 'civilised' classes. Accordingly, they made numerous efforts to imitate these lifestyles. But since the actual conditions of their daily lives were far inferior, they ended up constantly deprecating themselves and became haunted by a sense of inferiority.[22]

Early ethnographers observed a 'wave of custom transmitted by imitating the upper classes'[23] in the 1920s, the period in which Kon Wajiro collected his detailed data and made his hand-drawn diagrams documenting the emerging material culture, fashions and lifestyle of ordinary men and women in the capital.

The centre of girls' fashion in Tokyo in the 1990s was local labels and outlets. For *kogyaru* these were clustered in Shibuya and in Tokyu's cluttered and teen-oriented '109' department store (known colloquially as *marukyū*). Favoured local brands such as Love Boat, Vivitix and Alba Rosa were sometimes mixed with both fake and real items bearing the brand logos of international brands such as Vuiton and Prada. In the case of real items, this was usually a small but visible accessory such as a key fob, purse or make-up bag. Throughout the 1990s the price of cloth items reviewed in *kogyaru* magazines (*kogyaru zasshi*) was typically lower than 10,000 yen (about $100) and regular editorial features provided ideas about how to assemble outfits for less money. *Popteen* featured a regular review of 'good value fashion' (*negoro fashion*), with each item typically priced at between ¥1900 and ¥7900; or, for example, in 1997 *Cawaii!* featured an article on where to buy cheap sandals, one-piece swimsuits and shorts, for ¥4900 to ¥8900,[24] while *Tokyo Street News* (*sutonyuu*) encouraged its readers with 'Buy cheap coordinates!' (*Yasukau kooridinate*), all below ¥10,000 in 2002.[25] As the chief editor of *Cawaii!* observed, 'Girls like cheap things as well as brand name products. They don't want to look the same as everyone else so they buy non-brand goods to get variety.'[26]

Lumpen girls

Though the number of high-school girls going on to university instead of leaving school for work or moving on to two-year junior colleges increased rapidly from

1992,[27] and no significant shift occurred in the percentages of pupils dropping out of high school at this time, girls into the *kogyaru* lifestyle squatted in public doorways and stairwells as if they had run away from home (*iede*) and were homeless. Being low class, down and out, dirty and generally '*lunpenppoi*' (tramp-like),[28] was a more delicate element in the mixed threads of *kogyaru* style and behaviour. (See the stained school skirts and grimy blouses worn by girls in Kichijoji.)

In a society with relatively austere attitudes towards neat appearances and personal cleanliness, being a dishevelled and unwashed young woman required a quite particular audacity. Dirt suggested an unwholesome life outside of the bio-management of the maternal home and was combined with other shocking and coarse trappings borrowed from male behaviour and communicative style. *Kogyaru* squatted in the streets with legs open in a style reminiscent of lower-class East Asian men and of the working-class-style 'hard school' postures (*koha*) of *yankiis* and boys' bike gang (*bōsōzoku*) members during the later 1970s and 1980s as hand-drawings of motorbike gang member postures made in the early 1980s by anthropologist, Ikuya Satō, testify.

Greeting each other, some girls abandoned dominant patterns of feminine speech for low tones and masculine grunts of acknowledgement, 'ossu' and 'ohh'. Looking ugly and pulling gross expressions became a popular thing to do for the camera, and, framed on print club stickers, this habit became known as *yabapura* (Figure 5.3).[29]

Accompanying sloppy attitudes, girls were reportedly using coarse and masculine and sexually lewd language to address each other and the eavesdropping world. A great deal of media attention was paid to capturing

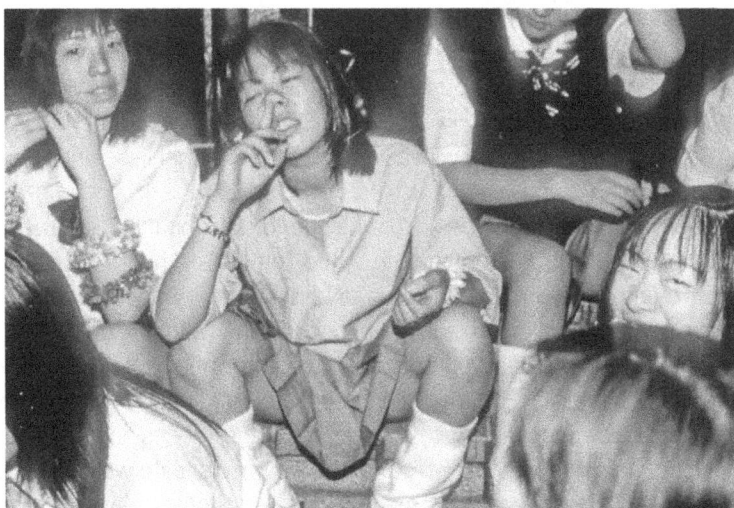

Figure 5.3 Girls sit around in the 'shit squat' (*unkosuwari*). Photo by Maggie Lambert, 1998.

what became known as 'kogyaru language' (kogyaru go): 'If you listen to the voices of the girls as they roam around Shibuya, they will horrify you with their toughness and terrible energy, as they rudely calculate everything with an almost flamboyant brutality.'[30] Many of the terms ascribed to kogyaru in lists published in current affairs magazines, for example, the phrase 'chō beri guu' (super very good), alighted upon early on, would appear in fact to be revived forms of rather dated, male slang. Published kogyaru go included the following coinages: iketeru (fly, good), ikemen (good-looking man), chōkawa (super cute), gekikawa (hyper cute) and onikawa (devilishly cute), raburabu (loved up), mecharabu (deep in love), enko (compensated dating), uri (prostitution), geto suru (to get something you really want), buya (Shibuya), bukuro (Ikebukuro), yabai and yabukanai (risky, not cool), teman (female masturbation or 'fingering'), chūpuri (kissing on a print club sticker), uzai (boring), chōza (very boring), baibingu (using a vibrator) and gyakunan (reverse flirtation, 'nanpa', meaning a girl picking up a boy). Some of these terms may have been invented by schoolgirls, but evidence also points to male cultural producers and editors as the source of this gutsy and sexual slang.[31] Journalist Fujii Yoshiki concurs that so-called 'high school girl words' and 'kogyaru language' were a fiction invented by the mass media.[32]

Media inspection of the dirty theme connected to more extreme yamamba fashions by the end of the twentieth century was condescending and literal. In May 2002, the popular TBS primetime television show 'Let's Go to School!' (Gakkō e ikō) introduced a new slot titled 'Dirty Girl Busters' (Oogyaru baasutazu), which lampooned this stained and dishevelled look. Each week its celebrity young male hosts broke in to the rooms of teenage girls suspected of being 'Dirty Girls', frequently yamamba, and ridiculed their slovenly habits. Though attracting some prudent internet discussion about the extent to which dirty girl busting was actually 'staged' (yarase) and not authentic documentary, the 'Dirty Girl' feature did not appear to attract criticism specifically for its nosy invasion into the personal lives and rooms of anonymous young women.

Kogyaru magazines and their editors helped to transmit this raucous ladette aesthetic to girls. In Popteen magazine in the first half of the 1990s there was a distinctive emphasis on the earthy fun of ordinary life. Readers' photos show teenagers playing pranks on each other, cavorting with their toddlers and embracing. Unsophisticated young couples squat on the ground in the yankii school dropout manner.[33] Egg magazine also featured a great number of photos of readers' pranks – teenagers with chopsticks up their noses and rows of boys or girls doing 'moonies'. This bawdy and anti-bourgeois taste was incubated in the physical carnivalesque of porn magazines, the editorials of which connived to launch a new range of sexy magazines for girls – later to become known as 'kogyaru magazines' (Figure 5.4).[34]

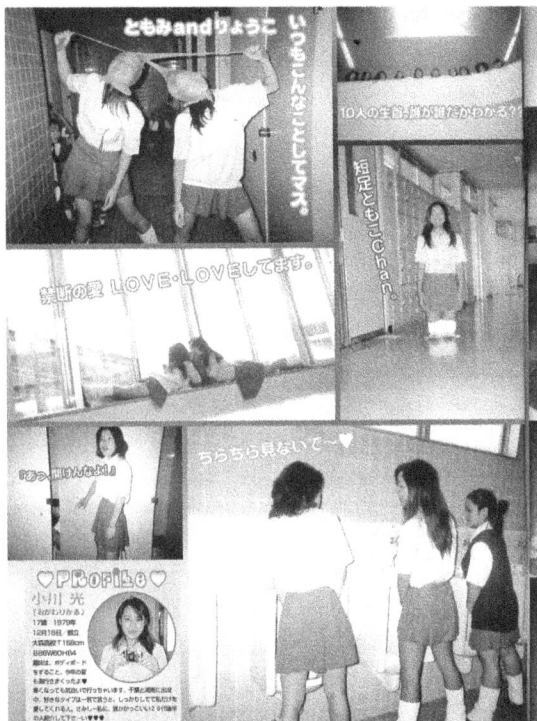

Figure 5.4 Girls goofing around in boys' toilets and wearing nylon tights on their heads in bawdy horseplay around the school gym, framed in *Heart Candy* (15 October 1997).

The class reaction

Attitudes towards *kogyaru* amongst their peers reveal an overall picture of the class feelings lurking in reactions to the style.[35] *Kogyaru* looks fascinated a minority but enraged and repelled the majority of their teenage classmates. Their peers confirmed that the *kogyaru* look was, if nothing else, sexy: 'They are sexy and have a good time'; 'they have got no modesty whatsoever'; 'I like it, but the stuff which shows off everything for all to see, is horrible'. This was linked to a suspicion that *kogyaru* behaviour was culturally inappropriate: 'You should be free to wear what you want, but they try to grab attention from other people, by exposing a lot of skin'; 'they wear showy clothes that don't suit their age'; 'they look like they're going to get skin-cancer'. And in fact there was a feeling that *kogyaru* were immoral: 'They're disgraceful'; 'they've got no decency'.

Kogyaru style was garish – 'I like that stuff that stands out'; 'the colours they wear are too heavy'; 'I'm too childlike to wear that glitzy stuff'; 'they have no taste'... – and dirty: 'they are sloppy, not like the ones that get a lot of media exposure'; 'they all look the same, and they're messy.' *Kogyaru* apparently also talked and acted coarsely: 'Though it costs a lot of money to send them to high school, they don't act worthy of it'; 'I hate their tone of voice when they speak'; 'they make a racket'; 'they can't use words properly'; 'they clutter up the pavements, and they're noisy'; 'when I hear the way they speak I am ashamed'; 'the way they talk is awful'.

Other young people thought that they acted stupid: 'They all have the same make up on and the same clothes, not one of them has got any individuality, in short they're rough'; 'they all look identical, it's grotesque'; 'dumb'; 'they've got no individuality, they're idiots'; 'they look stupid'; 'they're all identical'; 'they look a bit thick.' In an educationalist society (*gakureki shakai*) in which social class is refracted through a tiered system of educational accreditation, to be 'thick' can also imply poorly educated, and poorly raised, and, by implication 'poor' in social rank and status.

In response to the question, 'Do you like or dislike the behaviour of *kogyaru*?', young women were more cautious in their condemnation, suggesting that 'I can't just say whether *I* personally like or don't like it' and that 'it would depend on the person'. Three young women between 15 and 21 years old gave encouragement to the subjects under discussion in suggesting that 'to put it simply they have a will of their own'; 'they're relaxed'; 'they are frank and open', but about two-thirds of this small sample of 36 teenage girls and boys, all of whom were middle- and high-school students at the peak of *kogyaru* style in 1995 to 1998, also said that *kogyaru* were rough and uncultured: 'crude'; 'boring'; 'trash, criminal people'; 'they're scary'; 'when they gather up into gangs they are scary, and when I can't get past them, they force me to look up at them from somewhere down below'; 'they don't give a damn about disturbing other people'; 'they have no respect for adults.'

Several responses implied that *kogyaru* behaviour was a kind of performance: 'They look like they are just playing'; 'they don't even understand themselves and yet they are acting like they are adults.' What is more, others commented further that they thought that the *kogyaru* they saw on television had been duped by a manipulative media system: 'They got invitations and it went to their heads, it's absurd!'; 'there is no way *I* would ever appear on one of those shows!'

Being a *kogyaru* was perceived as an uninhibited, tasteless and lustful posture; a style other teenagers distanced themselves from not least because of their discomfort with how the *kogyaru* look seemed to play into media portrayals of 'trollop' schoolgirls. The feeling of their peers when they saw schoolgirls presented in the media ranged from distance – 'I did not really understand it, but some of it looked like fun to me'; 'I was just watching it for the sake of it, didn't think much about it'; 'how ridiculous'; 'silly – it seemed very remote from me' … – to contempt: 'what rubbish', 'haven't you got anything better to show?';

'it is contemptible but still interesting to watch'; 'I don't know why they make those kind of programmes'; 'it looked like adults condemning schoolgirls for their appearance'; 'all they ever put on television *is* high school girls'.

Kogyaru fashion brought to light a more closeted vein of bawdy and working-class girls' culture and experience in Japan. It was not for the faint-hearted and not a look most girls saw the appeal of associating with. In practice most compromised, with a nod towards the look, by donning, what some girls ironically categorised as the 'have to wear' (*sho ga nai*) loose socks.[36]

A history of feminine burlesque

Kogyaru magazines encouraged its readers to be pragmatic, energetic, unhampered by rules and engaged with the pleasures of the present moment. *Egg* magazine carried the slogan 'bakushō' (burst out laughing) on its cover, while an editor of the short-lived *kogyaru* magazine *Street Jam* suggested that 'if the editorial has a message to the girls it is – "Play now while you can, because you won't get the chance when you become adults".'[37] Sociologist Miyadai Shinji promulgated a more sophisticated version of this idea in his writing on pursuing *mattari* – the acquired art of feeling satisfied with 'never-ending everyday life' (*owarinaki nichijo*) – which he largely credits schoolgirls with pioneering. Miyadai Shinji suggests that by leaving behind illusions about family, work, school and conventional attitudes to sex, trend-setting schoolgirls have been able to embrace 'intensity' (*kyōdō*) and 'enjoy the here and now'.[38]

Historical sources of the tarty style

The coterminous proscription and description of *kogyaru* culture in the media was reminiscent of the 'gaudy legacy of escapism, titillation and outright sleaze' that historian John Dower suggests was left behind by the low-brow *kasutori* culture of the 1950s.[39] Audacious, earthy *kogyaru* were presented in a manner similar to 'the denizens of *kasutori* culture [who] also exhibited an ardour and vitality that conveyed a strong impression of liberation from authority and dogma'.[40] In the work of the *kasutori* literati was a return to humanity with 'impermanence, a world of no tomorrow, the banishment of authority'.[41] Impermanence and living for the moment with heightened energy and appetite was also something that underscored descriptions of independent 'modern girls' (*modan gaaru*) in the 1920s. Fashionable young women in the *gaaru* posture were described as 'brightly breezy', 'highly animated' and even 'a bouncing ball of reason, will, and emotion, thrown at full force'.[42] Novelist Kataoka Teppei expressed his notion of *gaaru* presentism in a short story published in 1928:

Boyfriend A to the modern girl: My philosophy is this: Today is today. Tomorrow is tomorrow. I want to be totally swept away by what I am feeling the very instant that I am feeling it. *Modern girl to Boyfriend A*: I'm with you 100 percent.[43]

Journalists documenting modern girls in the 1925 to 1930 period described them as independent and sexually promiscuous young women with a taste for masculine and shockingly frank speech.

A few decades earlier still a fondness for unfeminine sexual *double entendre* and lewd jokes and gestures had also been observed in the repartee of young female factory hands. In 1898, educational reformer Miwada Masako recorded her opinion that factory girls

tend to be crude in their personalities. Working all day long away from their parents, they tend to sing vulgar songs and engage in obscene talk. Unless someone teaches them 'women's morality' *(joshi shūshin)* it is natural that they will be confused and tainted with vice.[44]

In a similar period of emergent industrialism, girls from the poorest families, particularly drawn from economically depressed areas such as Niigata, Gifu and Toyama, were contracted as *komori* to take charge of the youngest offspring of hard-working rural households, but the long-suffering *komori*, generally forced to tend to and entertain their infant charges outside and away from the parental home in all weathers, were described with increasing horror as a workforce of resentful and delinquent urchins. One 1893 account described how the *komori* 'sing vulgar songs, damage carts and horses, and even make fun of people passing by them. One cannot even mention their behaviour, which is too crude, nor their language, which is too rude.'[45]

The coarse and jolly behaviour credited to *kogyaru* echoed these earlier accounts of the behaviour of local Japanese women of the lower orders and also correlated closely with what might be considered an international archetype of the prostitute character. Writing on *kogyaru* in their *ganguro* phase in 2000, male photographer Ohnuma Shōji said, 'In one day, I witness in one blast, their materialism, their sexual desire, and their appetite for food.'[46] A description – if not a projection – of unbridled physical desires, which bore extraordinary similarity to comments written by the earliest formal student of modern prostitute behaviour and phrenology, the Frenchman Alexandre Parent du Châtelet. Researching new urban prostitute populations in the mid-nineteenth century du Châtelet observed that they were 'filthy, and spoke in a harsh voice' and 'lack concern for the morrow', while having an 'energy of body and spirit that is truly remarkable'.[47]

6

THERE'S NO B'NESS LIKE 'HO' B'NESS: DECONSTRUCTING THE HIP-HOP 'HO'

Alex Franklin

Fashion has long been used to differentiate between prostitutes and 'respectable' members of society.[1] Whether through state-enforced sumptuary laws or less formally imposed but equally codified visual markers, the identity category of 'prostitute' has been constructed in such a way as to annul all others, defining the bearer of the title according to their illegality, sexuality and perceived immorality. Nowadays, however, from the mainstreaming of the thong – a garment devised to censor the bodies of 'exotic' dancers – to the street walker chic of wet-look leggings, few areas of Western popular culture today remain impervious to the power of the aesthetics of the sex industry.

Nowhere is this influence more acutely apparent than in the products of contemporary hip-hop culture, wherein the hegemonic hyper-sexualised caricature of woman as 'ho' belies the early emancipatory messages of female artists such as Salt-N-Pepa, Queen Latifah and MC Lyte. Hip-hop is a multi-million-dollar global phenomenon and – when the combined revenues of music sales, fashion labels, films, television series, advertising endorsements, video games, cars, jewellery and other 'lifestyle' accessories are factored in – it generates more money annually than the GDP (gross domestic product) of a small country.[2] Its influence can be felt worldwide, with distinct hip-hop cultures evolving on nearly every continent and with the dichotomous gender roles that it endorses embedded in all its various manifestations.

The 'ho', as one of the dominant representations of womanhood discussed by male hip-hop artists, presents a paradoxical image that is both threatening and desirable; 'hoes' are needed in order to effect a 'pimp' identity and display the 'pimp's' business and sexual prowess, but the seeming avaricious nature of the 'ho' threatens the 'pimp's' financial and social status if not perpetually kept in check. The 'ho's' complex contemporary signification, from the 'pimp's' reliance on her as a defining status symbol to her implied mastery of both male and female sexuality will be examined here. Further, the ambivalent role that high-end fashion labels play in indicating both her 'keptness' and her acquisitive autonomy will be explored; for as 50 Cent states in his 2003 single 'P.I.M.P.', 'she got a thing for that Gucci, that Fendi, that Prada / That BCBG, Burberry, Dolce and Gabbana / She feed them foolish fantasies, they pay her cause they want her'.

The 'ho'

The 'ho' is a staple component of the mise-en-scène of the mainstream[3] rap video. She is a young, full-figured woman who is to be found gyrating alongside of or draped across men, expensive cars, boats and bikes, sporting scanty but expensive outfits and accessories. For the vast majority of the audience, the 'ho's' symbolism is disconnected from the realities of the sex trade and her specific roots in American urban prostitution and criminality. To an audience not versed in the histories and subtexts of hip-hop culture she is read as one more exotic, ideal 'thing' to be desired along with the diamonds, cars and mansions similarly presented.

The 'ho' is a fantasy figure: a pneumatic, adolescent imagining of an ideal woman; beautiful, predictable and constantly ready to put out. She is an assemblage of desirable body parts that can be gazed upon and symbolically dismembered by the viewer's proxy, the camera, without fear of retaliation. Her personal history, identity and voice are irrelevant to her function; she is denied individuality or agency as her sole purpose is to serve as constant iteration of the male star's virility and heterosexuality. The beauty and physicality that in another context would make her stand out, here are unremarkable and result in her being positioned as uniform, interchangeable and ultimately disposable. She is presented as an object whose function it is to be displayed, consumed and discarded as and when her symbolic value starts to wane, i.e. when she starts to age or to otherwise become undesirable.[4]

The 'ho' is fashioned to appear perpetually in oestrus and receptive to male advances. This effect is achieved through a combination of make-up contrived to mimic the signs of sexual excitement – flushed cheeks, moist lips, darkened eyes; hair – a traditional symbol of female sexuality – typically left long and loose to suggest a similar sexual abandon; revealing and/or skin-tight clothing that draws attention to the most erotically coded areas of the body; similarly messaged 'fuck me' heels and deportment derived from lap dancing moves and designed to stimulate male sexual arousal. Within the narrative of the video the 'ho's' function as a passive, scopophilic spectacle there to be visually consumed while the action goes on around her or to her, but not because of her, is nothing new: what makes the 'ho' stand out amongst myriad other such objectifying images is that she does not just connote *to-be-looked-at-ness*. The 'ho' is imbedded in visual and aural narratives that consistently impress upon the audience that her sole worth is based in her physical availability; she is presented as the ultimate object of the male gaze, coded to connote repercussion-free *to-be-fucked-at-will-ness*. Even when compared to mainstream pornography, wherein the majority of narratives are constructed to (weakly) suggest that a woman might have a life outside of sex – albeit as housewife, schoolgirl, secretary, teacher or nurse, for never let it be said that the porn industry has moved beyond the 1970s in terms of its definition of acceptable female occupations – the hip-hop rap video's representation of the 'ho' is painfully one-dimensional.

The 'ho' embodies a willing, ever-ready, potential conquest; however, her value lies not in her sexuality but in her docile receptiveness. It is her role as reification of a limited form of male heterosexual desire that defines her, not her own sexual drives or desires. While she might present a facsimile of liberated sexuality, she is, rather, sexualised and, as a result, poses none of the complex negotiations necessary to an equitable intersubjective meeting of individuals and hence none of the rewards.[5]

For the 'ho', however, sex is framed as a means of social ascension, a tool to be deployed strategically to achieve material ends, and stripped of any promise of intimacy or bonding. In turn, her body is conceived of as social equipment whose principle value is determined according to what it can get rather than the experiences it can have. The 'ho' is encouraged to assess her body against an ideologically defined schema which determines the body's usefulness according to its appearance, i.e. form is its function. This focus upon what the body looks like rather than what it can do can disrupt an individual's stream of consciousness to the point that it limits their ability to fully engage in other activities.[6] Sex is the obvious example of an activity that is negatively affected by an over-abundance of body consciousness; an individual can either 'live' embodiment or be conscious of being embodied but cannot do both at the same time, and to attempt to do so is to invite dysfunction.[7] Therefore the emphasis that is placed upon the appearance of the 'ho's' body means that those who repeatedly enact the persona can no longer fully experience their own body in action no matter how much sex is performed. The process of vigilantly monitoring her external appearances leads to unstable self-objectification, as the image smothers the real and the 'ho' becomes an unsustainable caricature periodically inhabited by different women.

The 'pimp'

Within the 'ho's' cultural matrix, a facsimile of male heterosexual desire is taken as the benchmark of normality, and the 'pimp' is this virile masculinity personified: dominant, violent, self-assured and volitive; the 'pimp' is the polar opposite of the 'ho's' mute, submissive vacancy. The one-dimensionality of the 'ho' is due largely to her function as avatar of the 'pimp', inasmuch as she is a mannequin on which his values and tastes are displayed and through whom much of his power and material wealth is projected.

The brands that the 'pimp' sports himself and in which he dresses his 'hoes'[8] are often those associated with a specific cultural capital that has previously and, arguably, actively excluded urban Black consumers. Gucci, Fendi, Burberry, Tommy Hilfiger, Dolce and Gabbana, Prada – the list goes on – are all brands primarily associated with upper-class, white money. Such strategic consumption by the 'pimp' is not limited solely to clothing but extends to the appropriation of other luxury branded items such as Bentley cars, Tiffany diamonds, Cristal champagne and Courvoisier brandy. This expansion of their consumer base has not always been well received by the brands in question: comments from Cristal's MD, Frederic Rouzaud, in *The Economist* in 2006[9] led to accusations of racism and the boycotting of the champagne by powerful figures within hip-hop. When asked if Cristal's association with hip-hop's 'bling' lifestyle could be detrimental to the 230-year-old brand's image, Rouzaud replied, 'That is a good question but what can we do? We can't forbid people from buying it. I'm sure Dom Perignon or Krug would be delighted to have the business.'[10] Similarly, and despite its promotion in song lyrics (such as in Foxy Brown's 'Styles'), Burberry has largely failed to embrace its popularity within this unanticipated demographic. Burberry's Spring/Summer 2011 campaign featured Jourdan Dunn and Sacha M'Baye as part of what Christopher Bailey, Burberry's chief officer, described as an 'evolving campaign that reflects the diversity of [the brand's] broad global consumer';[11] however, they were the first Black models to be used in such a prominent position since Naomi Campbell in 2001, and the models used to display its products on the brand's website remain overwhelmingly white.

Conspicuous consumption – the active and overt display of social power through the acquisition of prestige items – is part and parcel of the 'pimp' lifestyle. Likewise, conspicuous leisure is reserved for him and him alone, for the 'playa' who's got 'game' and who's not being played by anyone, whose wealth is achieved through playing others and exploiting their weaknesses, whether through drug dealing, the sex trade or general hustling. Real (i.e. legal) work is presented as being the preserve of 'suckas' – which is somewhat ironic given that breaking into the music industry is incredibly hard work, and, once there, involves working long hours, lots of responsibilities, pressures and deadlines, and generally working for 'The Man'. This type of contradiction lies at the heart of the 'pimp's' existence: he must work hard, but without being seen to; he must appear borderline sociopathic, rejecting many dominant social mores and sticking it to 'The Man' who's trying to keep him down, while all the time abiding by the restrictive contractual obligations that ensure that his work reaches his audience. The material wealth thus acquired must be constantly on display but in bragging of his financial worth he identifies himself as a potential target for gold-diggers; yet his sense of self-worth is so constructed around the notion of financial power being the sole means of determining personal value (a construct normalised by 'The Man'), that he cannot conceive of a relationship that is not grounded in some way on an attempt to benefit from his money and influence. So the 'pimp' must constantly appear at the centre of an entourage of men who respect him, as without the perpetual circling of other 'pimps' and 'playas' trying to muscle in on his act, his status as someone to envy would be undefined. Likewise, he must be surrounded by women who desire him, and that must be done explicitly, lest his hyper-muscled, carefully groomed body be seen as inviting a scopophilic reading by the male audience. Therefore the 'pimp' can never be at ease, even when at leisure, as he must always be guarding against those people trying to play him, i.e. everyone.

The 'pimp's' isolation and alienation is concealed beneath a facade of aggressive bravado and barely concealed contempt for anyone not engaged in the 'pimp' lifestyle that he understands, and yet he is utterly dependent on the ongoing approval of his law-abiding fans – and their legal purchasing of his product(s) – for his continued power. His utter dependency on people outside of his immediate control and realm of experience makes for an unstable world in which any drop in music and product sales would equate to the ultimate emasculating rejection.

To militate against this threat, the 'pimp' speaks to his audience. The narrative fiction of the music video is like no other, the audience is frequently addressed directly and consistently, eye contact is made and maintained with the audience, and the fourth wall deliberately shattered. Via the direct address, the viewer is positioned as known and knowing interlocutor and as such is invited to attest to the reality of the image presented – a collusive tactic most frequently encountered in news reportage or documentaries. By making the 'invisible guest'[12] visible, their otherwise voyeuristic gaze is both normalised and exalted as part of a shared experience. The (male) viewer is repositioned, moved from having to project his repressed desires onto his surrogate, the male performer, into the role of confidant and confederate. In some cases this relationship is equitable, with the artist manifestly seeking the approbation of their audience, but in mainstream rap videos featuring male artists the audience is often actively characterised as inferior and envious, with the low camera angle forcing the viewer into the role of supplicant. However, even in these instances there is a clear presupposition of shared value systems and desires, and in positioning the (male) audience as both threatened and threatening their agency (and hence masculinity) is acknowledged and their fundamental equality established. The 'ho' plays a key role in defusing any tensions that this hierarchical structure might cause inasmuch she is positioned as inferior to and less powerful than both the 'pimp' and his (male and female) audience; she unites them in their superiority. She is the symbolic whipping-boy on whom all frustrations and fears are enacted; she can never be at leisure.

The 'ho' can never be seen to be at rest for that would imply that she had free time, time where she wasn't concerned with the 'pimp's' interests. None of what she displays belongs to her; everything, including her body, is a symbol of her obligation to the 'pimp', and to be seen to be at leisure would imply that she was no longer in his thrall. The 'ho' also has to be carefully coded so that the 'pimp' isn't seen to be 'keeping' her, for to be seen to be supporting a woman with no financial return would be to suggest that he was being taken advantage of or, worse still, it could suggest an emotional attachment on his part, a point of vulnerability, of weakness, one that could undermine his whole persona. The idea that the 'pimp' might form an emotional, rather than transactional, relationship with a woman is hugely problematic for the style of aggressive machismo that he promotes. Typically this type of bond is reserved for 'baby mommas', women who have had the good fortune of bearing him a child and with whom he is obliged to maintain some form of civil relationship so that he might retain contact with his progeny, who in turn act as constant symbols of his virility and heterosexuality. This type of relationship with the 'pimp' is forever denied the 'ho', for once thus labelled a woman's social utility and cultural capital is capped and, in the words of Ludacris, 'once a ho always'.[13]

And yet despite the emotional distance that he endeavours to maintain, the 'ho' necessarily violates the 'pimp's' self-containment and much lauded independence: she is the means by which he is able to prove his heterosexuality and uphold the affluent lifestyle on which his power and position depend. In this she is both violator and victim, for without the 'ho' or his stable of 'hoes' the 'pimp' is rendered powerless, and so he lives in fear of their abandoning him: 'I holla at a ho til I got a bitch confused',[14] because if she were to have time to get her head straight she'd realise that 'Ho make a pimp rich',[15] while she gets nothing in return except a physical and psychological battering, only to be cast aside when she can't work anymore: 'Man this ho you can have her, when I'm done I ain't gon keep her.'[16]

To many adult viewers the 'pimp'–'ho' dynamic and identities that are presented via mainstream hip-hop music videos might appear somewhat crude and unappealing; the gendered performances that they present are so exaggeratedly one-dimensional that their fantastical natures are both obvious and compelling – in the same way that performances offered up by the porn industry are. However, it is worth noting that many of the viewers of these videos are not adults: market researchers identify Young Urban Consumers (YUCs), 'trendsetters and influencers who affiliate with hip-hop culture [and] exercise a powerful impact on the direction of the fashion, media, entertainment and other key consumer-focused industries',[17] as being aged between 12 and 34. The type of music videos that these YUCs watch have been singled-out by UK parents as being a negative influence on 'their sons' behaviour towards and perceptions of women and girls',[18] for even as they ape the styles and language of their idols so they endorse their value systems.

While acknowledging that interest in these issues is 'fanned by a sometimes prurient press',[19] the same report identified 'sexualised and gender-stereotyped clothing'[20] as also being a major source of parental concern. Hip-hop is by no means alone in its promotion of such modes of dress, but its videos do include 'topless lap dancing; strip tease routines; other sexualized breast nudity; and sexualized violence',[21] and in the 'pimp' and 'ho' personas it presents it glamorises and normalises what is effectively a criminal subculture. In a very real sense, in this context 'fashion is entirely on the side of violence, the violence of conformity, of adhering to models, the violence of social consensus and the contempt it conceals within it'.

The 'pimp'–'ho' paradigm

The 'pimp'–'ho' paradigm could arguably be seen as indicative of an endemic and unhealthy neoliberal romanticism present in contemporary mass culture; one that equates personal happiness with the acquisition of material things and mature relationships with romantic infatuation. In a culture that presents self-gratification as a fundamental right and in which the dominant relationship narrative is that of romantic love and perpetual romance, when faced with the realities of an equitable intersubjective relationship that necessitates compromise and deferment, it is perhaps unsurprising that the brutal simplicity of the 'pimp'–'ho' dynamic could seem appealing.

The 'pimp'–'ho' paradigm is coded as a masculine–feminine binary performance, one that promotes an artificially exaggerated gender-dimorphism via the hard, disciplined, muscled form of the 'pimp' and the soft, seductive body of the 'ho', and one that continues to equate masculinity with the active subject and femininity with the passive object. Its influence resides in its ongoing enactment, rather than in biologically determined roles, and the 'ho' identity is problematic in that it both continues the role historically cast for the prostitute as someone who exists on the periphery of society – an outsider, denied individuality or voice – as well as becoming a normalised and desirable performance of femininity. The sexualised image that the 'ho' presents is an example of consumerism's institutionalised desublimation of desires, wherein a limited male fantasy is given form and in doing so promotes an unhealthy process of self-objectification and sublimation of female sexuality in those who would ape her performance.

The 'pimp's' treatment of his 'hoes' is not simply tolerated; it is implicitly lionised: any woman who is seen to trade upon her sexuality is considered to have tacitly rescinded her right to freedom from objectification and abuse; the 'pimp' is simply helping to realise the consequences of her actions. This attitude is not restricted to the seemingly exaggerated fantasy world of the music video; a poll carried out by Amnesty International in 2005 in the UK found that 26 per cent of respondents 'thought a woman was partially or totally responsible for being raped if she was wearing sexy or revealing clothing'.[22] The normalising and mainstreaming of the 'ho's' performative identity can be seen to have real-world consequences: young women who mimic the modes of dress and dance on display in hip-hop videos can be seen in clubs and bars around the world and in doing so they are viewed as actively inviting objectification by presenting an image that – in the infamous words of High Court Judge James Pickles – is 'asking for it',[23] effectively signalling that they waive their right to say no.

By comparison the 'pimp' identity appears an empowering one, with its associated wealth, luxury and personal agency; however, in many ways it is as limiting as that of the 'ho', promoting a similarly disrupted relationship with sex and the body and a similarly limiting, prescriptive form of masculinity. Likewise embedded within it is the perpetual threat of violence, not the sexual violence that threatens the 'ho', but the gun and knife crime that is glorified within gangsta and thug rap. Also, where the 'ho's' ongoing value is determined by the 'pimp', the 'pimp' is similarly dependent upon the recognition of his performance by others – his 'hoes', his fellow 'pimps', his audience – for without their acceptance his identity would cease to exist. His audience in particular contribute to the instability of his sense of self: in a variation of Heisenberg's Uncertainty Principle, the 'pimp' doesn't know whether he will continue to exist until he is observed; his persona is neither alive nor dead until it is witnessed, judged and purchased – possibly making him Schrödinger's prat. The 'pimp' persona is defined by its fearfulness; he understands himself relationally and negatively, according to what and who he's not, rather than what he is, so that when those boundaries are removed his catastrophic isolation is revealed.

7

FEAR AND CLOTHING IN ADIDAS: BRANDED SPORTSWEAR AND FASHIONING THE 'HANDY DANDY'

Joanne Turney

Football hooliganism, emerging in the 1970s, is largely seen as a British phenomenon, yet it arises in every country where football is played. As with all sporting activity, the concept of combat, of man against man (and football has been a predominantly male domain), is exerted, and victory over an opponent becomes an indicator of both prowess and power. For football fans, on-pitch dominance spreads to and is sometimes surpassed by that on the terraces, and a group mentality and behaviour becomes an expression of power through aggression. In Britain, football spectatorship is performative, an indicator of the carnivalesque,[1] chanting and face painting in order to dislodge social norms through ritual, but it is also about style and the re-appropriation of signs of class, wealth and power through dress in order to articulate dominance that goes beyond the game. Here, power is obtained through subversion; both social and cultural norms are upturned, the ordinary becomes extraordinary and vice versa, and innocuous clothing becomes invested with fear and violence (Figure 7.1); it becomes a sign of the 'hard man'.

This chapter aims to address the ways in which clothing intended for organised sporting activity was appropriated as leisurewear in the 1980s and redressed to accommodate informal street sports, such as inter-group combat. Focusing on the Casual subculture, themes will discuss the ways in which masculinity was performed through sartorial coding and gesture, and how these elements were presented as indicative of the 'hard man', elevating clothing as a 'badge of

Figure 7.1 Casuals. From the Chelsea FC collection. Photo by John Ingledew/Chelsea FC via Getty Images.

honour'. The discussion therefore pivots on how and why innocuous, everyday garments were transformed by a specific group at a specific time, into indicators of dominance and fear. We might consider this as a means of presenting a traditional and violent coding of masculinity, dominated by power through combat on and off the sporting field or pitch (football hooliganism), alongside one that is driven by narcissism and a consumer culture more befitting of the times (designer goods and sportswear) and thus propose the visual and performative elements of this subcultural style as offering a means of negotiating or solidifying masculinity in flux. Ultimately, this chapter considers the ways in which the performance of male aggression and dominance was articulated through dress.

A recent revival of interest in the casual style[2] and 'old school' sportswear[3] has developed alongside a new form of literature aimed at a male reader. The memoirs of football hooligans have become bestsellers, and although akin to the biographies of criminals and gangsters, the glamorisation of violence in these texts is combined with detailed, almost fetishistic analysis of dress. Glamorising acts of violence and exalting branded clothing, these books propose identification and objectification through consumption and behaviour, heightening a sense of what it is to be a 'man' in the contemporary world (specifically the 1970s and 1980s). Drawing from this popular literature and supported with critical readings in psychoanalysis, masculinity studies and fashion theory, the chapter considers clothing, and its role in the presentation of masculinity as fluid, and thus posits sportswear and reminiscences of wearing specific clothes at specific times, as a transient or retrogressive form of gendered performance. 'It's the dressing up. It's becoming someone else. It's walking up and down and showing everyone what you are made of. It's being proud of who you are. It's not caring at all. It's not giving a fuck anymore.'[4]

In response to the influx and popularity of football hooligan memoirs[5] (hoolie lit, hit and tell or 'dick lit') this discussion returns to the scene/s of the crime/s, the 1980s, and, in case studies, takes the football casual as an indicator of a transient masculinity, which embraced and fused the dandiest tendencies of luxurious sartorial coding through the consumption of specific branded sportswear. One might posit this as merely another foray into subcultural identity, and although there are obvious crossovers, the focus here is to uncover the ways in which largely working-class men acknowledged and subverted concepts of 'new' masculinity and the emergent consumer market during the period, through the clothing of the male body. This is therefore as much a study of redressing the 'classed' body during a time in which masculinity was considered to be in 'crisis' and one in which traditional forms of blue-collar work were threatened by mass-scale de-industrialisation.[6] So, renegotiations of what it was 'to be a man' drew from traditional and new means of identity building. This chapter addresses two of these, 'hardness' (aggression, violence and physical domination) and dress (new consumer cultures and the appropriation of 'middle-class' sportswear).

By investigating the concept of masculinity and its display through dressing for violent behaviour, incorporating the increased awareness of and access to luxury consumer goods by a 'new' male market during the 1980s, the ways in which innocuous garments such as sportswear, became indicators of power and terror are uncovered. The chapter therefore emphasises new approaches to the male dandy, or the hard 'handy' dandy; expressions of masquerade through (often enforced) leisure, consumerism and a sartorial expression of cultural capital evidenced through the iconography of violence.

Regardless of what one might read in the tabloid press, the relationship between menswear and group violence is not a twenty-first-century phenomenon. The term 'hooligan', for example, was used in the 1890s to describe groups of young men who engaged in criminal, violent and antisocial activities, recognisable through group sartorial styling.[7] Likewise, the Casuals were not the first group to link 'fashion' or specific styling with football club allegiance. However, the Casuals were different, predominantly because they didn't look like outsiders, nor did they look threatening (they were often smart, well groomed), and consequently the violence wreaked on opponents came as a nasty surprise to onlookers. If one can't identify potential threat, how can it be avoided or combated?

Emerging in the mid-nineteenth century,[8] football, although attracting decidedly middle-class players, appealed to the masses. By the early twentieth century, working-class men were increasingly determining both the nature of the game[9] and formulating their own identities around it. Indeed, for historians such as Brad Beaven, the rules of society were enacted on British playing fields,[10] and from this perspective, one can see the fusion of sport, class, regionality and power, in the establishment of civic pride. This implies that on-pitch dominance is translated to a certain extent, into civic and social dominance, which in turn exerts a sense of collective and group belonging. Indeed, time has changed very little.[11]

Consequently, the most successful football clubs emerged from the most deprived regions,[12] suggesting that sporting prowess and league-table dominance had the obscure potential to subvert normative assumptions relating to power, such as wealth, and, in relation to the spectator, notions of one's position within a social hierarchy.[13] This Marxist perspective, adopted by Ian Taylor, poses football as a vehicle for overturning the status quo; the acquisition of dominance for those who ordinarily have none, whilst simultaneously reinforcing it once the full-time whistle has been blown.[14] This is the carnivalesque manifest; the world is turned upside-down only for its later reinstatement.[15] Such short-lived grasps at power are perpetuated by the language of masculinity, which promotes the constituents of maleness as competitive, strong, hard, dominant and aggressive. As the sociologist Jean Lipman-Blumen acknowledged,

> Even as small boys, males are trained for a world of independent aggressive action. … Males are groomed to take the universe by storm, to confront the environment directly. Males learn that society's goals are best met by aggression, by actively wrestling their accomplishments from the environment. Force, power, competition and aggression are the means …[16]

Dominance through aggression and control is explicit in the iconography and iconology of the sportsman, exemplifying prowess through the ability of the mind to discipline the body.[17] Sporting activity involves mastery, of the game and the self over others. In sport there are winners and losers, and competition becomes emblematic of the duel, a fight to the 'death', man against man, sustaining injury along the way, and competitively consuming vast quantities of alcohol once the fight has ended.[18] These are exercises in stamina, and participation in sport expresses a sense of heroism and superiority, the strength of the individual to gain mastery over the weakness of the flesh. In psychoanalytic studies, Michel Foucault discusses the significance of these images of 'hard', disciplined bodies, concluding that a phallic body is a body that demonstrates the ultimate masculinity; not only actual muscularity and strength but the triumph of the will over nature and pain.[19] Masculinity is presented therefore as a means of perpetuating the ideals of patriarchy.[20] These hard bodies cannot be penetrated and, like an armour, show masculinity as untouchable and superior.[21] Sporting (or hard) bodies are therefore signs of achievement, examples of a masculine ideal to be celebrated and emulated.

Fans are not sportsmen, but spectators, and, by definition, are a passive group, voyeuristically embodying the 'hard' sportsman's armour. One does not have to discipline and punish one's body to watch others compete. Yet for the Casuals, and other 'hard men', 'hardness' was not merely attributable to size or developed muscularity but to the ability, or allusion, to fight, to stand ones ground and to assert aggression.[22] Tommy, in Simon Winlow's *Badfellas*, noted,

> That's what I liked: big blokes being scared of you, everyone being nice to you and that. Nobody would fuck with me when I was a young 'un. It's a good feeling, hard to talk about, you know? Like always being ready … on your toes.[23]

The performance of 'hardness', as indicated in Tommy's memoir (above), is not limited to actual violence – although violence is emphasised within memoirs of football casuals – but through its potential, as articulated in gesture and stance.[24] Aggressive posturing amidst the group, such as arm folding, walking with a specific gait and bawdily behaviour, implied threat and chants, jokes and taunts all become weapons. Indeed, Caroline Gall notes that in these instances the 'hard man' was not easily distinguishable from their more respectable counterparts:

> It wasn't as if they were flash-git hard men showing off with loads of money and glamorous bitches in tow, or bad boys who had rushed the doors and were now moping around with fingers tucked in their waist-belts pretending to toy with their imaginary guns. No, these guys exuded silent authority and appeared to be respected in equal measure …[25]

She continues, 'He was the perfect gentleman, charismatic, charming, gentle and polite and he knew a lot of people who all seemed to like and respect him.'[26]

What is described here is an aura, something that is seemingly invisible, but was as developed as muscles through physical exertion; a reputation built on mythology and appearance. Much like the style of the early cinematic gangster, for whom clothing – the suit – represented an air of respectability – thus 'respect' – combined with the aspiration of social mobility along with the wealth and power that this would bring, 'hard men' and indeed, the Casuals, appeared un-threatening, even charming. For example, Stella Bruzzi states that gangsters occupy an 'identifiable school of stylishness', and therefore their dress can be seen not only as camouflage or 'warrior dress', suitable for the battle ahead, but also mirroring a hierarchy of clothing already at play within the social strata.[27] Clothes, through wearing 'make the man'.

Likewise, the Casual's adoption of luxury branded clothing and sportswear, and particularly that which was associated with heritage brands or middle-class sports such as tennis, sailing and golf (Pringle, Fila, Lacoste), frequently enjoyed by a leisured class as well as wealthy retirees, communicated a sartorial coding of wealth, age and non-aggressive competition. The dress and its meaning not only seemed benign but also communicated a sense of longevity and belonging.

In Casuals memoirs, dress is highly significant. It not only demonstrates connoisseurship, as one might expect from a subculture, but also indicates levels of 'hardness' hitherto unseen.

> 1984: 'We got Spurs out of the Railway End later and I clearly remember a half-caste guy in Burberry raincoat, one of their top lads I later found out, come striding past us. He was the last one out. He looked at us and nodded. We knew what that meant; they got the result. They looked good as a firm and were the first ones I noticed wearing Stone Island and Armani.'[28]

As this recollection outlines, a 'good firm' is a well-dressed one. So, we might consider dress as a form of sartorially coded but fluid, uniform. In this instance, 'uniform' takes the form of a recognised style, but one only understood by those within, or in conflict with the group. This adds to the 'ordinariness' of the mass; these men can be seen as merely being well-dressed football fans.

In addition to dress, the gait and behaviour of the Casuals added another dimension to the performance of 'hardness'. Hanging around and visibly doing 'nothing' can be read as a precursor to doing 'something', in particular something antisocial in the near future.[29] As with the appearance and demeanour of the gangster, as Bruzzi noted, a sense of readiness and adaptability, or the potential to reveal one's true intent or identity, increases a sense of anticipation:

> Dressed in Fila, Burberry, Lacoste, Tacchini and Farah, the dapper looking lads spent their days hanging around Birmingham's infamous Bullring shopping centre and at a nearby café called Gino's with some of the older Blues lot, just waiting for the next opportunity to bash some away supporters.[30]

Such behaviour suggests the moment before the spark hits the tinder box; anticipation, anxiety and expectation, awaiting the curtain to rise and the performance to begin. As a respondent in *Yob Culture* stated, 'We knew if we approached people in the street they would be scared of us. And we loved it! It was a laugh to watch them cross the road or run away as we approached.'[31] The aim is mastery and domination; the body is both the medium and the target, and in some cases, the message.

For early Casuals the hard exterior of the male sporting body was to be hidden beneath baggy 'sportswear', demonstrating leisure and a concealed prowess, in a soft wrapping. Here, the sportswear became an indicator of 'readiness', to leap into action or battle at a moment's notice, and can be seen as a sign of the 'resting' competitor. The clothing therefore is a sign of transition, of the calm before the storm and of the ever-present potential for violence. Under these circumstances, everyday life becomes an arena for competition, for sport, and the accoutrements of leisurewear emphasise a state that is 'not work' but one of pleasure.[32] Likewise, football spectatorship, particularly in deprived areas, encourages participation in violence[33] as part of the 'sport', a form of pantomime in which the audience contributes to the entertainment. As Jay Allan notes, 'For us fighting is the game.'[34] Fighting therefore becomes 'fun',[35] a sentiment validated by the sociologist Dick Hobbs, who suggests that 'the hedonistic strand to serious criminality reflects a division of labour that is rooted firmly in traditional practices and traditional proletarian notions of leisure and pleasure'.[36]

The myth of the 'hard' man is therefore perpetuated through sartorial codes that imply waiting for battle, the dress of the mob, of the anti-establishment[37] (through a disregard for 'work' clothes). Indeed, the rejection of working attire emphasises a non-productivity, a space where the spectator becomes performer, or as Hobbs indicates, a stage for hedonism.[38] This exemplifies the distinct relationship between performance (wearing sportswear for sport) and performativity (sportswear as a sign of display).[39]

This performance of 'hardness' is not costumed by just any form of sportswear, as sportswear is a decidedly democratic form of casual clothing, worn by everyone, regardless of their income, age or gender. In relation to violence and dress, very specific items of clothing were worn as signs of belonging, exerting a cultural capital that extended way beyond the high street. Branded goods such as Lois, Lacoste and Adidas were de rigueur, with specific items gaining cult-like status.[40] The favoured branded goods took influence not only from the clothing worn by professional sports stars,[41] i.e. Bjorn Borg in Fila, but also from class-coded leisurewear such as Pringle, Aquascutum and Lyle & Scott. Borg, a young, stylish and successful tennis player in the 1980s, was emulated by his peers, whilst the leisurewear of the wealthy establishment, golfing sweaters, tennis shoes (Stan Smith's[42]) and the like were re-appropriated as signs of dominance and of a new power that existed outside of traditional hierarchical frameworks. Such clear class-based re-appropriation of consumer goods provides an exemplar of contemporary critical debate that questions the validity of either class or consumerism as linchpins for the formation of personal identity and therefore the representation of the 'self'.[43]

> Pringle lambswool jumpers were a definite part of the uniform, although by the time I had started dressing the diamond pattern had been and gone, which is a real shame because I loved the look of those. I did, however, get in on the block-pattern Pringles and also had a few plain coloured ones too. … Lacoste was a favourite. These came in the same sort of bright pastel colours as the Pringles, with lemon and pink being the favoured colours.[44]

The styling of the contemporary with the established, professional with the leisured and the upturning of class indicators, created a look that was both inclusive and exclusive in terms appropriation. Such dress, therefore, enabled the group to blend socially sartorially, whilst they simultaneously terrified potential opponents.[45] Being well-dressed became a coded sign of 'the hard man', and therefore sartorial norms hitherto associated with effeminacy (pink sweaters, 'soft' middle-class sports like golf, polo and tennis) were subverted. Dress codes enabled these perpetrators of violence to simultaneously fit in and stand out, blurring the boundaries between the harmless and the harmful, the soft and the hard, the weak and the strong.[46] Likewise, class codes were also subverted. Indeed, Gareth Veck, a Nottingham Forrest fan, notes,

> Now, everyone and his dog thinks he's a top dresser but if you dressed (as a Casual) then you looked like a fucking freak, especially in a mining village. I remember me and my mate walked in the pub, there was only two of us in the whole village, and I had a mullet right down the neck and a crew neck Boss sweatshirt, a denim shirt, Levi's flares and Nike Joggers. They're stood there in their half-mast kecks and they think I looked a cunt, but that was half the fun of it. You looked different, totally different. They were all industrial workers who'd flog themselves to death in some shite factory for shite money, piss all their money up the wall and club each other to death at closing time. It sounds bizarre, but we don't mind having a row but we thought we were having a row in a stylish fashion. … We didn't know what we wanted but we knew it wasn't that.[47]

Veck's recollection implies a continuation of working-class traditions, distinguished through the appropriation and styling of specific branded garments. Yet the mentality of distinction, of escaping from the constraints offered by 'traditional' modes of living in post-World War II Britain, is classically subcultural.[48]

For subcultural theorists[49] distinction from the mainstream is marked through dress and the ways in which it becomes symbolic, sending coded messages within the group whilst simultaneously acting as a form of separation from those outside it.[50] This form of resistance becomes ritualistic in as much as it is a collective activity that has a political intent: to recapture that which is lost.[51]

> Pumas were the business, as were Reebok with that British flag that reminded you that you were part of a scene that was a white working-class British phenomenon and there's fuck all wrong with that. But Adidas were the mother superior of footwear, still are.[52]

Yet one might see such behaviour as the instigation of wider cultural trends: the combination of consumerist display and posturing, with the celebration and communication of violent and criminal activity, as the expression of postmodern carnival – a desire for deviance and an upturning of social norms of acceptability. As Sophie Woodward acknowledges,

> Identity as expressed through clothing emerges through the relationship between the individual and particular social groups, and what is at stake is credibility, belonging and standing out. It may be articulated through a desire both for sameness, to 'fit in', and for differentiation, since self-identity comes through an understanding of being different from others.[53]

Difference, in this instance, was somewhat determined as a redefinition of leisure and new sociocultural approaches to sports spectatorship. For example, in the 1980s leisure paradoxically became more privatised and commodified.[54] In relation to watching football, spectatorship was no longer limited to the terraces and could be viewed at home on television. The prominence of the television cameras at stadiums facilitated overt marketing and branding including that of major sportsmen and their clothing, which, alongside more showy half-time entertainment, added to its visual appeal.[55] Likewise, a trend towards what Ian Taylor calls the 'bourgeoisification' of football, a move by clubs to attract more middle-class and affluent working-class fans to matches, combined with increased professionalism within the game, widened the gulf between football and its grass roots.[56]

Concurrently, discussions of masculinity in the broadsheets emphasised what Pierre Bourdieu would have described as a cultural crisis; a grappling with changing systems of sociocultural classification that ultimately redefines positions from which to speak.[57] This uncomfortable blurring of gender, sexuality and lifestyle offered the fashion and communications industries the opportunity to exploit new consumers and develop new products. For example, the lifestyle magazine, *The Face*, a clear example of cultural and lifestyle fusion, although aimed at the 'Avant Guardian'[58] or 'new' man,[59] was read by a vast number of casuals. Indeed, many complained (in their memoirs) that when *The Face* featured the football casual as an exemplar of high contemporary style; the magazine misrepresented the group/s.

Within the constructs of the new man, the language of dress became a signifier of personal identity, communicating a sense of self or legitimacy through the consumption of goods and body display.[60]

> I was part of the label madness that was the world of the Casuals. Everyone in my immediate circle was. You *had* to be one. You were either a Casual or classed as a State (i.e. in a state, badly dressed).[61]

Again, this underlines a new reliance on the acquisition and display of cultural capital;[62] by knowing what was 'in' with a particular group and by wearing it,[63] by even setting trends and in particular by acquiring new styles from overseas, one could establish oneself within the hierarchy of that group. This can be seen as a form of ultra-non-class-based conspicuous consumption, a critical regionalism[64] in which identity is communicated through the display of specific and excessive goods in public, particularly in leisured environments and through ritual behaviour.[65] One might therefore align this form of masculine consumerist display with Bill Osgerby's analysis of the American gangster: the correlation of sensual pleasure and individual fulfilment with the rejection or re-negotiation of societal norms.[66] From this perspective it is possible to consider the soccer casual as a product of Thatcherist laissez faire politics, rather than distinct from the mainstream, i.e. representative of a self-interested, affluent(ish) brand led, culturally aware, new working class.[67]

> I had slipped into my new gear. As you do with any new clobber, I studied myself in the mirror, turning this way and that, swivelling my head over my shoulder to see how I looked from behind. Did it look okay? We're worse than fucking women, us blokes …[68]

This new-found self and sexual awareness as demonstrated in King's testimony (above) demonstrates the male body as a site of consumption, a vehicle for the performance of a male sexuality that was both narcissistic and an aspiration, a fusion of the old, aggressive and competitive man, with the new label slave. Men seemed to demonstrate their affiliation to the ideals of masculinity whilst alluding to their power through the accumulation of goods and knowledge of sartorial styling;[69] the dandy got handy.

Luxury sportswear, as worn by groups of football fans in 1980s Britain, can be understood as an expressive reaction to a variety of contemporary sociocultural issues. Firstly, the re-adoption of class identities as expressed in affiliation to a football club, the resurrection of a working-class understanding that acceptability is based on 'fighting' for your beliefs, territory, pride and so on, combined with the correlation between violence and entertainment, brought to the fore what it was to be a man in a post-industrial world rife with unemployment. Reclaiming a working-class identity, young men gained a voice, previously silenced. Likewise, the re-appropriation of exclusive leisurewear made an ironic comment on unemployment; leisure had always been the preserve of the rich, those who could afford to pay for it, and here, young men facing enforced leisure were wearing the clothes of the elite. Indeed, the dandyish re-appropriation of clothing by these groups provides an exemplar par excellence of the postmodern commodity; a fluid entity that is valued in terms of the cultural signs bestowed upon it, fusing the dual mainstays of identity formation in the late twentieth century, class and consumption. Sportswear became not merely a sign of institutional competition and leisure, but of its converse, of informality and antisocial discipline. By fitting in, and standing out, the meanings of dress as symbols of modesty, conformity and rebellion were embraced and applied to new ends. Fashion here became the embodiment of expectation and anticipation; the wolf was wearing the sheep's clothes, and the sheep knew.

CRIME AND FASHION IN THE 1950s AND 1960s IN SOCIALIST HUNGARY

Katalin Medvedev

Gilles Lipovetsky declares in the *Empire of Fashion*[1] that fashion can only thrive under democratic regimes and market conditions. British Cultural Studies scholar, Malcolm Barnard, in his treatise *Fashion as Communication*, citing French sociologist Jean Baudillard,[2] concurs with Lipovetsky, stating that fashion can thrive only in a flexible social and economic environment. Although it might ostensibly be difficult to counter the arguments of the above theoreticians, a close examination of Hungarian socialist fashion in the 1950s and 1960s modifies their observations. It appears that in Hungary at that time people's increasing desire for a fashionable appearance was instrumental in the democratisation of the regime, and eventually led to the first step towards a consumer-oriented economy.

A thorough examination of fashion under socialism is an exciting scholarly endeavour, because contemporary attitudes towards fashion mirror the historical shifts in socialist mentality and the gradual transformation of the socialist value system. Fashion and politics are usually regarded as incompatible concepts. However, as this study demonstrates, overlooking such 'trivial' things as fashion might turn out to be a grave political mistake.

A close analysis of socialist fashion practices demonstrates that the attempts at a socialist restructuring of the social and moral fabric of the society fell short in people's private lives. For example, fashion continued to remain more significant in women's lives than men's. Dressing fashionably actually became an even more important gendered expectation under socialism, which highlights that full gender equality existed only at the level of rhetoric, whilst socialist society remained partly entrenched in patriarchal practices. Socialist fashion practices also reveal that material realities continued to play a very important role in people's lives; in fact, their overly ideological existence made the general population more materialistic than before.

In the literature on existing socialism, if there is any mention of fashion at all, the main emphasis, at least until recently, with notable exceptions,[3] was on the fact that there was 'no' fashion. I, however, arrived at a very different conclusion, based on numerous interviews with Hungarian socialist women. According to my interviewees, fashion played a central role in the lives of Hungarians. One of them said this in her account of fashion:

> They like to say that fashion under socialism came to a standstill. But nothing could be further from the truth. Those who cared about fashion, one way or another were able to get a hold of smart clothes even then. We learned about fashion from one another. Paradoxically, the difficulties of life made us resilient and increased our creativity. We made fashionable articles from anything we could get our hands on. I, for example, assembled a cute blue summer handbag from film used for slides or made stylish earrings from cheap pearls and beads available in state stores. People either made their own clothes, so they at least fitted them well or had a skilled dressmaker copy a stylish item from a Western fashion magazine for them. Some would re-cut clothes bought in the state sector according to the latest Western styles or re-dye them into the hot colours of the season. Back then, fashion did matter. In fact, it mattered a great deal. So, people did everything that was humanly possible to look stylish and well put together. A lot of people also strived to look distinctive or special.[4]

Another interviewee, talking about the importance of fashion, explained,

> A well-dressed individual was the target of envy, because there was a huge shortage of high quality fabrics and accessories in the 50s. Ordinary people had few clothing items. Therefore, if they managed to acquire a stylish item they would go out of their way to protect it. I, for example, at work, always wore a drab lab coat over my outfit to extend its lifespan … Clothing and appearance was our favourite topic of conversation at the firm. Most women knew how to sew, so we often shared tips about how to refashion old clothes and regularly discussed the latest styles. Back then, people were closer to one another, they shared more. So, we always commented on what looked good on one another and gave each other advice on what types of outfits complemented our body types. … If somebody came into the possession of a Western fashion magazine, she would circulate it among colleagues. The most famous actresses of the time had a huge influence on our appearance and style. We scrutinized their images published in the magazines and copied their styles in the minutest detail. Because access to fashion was limited, fashion was much more important in people's lives than it is today. One had to be imaginative and creative to make the best of the existing resources.

Stylish items were expensive and hard to come by, so one could not afford to make any fashion faux pas. Women made every effort to look fashionable because fashion, above all, granted them popularity among friends and peers or supplied them with important social contacts.[5]

Nothing demonstrates the relevance of Hungarian fashion more than the fact that complete strangers would routinely stop people walking by to ask, 'Excuse me, where do you get *that*?' Because fabrics were scarce, people had to become knowledgeable about fabric properties, functionality and care. The popularity of tailors and seamstresses was immeasurable; there was fierce competition to be included in their inner circle of friends.

During World War II, the majority of people's basic clothing items were destroyed. In the war years and its aftermath stealing clothes became a frequent crime. People were regularly held up in the street and stripped, sometimes even naked, which suggests that clothing items must have been extremely valuable.[6] There was a serious shortage of clothes in the stores, whilst the black market was thriving, and quality items were fetching exorbitantly high prices. An article published in *Asszonyok* in 1946, titled 'We protest', reported that the situation escalated to such a degree that an angry female mob marched on the parliament building in Budapest demanding no less than the death penalty for the black marketeers, referred to on their banners as 'hyenas'. Because post-war living standards did not even reach two-thirds of the pre-war level at this time, it is not surprising that one of the first goals of the new socialist state was to provide basic garments for all its citizens. To meet this challenge, they launched the production of a ubiquitous, inexpensive and unattractive flannel fabric, which was used for all types of garments: blouses, trousers and skirts and so on. It is likely that the pervasive phenomena of hoarding fashion items among socialist women in later periods stem from the painful sentiments of post-war deprivation. The state sector also mass-produced a single shoe style, called *típus cipő*, (uniform shoe style). So that the price of the shoes could not be manipulated, the cost was carved into the sole.[7] Because clothing shortages reached a critical level at this time, such steps were met with general approval and were viewed as progressive.

Although one of the primary causes of fashion stagnation is poverty,[8] and fashion was not able to thrive because the country's economy and infrastructure was in a shambles, another cause was ideological. Because socialism was brought about by a brand-new worldview and entirely different socioeconomic parameters, socialist fashion was expected to be different from capitalist fashion. It was treated as a means of reification of ideological principles, shaping them into a visually accessible form. The primary purpose of socialist dress was to provide comfort and enable a working-class lifestyle. Socialist dress was also a hallmark of the 'proper' socialist mindset. Fashionistas were often publicly humiliated and ridiculed. In other words, dress, in the first, totalitarian phase of socialist development, was not a tool of individuation – on the contrary, it was a symbol of self-sacrifice and showcased one's belief in the collective good at the expense of personal desires. This is the reason why the most important features of socialist dress were not style, but function, comfort, cleanliness, simplicity and a non-wasteful use of fabrics, all of which tend to be incompatible with the true concept of fashion.

The primary function of the ideologically conceived, simple, unadorned and comfortable socialist dress was to increase people's productivity on the labour front. The shapeless and colourless clothes available in the stores did not enhance one's sexual desirability or accentuate one's bodily features – this, conveniently, kept people's focus on their work tasks. The simple silhouettes and styles conveyed the message that the new regime had broken with the extravagant and non-productive lifestyle of the preceding regime. They conveniently masked still-existing class differences as well. At the same time, because of the low level of garment manufacturing capabilities, it was also easier to produce uncomplicated styles.

Initially, the general population did not contest this state of affairs. They had more immediate concerns, such as putting food on the table, finding work, educating their children, having access to health care and so on. Consequently, they did not give much thought to the symbolic, psychological or aesthetic aspects of appearance. However, less than a decade later, things began to change dramatically. The trials of everyday life and the bleakness of the material environment surrounding people increased the importance of such 'trivial' things as fashion.

Although accounts in socialist social history[9] provide detailed information on the sartorial circumstances of the population, they lack a discussion of the emotional aspects of people's sartorial deprivation. Feelings of envy, shame, humiliation or the desire for sexual self-expression, I believe, played a primary role in changing fashion's social significance. However, this oversight is critical. From the second half of the 1950s the sentiments surrounding dress became so intense that even harsh prison sentences could not deter a considerable cross section of the Hungarian population from entering into illegal activities in order to satisfy their insatiable appetite for fashion. The contemporary press was full of reports of serious customs violations involving dress articles. These accounts went into great detail listing how many tracksuits, pairs of shoes, bottles of perfume and so on were smuggled into the country, mirroring the socialist state's obsession with statistics. People of all classes and social backgrounds, such as housewives, factory workers or teachers, became involved in clothes smuggling, some as perpetrators but many more as clients. Although people were frightened by the humiliating encounters with customs officials sifting through their personal belongings, and dreaded being patted-down, the fear of degradation did not deter them. This contradiction can be explained by the emotional value of the smuggled items.

To prevent widespread smuggling, contemporary newspapers provided detailed accounts of Hungarian tourists caught with half a dozen watches, which were the most coveted status symbol at the time, duct-taped under their armpits, or of tourists putting on several coats at the same time or wearing under their clothes purpose-built belts featuring large inside pockets capable of hiding a plethora of smuggled goods.

Soon, customs officials became the most hated members of Hungarian society, not only because they stopped Hungarian subjects from satisfying their burning sartorial needs or prevented them from making some money on the side but also because the employees of the Customs Office stood for all that was wrong with the regime. Whilst the official media made heroes of them, the average Hungarian was well aware that they were far from saints.

Every package arriving at the Austrian–Hungarian Border was cut open and ransacked. In the process, to the bitter disappointment of the addressees, the most valuable pieces either disappeared or were routinely exchanged for inferior items. This especially hurts the fashion conscious, as these Western packages were the primary source of fashion in Hungary well into the 1960s. Although one had to pay a fee of 800–900 forints for a package weighing 20–25 kilos – an extremely high sum at the time – it was still worth it, as one could sell the contents for a couple of thousand forints.[10] Whilst the population was convinced that they had been robbed by the employees of the Customs Office, their spokesperson asserted that the pilferage took place after work, ostensibly by postal employees, whilst the package was en route to its final destination.

Because of the relaxation of travel rules during the 1950s, clothes smuggling became widespread. Traffic both into and out of Hungary increased considerably. The exposure to fashionably dressed Westerners in large numbers fuelled the envy and the desire of the locals. The contrast between the locals and their Western counterparts was so obvious that 'Hungarians concluded that Westerners were more attractive than them'.[11]

Because the vast majority could not even dream of buying an apartment or a car, clothing became the most important status indicator. Decent clothing was expensive. For example, the clothing expenses of a family of three in a rural town were almost equivalent to their housing expenses.[12] Therefore, a winter coat, for example, was considered a major investment, and its expected life span was close to a decade.[13]

The lingering product shortages led to the demoralisation of the population. As soon as a Western tourist bus rolled into downtown Budapest, it was surrounded by locals demanding that foreigners sell them the most current fashion items. These included thin windbreakers, called *orkánkabát*, inexpensive nylon scarves, Terylene pleated skirts and cosmetics. Because dress items were generally perceived to have huge social and economic value, many young women were compelled to enter into sexual relationships with Westerners, because, unlike local men, they could supply them with fashionable clothes. According to contemporary documents, the most important gift items received in exchange for sexual favours were nylon panty hose, Western cosmetics and perfumes. Rumour also had it that even the country's top actresses were prostituting themselves for stylish clothing items, which in their case were a professional necessity.

Not only the young and the cultural elite but working-class people as well had an enormous appetite for fashion. The theft of clothing items was rampant in factories, especially in factories manufacturing clothing items for export. The workers in such factories were particularly irritated by the glaring disparity between the quality of clothes available on the local market and those produced for export. It was also disheartening that ordinary citizens could only acquire high-quality fashionable items by travelling abroad or buying things from packages sent from the West, or from the black market, whilst the members of the bureaucratic class were free to visit export facilities and pick out the latest styles. The same people also had the privilege of purchasing fashions in the so-called IKA shops, where purchases could only be made in foreign currency.

Thus, the members of the political and cultural elite, if they had the inclination, could dress fashionably with relative ease. The wealthy could also enlist the services of such famous establishments as the Klára Rotschild Salon, where everything was made of the finest fabrics and the latest styles of the major Parisian fashion houses were copied. The clients of this salon even included foreign dignitaries. For example, the former First Lady of Yugoslavia, Jovanka Tito, kept a life-size mannequin at the salon so that custom-made items could be produced for her in her absence. The clients of this salon also had access to the major fashion journals of the West, although, rumour had it that even Klára Rothschild had to get these on the black market.

The majority, however, were excluded from the exclusive fashion channels, and as a result, stolen and contraband items were in tremendous demand. Everybody who could afford the steep prices would buy their fashions on the black market, where almost everything was available. Because even the most law-abiding citizens enlisted their services, the black marketeers were often left to operate without police harassment.

Athletes were the other major suppliers of fashion. At the height of the Cold War in the 1950s and 1960s, government-sponsored athletes, whose role was to demonstrate the superiority of the socialist regime in international sporting events – the peaceful substitute for military conflict – had major privileges, including frequent trips to the West. They would even take special clothing orders. Whilst customs officials were aware of their illegal activities, they turned a blind eye. 'Even then, some were more equal than others', one of my interviewees commented. She also had this to say:

> When the athletes returned from abroad, women at the firm would gather in their offices to go through the new selection or pick up their orders. They worked with a hefty profit margin. … When I first went to the West in 1964, in Italy, I bought a similar mohair sweater for my sister as mine, purchased from a fencer at the firm a couple of months earlier. I paid 90 forints' worth of currency for it. But, back home I paid ten times as much, which was more than my monthly salary. So, you can imagine how financially advantageous this business might have been for them. Truth be told though, we were still elated at being able to deal with them because they brought in things which were missing from the shelves of local retailers. The products one bought from them were light years ahead of local products in fashionability. By the way, the illegal transactions took place right under the bosses' noses; they were considered to be 'company perks'.[14]

These practices threatened the sanctity of the socialist workplace by violating the most sacred principle of the socialist work ethic – smugglers earned income without labour. It was also a violation of socialist labour rules that the transactions took place during regular working hours. It was equally troubling that the most skilful smugglers left their jobs for a career in smuggling and became delinquents. It was also not unheard of for these individuals to pay others to work instead of them. Thus, on paper, they were at work, but in reality, they were either travelling, searching for new fashions or peddling contraband, according to the contemporary daily, *Esti Hírlap*, in its 25 February 1967 issue.

Another aspect of the smuggling enterprise, reported in the 13 September 1961 issue of *Kisalföld*, was the fact that professional smugglers often came from the ranks of former private entrepreneurs, such as watchmakers, tailors and jewellers. These small entrepreneurs despised the regime because their businesses had been nationalised. It was also reported by the paper that one could buy clothes from the smugglers on an instalment plan, a service that the state sector was not able to offer.

The smugglers' network was getting bigger every year. Both international and local teams of smugglers operated in Hungary. Among the foreign perpetrators, Austrian and Yugoslav smugglers were the most active. Because people in Yugoslavia were not subjected to such strict travel restrictions as the Hungarians, they frequently travelled to the West, especially to neighbouring Italy, and returned from their trips with suitcases brimming with the latest fashions. According to the 16 June 1966 issue of *Csongrádmegyei Hírlap*, the Yugoslavs were the main suppliers of the most coveted contraband – *orkánkabát*, which was a thin windbreaker.

Népszabadság, the highest circulation newspaper in Budapest, reported that 32 people, tenants of the same apartment complex in Budapest's 10th, a working-class district, formed a team of smugglers. Within 8 months the members smuggled clothes worth 2.5 million forints into Hungary from Bratislava. This incident, however, was an anomaly. Most clothes smuggling took place on a small scale by private individuals who involved only their closest friends and family members in the illegal transactions.

After the 1956 Uprising, travel restrictions for Hungarians were considerably relaxed. People were allowed to join organised trips to the West in increasing numbers. During their visits, Hungarian tourists were confronted with the painful schism between Hungarian and Western living standards, but what angered them even more was they found lower costs and a wider assortment of consumer goods in some parts of the East, too, which led people to question the validity and effectiveness of socialist economic cooperation. Soon, in the population's mind, every socialist country became equated with particular products. One was supposed to get knitting yarns, fabrics and shoes from East Germany. Quality cosmetics and fur came from Poland. People would shop for gold in the Soviet Union and leather products in Romania and Bulgaria. Yugoslavia was a paradise for the average Hungarian because 'one could buy everything there'. However, travel to Yugoslavia remained limited.

On the whole, the most popular travel destination of clothes smugglers was Czechoslovakia, because the Czechs considerably lowered the price of consumer goods in 1964; various wool products and textiles, yarns and shoes were discounted as much as 20–40 per cent.[15] The news of the drastic price cuts reached neighbouring Hungary in no time, and Hungarian travellers flooded the Czech stores in search of cotton babies' nappies, handkerchiefs, leather shoes, slippers, gym shoes and clothing articles. They bought up everything they could put their hands on. Initially, the Hungarian authorities were taken by surprise by the mob-like behaviour of the otherwise passive population. The situation was delicate, because the misconduct took place outside the borders of Hungary. Eventually, however, to put an end to the shopping frenzy, the National Bank of Hungary introduced restrictions on foreign currency access for travel purposes.

The bank's official announcement made it clear that the reason for the new regulations was the fact that the majority of Hungarians used their money not for sightseeing and tourism – for which it was allocated, but exclusively for shopping purposes.[16] A series of condescending and moralising articles in *Csongrádmegyei Hírlap*, especially the 16 June 1966 issue, disclosed that when socialist Hungarians chose a travel destination, their first question was not what could be seen there but what could be bought there. Needless to say, these contemptuous articles never discussed the gruelling reality of never-ending consumer shortages that fuelled people's materialistic leanings in the first place.

Despite the new travel regulations, the number of people travelling abroad steadily increased. It was a common occurrence that although people would only stay a maximum of two days in Czechoslovakia, they would purchase foreign currency for a much longer period, which was a violation of contemporary laws. In the end, to avoid rising tension within the socialist bloc, at the request of the Hungarian authorities, the Czechs limited the amount of goods that Hungarians could take out of the country.

The temptations for Hungarian shoppers were enormous, in both the East and West, and the smugglers' ingenuity was limitless. The 'amateurs' filled their pockets and suitcases with massive amounts of clothing articles and prayed for good luck at customs. The bold ones, counting on the prudery of contemporary society, hid their treasures, such as jewellery or wristwatches, in their bras or underwear. Some tried their hands at building suitcases with hidden compartments. Motorists utilised every nook and cranny of their vehicles. Customs officials found nylon scarves and stockings – the contemporary hot items – crammed into spare tyres, motorcycle helmets, even in car battery cells or in various boxes attached to the bottom of the vehicle.

A daring sailor chose a couple of logs to hide his contraband. First, he meticulously drilled long holes into the logs and placed 50 wristwatches into them. Then he sealed the holes with wood chips and smeared mud on them for disguise. His method was successful because he was only found out when he attempted to sell the watches.

Another smuggler, referred to as WN, took resourcefulness a notch further. He made tin pipes in the same size as the water pipes used in rail carriages. He painted them white, stuffed them with wristwatches and placed them next to the steam pipes in the lavatory on the train. Only an expert eye could notice that instead of the usual three identical pipes there was a fourth one as well, reported Jenő Gárdonyi in an article of *Esti Hírlap* titled 'Harsh verdicts await smugglers'.[17]

For obvious reasons, the most smuggled articles were the ones that took up little space, such as nylon stockings, thin windbreakers that could be folded up, small pieces of jewellery and wristwatches. If the worst came to the worst, one could always argue that these were not intended for sale, but as gifts for family members, and, needless to say, everybody had a large family. Others, when caught red-handed, would claim that they had bought the articles in question for themselves or that they had already been in their possession prior to the trip.

If one desired to look stylish or dress above the average, smuggling was not the only illegal activity. One also had to get foreign currency on the black market. In fact, the primary draw of organised tours was the fact that one could prepay the accommodation and meal costs in Hungarian forints at home, and then have more foreign currency left for shopping. The most popular destination for organised trips was Vienna, just a few hours away from Budapest, but beyond the Iron Curtain. On arrival, most people immediately headed for the stores specialising in clothes for Hungarians. Here, with the comfort of Hungarian-speaking sales assistants, people could satisfy their every sartorial whim. People were seduced by the aesthetically pleasing shop windows, the variety, the high quality and the polite service.

Abusing the travel currency quota per individual was another type of crime to which Hungarian smugglers resorted. Those who had used up their own quota would use their family members' papers to get additional foreign currency. They would also bribe officials to turn a blind eye to this practice.

Many people used their days-off for foreign shopping trips. They would leave early in the morning and come back with suitcases brimming with stuff in the evening. One of my interviewees said this about such quick trips:

> I have been on numerous such shopping trips. I was a housewife, so I had plenty of time to go. I mostly went to Poland and Czechoslovakia and made stops in Zakopane and Bratislava. In Bratislava I always stayed at one of the hotels frequented by Hungarian shoppers like myself. We would tell each other what was available, at what price, and where. I even took my kids with me. Once I wrapped a big piece of fabric around my son's tummy and he had to cross the border with me like that. To this day, he has not forgiven me for that. … Actually, I never thought of these trips as smuggling, but as a way to help my family. I did not feel any shame; I was only afraid of informers. I first I heard about these opportunities from my hairdresser. Her shop was a real clearinghouse for information. I learned that in Czechoslovakia one was supposed to shop for nightgowns, bras, underwear, socks, T-shirts for kids and bed linen. Their leather goods were also decent. Although these things sold at a higher price than at home, their quality was way superior, mostly because the Czech industry was much more developed than the Hungarian. Poland was good for sportswear, suitcases, and thick, hand knitted woollen jumpers, suits for kids and the like. In both places the locals wanted food in exchange, mostly cheese, sausages, and bananas. It was not difficult to sell these at all. The locals would know when the train from Hungary pulled into the station and every time a huge crowd would wait for our arrival. When we disembarked they gathered around us and asked: 'What have you brought? Did you bring any sausages, paprika? Do you have any *orkán* for sale?' … In 1968 I bought six *orkán* windbreakers and six nylon shirts in Vienna. I took these to Bratislava and sold them there. I got three times more than I had paid for them. I never priced my things too high. I wanted to get rid of them as fast as I could so that I could have enough time to buy the things I wanted … First, I only bought clothing items, everything from socks to suits for the entire family. Later, I bought household goods and tools as well. Actually, I collected the down payment for our cottage at the Danube Bend with these trips.[18]

The official consumer channels were also inundated with smuggled articles. The 18 January 1965 issue of *Népszabadság*, for example, reported that the employees of the Consignment Store Chain (BÁV) regularly accepted bribes from people bringing in foreign dress items without customs forms. The Hungarian authorities prosecuted not only the major offenders but also the 'small fry' because the customs violations could be interpreted as an indirect critique of the regime, which was ideologically opposed to wide-scale consumption. According to the contemporary rhetoric, it was 'morally questionable' to own a large wardrobe when a lot of people lacked even basic items. Everybody was supposed to have an equal share of the resources; the satisfaction of sartorial needs had to take place in the official, state sector. Materialism was not condoned; people's ideological existence mattered. Thus, the smugglers were clearly 'enemies of the socialist state'.[19]

The scale of smuggled goods flowing into the country highlighted the material inadequacies of the regime. Ordinary Hungarians resorted to smuggling primarily because the state sector was not able to keep up with the sartorial demands of the population. People were also infuriated by the fact that although high-quality clothing was manufactured in the country, it all went for export, which made Hungarian consumers realise that *their* interests were being disregarded.[20]

The physical properties of smuggled clothes made it evident that Western clothing manufacturers were light years ahead of local ones. Because high-quality products were available on the black market, the lesser-quality local products would not sell. It was also problematic to the regime that people's attraction to foreign sartorial items revealed 'cosmopolitan' attitudes, which people were not supposed to embrace. The stylish foreign pieces became targets of controversy because they conveyed alternative ideas and sentiments, which made them politically dangerous.

Michel Foucault argues that constant prohibitions and reprisals eventually make people stand up for themselves.[21] On the sartorial front, the totalitarian state demonstrated that it was against its own subjects. People at first obeyed the rules of the game, but in time they began to contest them. It was dangerous to express true sentiments verbally in public. However, it was relatively safe to do so through the silent medium of clothing. Clothing is a non-verbal means of communication that embodies desires, sentiments, values and political convictions, among other things. In fact, it was these expressive features of clothing that made dress so important in people's lives. Dressing stylishly required sacrifice, considerable financial resources and time commitment. A fashionable piece signified long hours of standing in line, spoke of the risk, fear and potential humiliation involved in acquiring it – which added symbolic meaning and value to it. The emotional aspects of clothing were intensified by the actual physical pain that the wearer experienced wearing locally produced, low-quality items. Several interviewees mentioned outright infuriation when they finally wore a well-made pair of shoes on their feet. One of them said this:

> I was on the verge of tears in a shoe store in Italy. I was completely overwhelmed by the huge selection. I wanted to buy every single pair. But, I could not decide. What if I make the wrong choice? In the end, I did not buy anything. I felt humiliated and really sorry for myself. Even today, it makes me sick to think about it.[22]

Only people who have had similar experiences can understand the intensity and lingering impact of these sentiments. Only those who lived through the sartorial shortages of the 1950s and 1960s can identify with my interviewees. Only those who also had to wear poorly made and uncomfortable shoes that literally cut into their flesh can understand what might have compelled people, against their social standing, values, personality traits and even political conviction, to debase themselves for a well-made pair. Although János Kádár, the General Secretary of the Hungarian Socialist Workers' Party, called fashion a 'trivial concern', the majority of Hungarians clearly disagreed. People's relentless desire for stylish clothes, their persistent search for trendy dress items and the scale of illegal activities carried out in the name of fashion were key factors in pushing the regime to create at least a semblance of a consumer economy by the late 1960s.

Acknowledgements

This paper is an abridged and translated version of the article '"Divat és Bűnözés" az 50-es, 60-as és 70-es években Magyarországon' ('"Crime" and fashion in the 1950s, 1960s and 1970s in Hungary') that was originally published in the edited volume *Öltöztessük fel az Országot: Divat és Öltözködés a Szocializmusban* (*Let's Dress the Country! Fashion and Clothing in Socialism*) published by Argumentum in Budapest in 2009. I would like to thank the editors, Ildikó Simonovics and Tibor Valuch, for their kind permission to allow me to publish the current article in English as well, making it available to a larger audience.

9

QUEER MATERIALITY: AN EMPIRICAL STUDY OF GENDER SUBVERSIVE STYLES IN CONTEMPORARY STOCKHOLM

Philip Warkander

Queer objects

Criminal behaviour is defined as actions carried out against the written laws of a society and is punished accordingly. During the last decades, Swedish law has been modernised to include also queer individuals in the protective custody of the law.[1] The aim is that no distinction should be made between citizens based on sexual preference or gender. However, homophobia and misogyny are still part of Swedish culture, existing alongside and intertwined with more liberal ideas of everyone's equal worth. Therefore, whilst it is perfectly legal to look and act queer, others might still reprehend one for overstepping invisible boundaries and breaking unspoken codes of conduct. Queer aesthetics are still often considered a cultural anomaly, viewed as so provocative that people are battered, beaten, even murdered because of the way they act and look. The consequence of this situation is of course a paradox, since the person attacking queer culture is actually breaking the law, thus herself becoming an outlaw, placing herself outside of the societal system. The queer-basher is, through her own actions, culturally queerified, making the relationship between queer styles, subversive actions and criminality a complex one, never fully transparent.

'Queer' is a fluid and dynamic term and must be understood as defined in relation to normative gender and sexuality expressions. What is considered a normative performance is under constant negotiation, which makes queer style a process, its manifestations ever changing.[2] Were queer to be formalised or ritualised it would lose its meaning; its most important contribution being the turn away from rigid politics of individuality to the more fluid concept of personal practices. It is also a political statement going against seemingly evident and ingrained opinions regarding ways of thinking about gender and identity; queer style is a strategy of opposition, created through subversive ways of aestheticising the body.

This aestheticised opposition is construed through complex systems of interaction; with other individuals, environments and also between different kinds of objects, both biological matter and cultural artefacts, always in relation to, and opposition with, dominant concepts of normativity. These interactions are part of an ever ongoing process, in which the meaning ascribed to the objects is under constant negotiation. A queer style is thus not to be considered a definitive or static phenomenon but is instead defined through its changeable character and appearance.[3] A style is dependent on the actual objects of which it is made up, as well as of the values ascribed to the actual garments and accessories that are being used, but the cultural meanings of the garments are activated, or made visible, when combined with other objects. It is in this interaction between different objects that a pattern emerges and a subversive aesthetic becomes discernable. These aesthetic patterns, based on a person's queer intention or desire, do not have the same appearance as heteronormative, as they contain different sets of values. Instead of listing particular garments or looks that I consider to be subverting the heteronormative aesthetic discourse, and to underline the importance of the combinations and interactions of objects, I use an abstract definition of queer aesthetics, as articulated by queer theorist Judith Halberstam: 'If straightness (masculinity in particular) is associated with minimalism, then excess (of form, colour, or content) becomes the signification of the feminine, the queer, and the monstrous.'[4]

My definition of objects is wide and also includes biological matter, such as the body. However, the body has a special position among objects as it is everyone's starting point in life – what all knowledge and all experiences are mediated through, as well as being the concrete entity others perceive us as.[5] Bodily sensations affect our experiences of reality; they orientate us in a certain direction, through touch, scent, smell and hearing. The body is not to be perceived as a neutral intermediary but as an active agent, determining our placement in, and perception of, the world. A white body will mediate different kinds of experiences than a black one; in the same way an older body mediates other experiences than a younger one. This is of course a result of the categorisation of bodies that we as a society continuously devote time to, where individuals are labelled and defined through gender, race, ethnicity, age, religion and sexuality.

However, it is also important not to view the body as something easily defined or as pure matter; the body is greater and includes far more than mere biological matter. As previously stated, the body is not simply a passive medium for sensation but rather one of many active objects, which together constitute the bodily self.[6] Instead of continuing the search for an exact definition of embodiment and bodily borders, I am more interested in the discussion of how meaning is produced through the interaction of a number of objects, biological matter being one of many entities involved, creating not simply a body but a body image which, according to philosopher Gail Weiss, 'informs us from moment to moment and in a largely unthematized way, [of] how our body is positioned in space relative to the people objects, and environments around us'.[7]

The context, by which I mean objects, places and people, is perceived and comprehended through the body, whilst the body is being created through the spatial and temporal dimensions in which it for the moment exists. The cultural artefacts that are around us create – along with more abstract ideals, dreams and fantasies as well as the actual bodies of others in our close proximity – our bodily image, and, as a consequence, our perception of our surroundings. The city, according to this line, is more than a backdrop or frame, it is an extension of one's body, it constitutes how you live your life and under what circumstances, constantly producing meaning on many different levels and scales.[8]

Subversive femininity and the power of plastic

Klara[9] is 25 years old and a self-identified female-to-female, who has lived in Stockholm her whole life. She is a popular burlesque performer and wears a feminine style also off-stage: with accentuated waist, big bows and frills, often vintage or with a mid-twentieth-century touch. Her look is consciously anachronistic; by dressing according to another time period's fashion ideals she wishes to show how transient and unstable femininity really is, that it is not – according to her – based on the idea of a biological truth but is actually a cultural construct. Her concept of the fluidity of gender is made visible through the ways she stylises her body, what kind of garments and other adornments she implements into her bodily practice, thus integrating her thoughts with the tactile sense of dressing and wearing clothes.

One early autumn day Klara is on her bicycle, on her way home from a political rally.[10] She is wearing a red dress with white polka dots, tightly laced corset, no bra and her hair dyed black. While cycling along a street in central Stockholm, she is suddenly hit from behind by a Coca-Cola can, right in the head. When she turns around, she sees that the can was thrown through the window of a van, which suddenly swerves and tries to force her off the road by pushing her towards the pavement. In the van there are two men, who start shouting death threats at her, calling her a communist and a feminist who deserves to die. Eventually they drive off, leaving Klara shocked and hurt but relatively unharmed, save for a few minor cuts on her leg.

The men's actions were triggered by Klara's appearance: the accentuation of the waist by the tight corset, the bare chest and black hair. The fact that she was alone, on a bike, made it possible for them to attack her in order to make her understand that her version of femininity was not only flawed but unwanted, and in the wrong place. This reproach is carried out physically, by cutting her off from the rest of the city with their van, which also hides her, as a queer subject, from view. The consequence of this situation is that her bodily contact with the city is lost; she is trapped and made invisible to others. Through their actions the city she is in is redefined, and suddenly it is no longer an ordinary summer's day but a threatening situation she is unable to control, her choices of action decided by others. By cutting her off from the city they take away her right to self-control; they place themselves in such physical proximity that they intrude on her space, her body.[11]

To the men, Klara's version of a female body has not only been provoking but also worth considerably less than their own idea of how femininity should look, which according to their logic gives them the right not only to intervene but also to take up her space. It is a matter of power being measured in movement; when they cut her off they also force Klara, as a queer subject in the city, to adjust to their terms. They confine her to a smaller space, whilst also shouting insults and threats, making the confinement even more threatening than had they remained quiet.

The incident happened in a place she had known since she was a small child, and was thus intertwined with many of her other memories of the city, from other points in time, making Stockholm into a multifaceted place where several (sometimes conflicting) discourses are present simultaneously. By adding this new and violent incident to her archive of memories of Stockholm as a particular place, the city is given yet another tonality, creating new dimensions and perspectives to the already known.

Attacking the tightly laced, black-haired Klara was part of a normative discourse where such variations on femininity were not allowed. The men were representatives of the hegemonic gender discourse and thus took it upon themselves to correct her, to make her aware of her transgressions. Two separate discourses collide, producing violent side effects for the person challenging the normative version of feminine appearances. Klara becomes aware of this collision in a very physical way, when the can hit her head. This is an intrusion into her personal sphere, as well as a derogatory act, made to make her aware of the fact that she is an anomaly, in need of correction. By using the words 'communist' and 'feminist', the men state that they see Klara's aesthetics as a political and subversive strategy, which they openly despise. Both words are heavily charged and the men's reaction, the act of physically hurting Klara, is to be understood as a stance against queer behaviour by claiming their own superiority, as expressed through their way of claiming the space that Klara was using for herself. The street where this interaction takes place is a prolongation of the discursive bodies of all three individuals, which explains the vehemence of the encounter; they all fight for their right to exist.

Klara says that incidents like this one are common in her life. She describes them as affecting her way of understanding the city she lives in, and her movements in and around it; events in her past determine what places she visits in the future. The past, present and future of the city blend together, creating a motion that is ever ongoing and continually changing how she relates to the place where she lives. Stockholm is full of not only queer possibilities but also dangers, or, in the words of phenomenologist Sara Ahmed, 'The question of orientation is … not only a spatial question.'[12] Klara turns from objects and places connected with risks, instead orientating towards safety and comfort. The actual facts of risk and safety are never known but rather felt, based on premonitions and recollections of earlier movements and incidents. She does this as an alternative to compromising with her looks, keeping her appearance intact but instead choosing alternative routes through the city.

Interestingly, the route of the Stockholm Pride parade uses the street where the attack occurred. The street itself has no one significant meaning but is charged differently depending on what actors are present, how they relate to each other and what kind of discourses they produce. Klara has walked with the Pride parade in Stockholm, making the street the site of two conflicting memories: one of injury, one of validation:

Klara: So then I noticed that there was, if I pushed it just a bit further, suddenly I was associated with something other than a woman. And very early, I got my first high heel shoes by my gay hairdresser, and I felt a strong connection to that kind of femininity. Because it felt like so much plastic, it didn't feel like it had anything to do with flowing menstrual blood.

Philip: No.

Klara: I felt strong, the culmination was reached at Pride 2005, when I'd got a strap-on from my girlfriend, we went through whole fucking Pride with … I wore corset, gloves, high heels and strap-on, and I was so fucking happy. And I felt, this is me. This is all fake, this is all plastic, this is me.

In the quote, Klara doesn't distinguish between artificial and biological matter, but 'fake' and 'plastic' define her body to an equal extent as biology, if not more, since the cultural artefacts – to her – reject the connection between nature and an imagined feminine authenticity. By identifying with, or possibly through, artificial objects (corset, strap-on, high heels), she emphasises the ever-changing character of the body, underlining the performative aspect of bodily matters. The body is viewed as a process where different kinds of artefacts and matter interplay to create meanings and context. In this case there is also an apparent resistance to heteronormative discourses, especially noticeable when Klara speaks of rejecting menstrual blood for the benefit of objects defined as 'fake'. She doesn't deny that the blood has female connotations but says that the femininity she identifies with is another, and that in the synthetic there is a relief from the weight of biology and nature. For Klara, there is not simply one version of being a woman, but several, none of them stable or constant. The emphasis on external objects is a way for her to visualise this notion; by placing focus on things outside of the body and claiming them to be the inside she demonstrates the flexibility of sex through a bodily and material performativity.

The objects emphasised by Klara ('corset, gloves, high heels and strap-on') are of the kind often fetishised in our culture. The power of a fetishised object is not traceable through the logic of ordinary causality but is instead to be understood as enchanted, or magical, creating a gap between the actual object (its shape, form, material and size) and the values ascribed to it.

Philosopher Bruno Latour has criticised this definition of fetishised objects, claiming its duality between actual object and fetish to be misleading. Instead of separating the object into two ('fact' and 'fetish') we should see it as a totality (a 'factish'), where object and inherent value go together, as one.[13] Transferring this line of reasoning to the example of Klara enhances the understanding of how her fetishised femininity is constructed, and the assembling of her bodily practice would be made clear. Agency is not limited solely to Klara's biological body; instead her femininity is constituted in an actual and real way by the values inherent in the attributes she uses and wears. The corset, the gloves, the high heels and her strap-on all carry values that interact with each other, their characteristics working together to construct Klara's version of what it is to be a woman. Klara is not a woman who wears high heels, gloves and a strap-on; she *becomes* a woman through the interactions of these objects, and through the queer style they create, as an assemblage. This kind of thinking is also aligned with Klara's Butlerian idea of the performative body as created through an assembling of objects.[14]

What values these objects possess is determined based on what context Klara is orientated in, and which individuals are in her close proximity. Creating the same version of femininity, by using the same kinds of objects, she is treated in very different ways depending on who is near her. The men who attacked her don't share her societal and cultural beliefs and thus reacted strongly to the values of the objects. The meaning was as obvious to them as it was to the people surrounding her during the Pride parade.

Present in Klara's choice of words and the way she describes her version of femininity is a political drive, which of course also shows in her Pride-participation. The context of the Pride parade is essential for the liberation aspects she describes, as shown when the same street where the parade passed through becomes the site of the attack. It is not the place itself, but how it is used and queerified by the Pride-participants, that makes it possible for Klara to act out her synthetic version of femininity. The space itself is thus to be considered neither heteronormative nor queer, but dependent on which actions are carried out in that particular place, at that particular time. Actions transform space, whilst space facilitates actions.

Power and politics

As explained, queer aesthetics is not about one particular style (such as the burlesque look Klara is displaying) but is instead defined by its political drive to oppose normative gender discourses. This is because queer aesthetics concern issues of power and resistance; looks, politics and theory are all part of a larger queer practice:

> If we want to make the anti-social turn in queer theory, we must be willing to turn away from the comfort zone of polite exchange in order to embrace a truly political negativity, one that promises, this time, to fail, to make a mess, to fuck shit up, to be loud, unruly, impolite, to breed resentment, to bash back, to speak up and out, to disrupt, assassinate, shock and annihilate …[15]

Queer is, by definition, indocile and difficult, linking it in an intimate way to the practice of subverting authority. However, to articulate resentment and question powerful discourses you need a potent voice, making the terms of power and resistance not opposites but prerequisites. Klara is violating unwritten codes of conduct, but the men are breaking the law, making her transgressions lawful while they would be the ones charged. This is blurred territory, and whilst both the men and Klara are in breach of societal norms only the men are breaking the law. Klara is well aware of the fact that some people are provoked by her appearance, and yet she continues to dress in this manner; what she compromises is how she moves through the city not how she dresses. This way, she is in a way limited by the men's actions while at the same time remaining uncompromising with her ideals.

The attack on Makode

Makode is a well-known artist and club host in Stockholm, often arranging events with a queer twist. One winter night he is walking home from a night out, dressed in tight jeans and a glittery sequined jacket, his long dreadlocks artistically placed on top of his head, when he suddenly hears someone shouting obscenities on the street behind him. He has almost reached the entrance of his building when he finally turns around and sees a man approaching rapidly. Makode hurries inside but the man, who is suddenly joined by another man Makode hadn't noticed before, apparently knows the entrance code and follows. With not a second to spare, Makode manages to unlock his front door and shut it closed when the men arrive, trying to break it down, shouting homophobic slurs along with death threats.

After that night he no longer feels safe, neither in his clothes nor in his apartment. What he used to wear on a daily basis without thinking about it has now become an issue. Was it his conspicuous appearance that caused the men's anger? This was the first time he had ever been subject to a hate crime, and he was confused; how would he know if a pair of jeans is too tight or a shirt looks gay? For some time after the attack he tries to downplay his queerness by wearing less flamboyant clothing, also avoiding going to queer venues. Since the attack happened right outside his apartment even this space seems unsafe, and he contacts his landlord for relocation.

The attack was aimed at Makode's person, and took place in his apartment building, thus marking two things in his life: his body and his home, both of which are to be considered as a point of origin for all his activities and experiences of the city. In a way, after the attack they blend together in Makode's attempt to leave them behind: by changing his looks and by changing his address. The place isn't safe because Makode himself isn't. Only by changing his looks and moving away from the place where it happened, removing himself from that particular spot, can he feel safe again.

Makode's reaction demonstrates again the agency of objects and how the notion of factishes works. The body is, in this case, constituted through the artefacts Makode incorporates into his body image; the tight jeans, the shiny sequins, as well as movements and gestures, but also the place where the body is contextualised. The body comes into being through the interaction of many different components, some of which stay in the body image a longer time, some only briefly. Makode's life is threatened by his display of a queer style; the ways the garments and accessories are combined create a queer presence in the city, which provokes others. The style exists because of Makode's desire for it to do so; it is through his will that the objects are put together. The tight jeans, the sequins, along with his extravagant dreadlocks, are all powerful objects, recognised as such by all three individuals in the example. The men who threaten Makode's life recognise his look as decidedly queer and act to silence him, to make him dress in other types of garments, to make him look less queer.

What the example shows is how the struggle between the two opposing value systems is articulated through materiality. Temporarily Makode chooses other garments than the most ostentatious, as a direct response to the violent attack. The garments are too powerful to use and for a while he has to wear less conspicuous clothing. It is important to not forget the temporal aspect of the production of meaning through interaction, as it is a constantly ongoing process. As such, the queer style is always changing in relation to all the different components involved: artefacts, places and biological matter. In the words of Latour, 'Objects appear associable with one another and with social ties only *momentarily.* This is quite normal since it is through their very heterogeneous agencies that social ties have been provided with completely different shapes and figures ....'[16]

The bodily process involves more things and is more irregular and more fluctuating than mere biological matters. By changing from the sequined jacket to a less noticeable one and relocating his home, he changes the terms for his body image in the city, which also, as a consequence, transforms his connotations of queer style. The body image is dependent on spatial context, as the space surrounding the body also defines the shape of the body image.[17]

The attack prompts Makode into moving to another part of the city, leaving behind the apartment now associated with the violence of the two men, and instead settling down in Södermalm, generally considered more bohemian and queer-friendly. What this move symbolises is how the attack is stretched out over time, including events taking place days, weeks or even months after the actual incident. No actions should thus be viewed as isolated or separate from each other; the attack affected Makode's way of dressing, where he lives and how he moves through the city. The city itself is in this manner also affected by the attack, by Makode's reaction to move from one place to another, creating a void where he once was and adding an extra dimension to the place he inhabits now. The attack did not delete or even diminish the queer presence in the city; it merely relocated parts of it.

Summary

The queer materiality I have described in the text is not about specific garments or objects but about combinations, interactions and assemblages, creating a style that makes sense in a specific place and point in time. The queer subversion of meaning exists in the shape and forms of the objects the informants use, but it is activated when objects meet and interact (as in the example of the corset and the strap-on). The biological body is one of many agents, working together to produce queer styles, containing strong political implications. In the extreme responses of some others, the provocation of queer styles becomes alarmingly apparent.

Inherent in the queer stance are a subversion of power positions and a questioning of the normative gender discourse. Not everyone likes to be questioned, which both informants were made aware of by others, who opposed their ways of looking queer. The right to visibility is central to questions of equal rights, which makes it a strong target for queerphobic individuals. Both Klara and Makode had been targeted by people objecting to their being visibly non-normative. The queer styles of Klara and Makode were transformed when they came into contact with their assailants; otherwise peaceful moments were interrupted when others suddenly reacted to their looks. Klara adjusted how she moves in and through the city, while Makode momentarily experienced a loss of security; his clothes weren't his anymore and he didn't feel safe in his own home. The power of the objects is strong and the social and cultural responses are equally powerful, something the wearer of the garments isn't always prepared for.

Though the objects, through their size and shape, carry significant cultural meaning, it isn't until it is put in a certain context, connected with other objects, that the desired, subversive style is created. Queer looks are often celebrated and its representatives considered outrageous and over-the-top. Both Klara and Makode are well-respected artists in their fields, which in large part is connected to their way of dressing and acting. But at the same time, it was their looks that made them vulnerable to attacks from others: their visibility placing them outside normative context and thus making them easy prey. In this way, the style they create holds a distinct meaning, at the same time playful and deeply political.

10

MATERIAL EVIDENCE: SEXUAL ASSAULT, PROVOCATIVE CLOTHING AND FASHION

Joanne Turney

Inspired by Mary Simmerling's poem 'What I was Wearing', Jen Brockman and Mary Wyandt Hiebert created an art installation as part of the University of Arkansas's RESPECT programme ('What Were You Wearing?', 2017) that literally redressed the pervasive myths surrounding rape in Western cultures. The installation combined student testimony of sexual assault, which was recorded and displayed next to garments that were representative of the clothing they were wearing during the time of the assault/s (and in some instances there was more than one). By exhibiting clothing worn alongside the words, memories and experiences of 'survivors', the exhibition aimed to demonstrate that popular conceptions surrounding dress and rape were problematic and inaccurate. Here, the focus was on debunking rape mythologies: myths that ultimately result in victim blaming, whilst simultaneously reinstate gender and clothing stereotypes that originate from perceptions of Victorian morality, i.e. women who dress 'provocatively' are 'asking' to be raped.[1] Indeed, by viewing the clothing on display, the spectator became acutely aware of the preposterousness of this statement or attitude; the clothes exhibited were bland, ordinary, mundane, jeans, t-shirts, jumpers, clothing that anyone, of any age, background or from anywhere, could be wearing at any time.

The significance of the 'What Were You Wearing?' installation can be read through statistics, with the Rape, Abuse, and Incest National Network (RAINN), recording that 11.2 per cent of all US university students (men and women) experience some kind of sexual assault, and an overall total of 23.1 per cent of women students experienced rape or sexual assault through force or coercion.

Sex crimes are the most prevalent of all crimes on campuses nationwide, yet 4 out of 5 students don't report the crime. Off campus, the situation is equally bleak.[2] Rape is a serious crime, and one that is endemic in contemporary society. RAINN state that 'every 98 seconds an American is sexually assaulted. Every 8 minutes, that victim is a child. Meanwhile, only 6 out of 1,000 perpetrators will end up in prison',[3] statistics that were apparent in the 'What Were You Wearing?' installation, which included a child's summer dress, and comments from respondents who, during the assault, just wanted to return to 'watching cartoons'.[4]

Likewise, in the UK, and in relation to statistics from 2009, Grubb and Turner note that 'approximately 4.2 per cent of women in the UK have been raped at least once since the age of 16 and that 19.5 per cent of all women have suffered some form of sexual victimisation since the same age',[5] although they acknowledge that these figures are likely to be grossly underestimated as very few victims report the crime.[6] In each example, the focus is on the ubiquity of assaults versus the infrequency of reporting, and this is a culturally constructed problem that is exacerbated by discussions of victims clothing, i.e. our attention is focused on the actions of the victim and not on those of the perpetrator. This is a much wider issue and one that cannot be addressed here but one that highlights a gender bias and disparity that favours male dominance (power/control over others) over female agency (choosing what to wear and getting dressed).

In the light of this statistical data, and in a climate where sexual assault has been central to Women's political activism and media debate (Women's March on Washington, January 2017 and the #MeToo# campaign, 2017, sparked by the exposure of serial sexual abuser and Hollywood media mogul Harvey Weinstein), this chapter considers the ways in which clothing has been considered an indicator of sexual availability, be it provocative or immodest, and how this has been used as a semiotic or sartorial clue in daily life as well as in courtrooms in the US and UK. As criminal acts are central to this investigation, legal representations and uses of clothing as evidence in the procedure from reporting a crime through to trial are discussed in relation to wider understandings of the meaning of clothes.

The significance of clothing as a player in the culpability of women as sexual predators or victims is important here, because dressing is not an unconscious act, whilst encouraging sexual assault is something considered horrific and not sought consciously. We are all accomplished semioticians and are only too aware of sartorial codes that allow us to project particular identities[7] that facilitate our 'dressing for success', that enhance our physical appeal, make us feel better about ourselves and ultimately allow us to fit in with or stand out from the crowd. At no stage do our clothes 'ask' to be violated, for crimes to be committed against us, yet these narratives dominate our understanding of sexual assault in the media, in general conversation and in the courtroom. In addressing how and why these concepts persist, the chapter will discuss how clothing is used in legal settings as a means of 'standing in' for the victim of sex crimes, and how undressing the victim allows her to be redressed as the representation of a particular kind of morality based primarily on the clothes she was wearing. Clothing here becomes a guise; a substitute for the real, lived body, a material witness that is also material evidence. The aim is to consider clothing not only as embodied and disembodied but also as representative of Eco's 'clues' that leave clothing and its meaning or intent open to misinterpretation.[8]

Finally, the chapter aims to consider why women might want to dress in a manner that might be considered 'provocative', and how this relates to notions of fashion, fashionability and attractiveness. By analysing sociological studies on provocative clothing and its perception by both men and women, the discussion aims to align fashion with sexiness within a post-feminist, neoliberal cultural climate, in which the objectified female body is central to mainstream expressions of beauty and female empowerment.

Material evidence: Clothing in court

Rape is defined as forced or coerced penetrative sex (oral, anal, vaginal). Most frequently, emphasis is placed on 'force' (the use of a weapon or injuries sustained by the victim) and 'may serve as a proxy for proof of non-consent'.[9]

In sexual assault, and especially rape cases, clothing is frequently used as evidence. There are many reasons for this, but primarily these can be reduced to two themes: a) to show physical evidence (blood, semen, violence, use of weapon or merely what the victim was wearing)[10] and b) to demonstrate the character and/or mental state of the victim (and sometimes, the defendant). Clothing is therefore a significant and continuous element of the reporting, recording and trial process. Clothes are listed and recorded, as if the victim were undressing, outer- to undergarments, with descriptions including damage, staining and, condition, de-personalising that which is considered highly personal: the way in which one presents oneself to the world. Embodied objects are disembodied, treasured possessions – favourite shirts, everyday underwear – are disembodied from a state of materiality to the form of words – words with meanings that are culturally, rather than personally, constructed. Likewise, the protective outer layer of clothing, one's social mask, is revealed, leaving the victim naked, bare, open to scrutiny. So, regardless of how the victim's clothing will be used or interpreted in court, clothing is not only evidence of but also witness to a criminal act; it bears traces of both the victim and the perpetrator that are both physical and metaphysical. Clothes are more than mere garments but are players in the scenario that will unfold and be told again and again.

Although clothing is often inadmissible as evidence in court cases, photographs of clothing are frequently admitted. This means that clothing, or the photographic representation of it, can be staged or framed to overemphasise specific elements, details or points (both the defence and prosecution exploit this). The act of photographing in these instances is almost like 'laundering'; it removes the personal or the 'human' connection, distancing it from the wearer and the experience of wearing, so 'my dress that I bought at my favourite shop', for example, is replaced with recognisable, generic words that are all open to cultural interpretation, i.e. 'skirt', 'mini skirt', 'bra', 'lace bra' 'shoes', 'stiletto heels' and so on. Not only does this imply that clothing and its meaning are not fixed and thus can be manipulated but the transformation of object to image further distances the 'evidence' from the 'scene of the crime' and the 'victim'. Although the clothing 'witnessed' the assault, that 'memory' has been eradicated and de-personalised, and embodied garments are reduced to everyday language.

In these instances, image and word become more important than the actual garment because it is presented as a series of semiotic clues that point to the linguistic assumptions of what that item of clothing should look like. This recognition is extended then to incorporate sociocultural assumptions regarding the 'appropriateness' of the garment to the circumstances of wearing/attack. These judgements then hint towards morality or intention of the victim, whilst simultaneously acting as a means of de-personalisation (through generalisation) and disembodiment (away from or 'undressed' in relation to the victim whose clothing is embodied and displayed in court). Clothing becomes a 'language' that can be read and understood, which is problematic inasmuch as it suggests something tangible or definite rather than a series of loose dress codes, manners and social conventions that are constantly under review, challenged and subverted. Regardless of this, within a courtroom setting the semiotics of dress becomes a foil for the victim – a state by which the 'covering' potential of garments is transformed not only as a 'revealer' of 'truth' as evidence but also as the symbolic tropes of popular concepts of a 'natural justice'.

The *just* world theory[11] promotes the notion that, as a general rule, people (society, communities, individuals) believe the world to be a fair place.[12] This implies that collectively there is a consensus by which personal responsibility is reciprocated with group responsibility or, perhaps more damning, one gets what one deserves (just desserts). Therefore, people/women who are raped are possibly looking to be raped, and those convicted of crime are more likely to actually be the perpetrators of said crime.

Such general belief systems are important in relation to the construction of social norms, especially if judgement is based primarily on perception and appearance, and might therefore emphasise other stereotypical characteristics emanating from 'understandings' of gender, morality and sartorial codes, amongst other things. We might consider these assumptions as popular 'truisms' and therefore give them more credibility than they deserve. So, in sexual assault cases, dress becomes a significant factor in the apportioning of blame because a) clothing is morally loaded and is frequently understood in this manner, b) getting dressed and making clothing choices is a conscious act, and if one understands the moral codes of clothing (a) then the act of dressing becomes one of personal responsibility/safety and c) the context of dress in relation to the location and circumstance of the attack – whether the victim put themselves in danger because they were inappropriately or provocatively dressed – again emphasises personal responsibility. Sometimes context offers a more favourable outcome, as although primarily understood as derived from internal causes (the role of the victim) crime can also arise from external forces, such as luck, in which the victim is in the wrong place at the right time, and it is these contexts that are articulated most strongly in the testimony of contributors to the 'What Were You Wearing?' project.

Dress becomes an extension of personal responsibility, of knowingness, whether in relation to sartorial codes and/or sexual provocation, as well as social norms of propriety, which firmly places the victim as complicit, thus challenging the concept of innocence. Indeed, many sexual assaults go unreported precisely for this reason; that the victim feels that she will not be believed or will have her morality and character questioned in the public glare of the courtroom. The private is made public; it is not merely her underwear that is on display, it is her reputation, sense of self and personal morality.

Therefore, the victim must appear as virginal or 'sexless' as possible, as morally upstanding, to counteract what will be revealed in evidence. So, the disembodied and de-personalised garments presented as evidence, dirty and stained, are presented as a direct contrast to the appearance of the victim in the courtroom. As Sterling notes,

> When her everyday clothes, including her underwear, appear piece by piece before the jury, the alleged victim appears to have violated the modesty imperative. Ironically, the violation is not her own act, but a function of the judicial system. Violating the modesty imperative places the victim in the territory of the objectifying imperative. The objectifying imperative invites society to treat her as deviant and therefore deserving of disciplinary abuse. The punishment is meted out as acquittal of the rapist.[13]

It is usual for the victim to appear in the courtroom in conservative dress. This is an intentional act to make the victim appear formal, in attire suitable for the very formal setting. This may not be clothing that she would normally wear.

Here, clothes are little more than a costume; like the evidence they, de-personalise, remove any sense of self from the victim and reduce her to a player, dressed appropriately, for her appearance in the drama of the courtroom. Her clothing, often overtly modest, mirrors the formal clothing of the judge and court officials, establishing gravitas and witness credibility by adhering to the 'rules'. We see before us an 'honest' woman, a woman who is stripped of personality and personal details.

The de-personalisation of dress within the courtroom is distinct from the de-personalised photographs of garments worn during the attack, and although courtroom dress may demonstrate social compliance, this can conflict unfavourably with the evidence presented in physical or photographic form. For example, in court modest dress will not reveal or indicate any sign of underwear, yet the victim's underwear is likely to be referenced in the case. In the William Kennedy Smith trial, the victim's actual underwear was inadmissible in court. However, photographs of it were, clearly displaying the label Victoria's Secret, linking the wearer with the brand identity, and through the use of photography associated the wearer with the sexy calendars the brand regularly produces. By association, the photograph thus implies that anyone who wears this brand of lingerie would be open to sexual activity, and, in turn, sexual assault.[14] This is important because the victim's underwear might not have been visible prior to the attack, and therefore its role in articulating any kind of sexual proclivity to an onlooker would be negligible or irrelevant. So, the photograph narrates a story based on a popular conception of what 'Victoria's Secret' as a brand represents, i.e. 'sexy' lingerie, soft porn calendars and catwalk shows and beautiful models and thus implies that consumers of this product wish to buy into this lifestyle. Therefore personal identity merges with brand identity, commodifying the individual.

If the legal system places so much weight on rather simplistic semiotic analyses of dress, then how will the victim's 'obvious' costumed and groomed appearance be met by jurors? Do jurors see the victim as 'dressing up' for court, and the clothing worn during the rape as a more authentic indicator of her own agency (or lack of it) in clothing choices? Indeed as Sterling argues,

> The prosecutor 'coaches' the victim to seem 'as virginal as possible', not only because she knows that the victim's dress at trial sends a message about her sexuality to the jury, but also because the prosecutor wants the jury to believe that the alleged victim is a modest woman, undeserving of the disciplinary abuse.[15]

This, of course, is a matter of perception that is constructed in response to a combination of somewhat fluid definitions of modesty/promiscuity and how this manifests as 'evidence' through dress, make-up, styling and the context in which these clothes were worn. The premise that clothing + context = attitude, intent, morality and provocation seems on the one hand to offer agency, whilst simultaneously placing a huge amount of weight on conjecture and somewhat outmoded semiotic, sartorial and behavioural codes. For example, the defence attorney frequently contextualises the clothing presented in evidence to the jury through the language commonly used to describe women's sexual availability and activity, thus making the near impossible visual and interpretative leap from virgin to whore (courtroom victim to disembodied underwear) reducible to a simple phrase or sentence, such as 'slutty'.

'Slutty' clothing, as described by Sterling in 1995, was described in the 1970s (somewhat more politely, but nonetheless significantly) as 'provocative' or 'seductive' dress. Examples of specific 'seductive' garments include, but are not limited to, the following: 'fitted, hip-hugger jeans',[16] 'midriff tops',[17] 'short skirts',[18] 'low-cut tops' and 'see-through' or 'clingy' garments and 'no underwear'.[19] What we might derive from this is that the ways in which clothing overtly reveals what lies beneath them, i.e. figure-hugging, flesh-revealing or see-through, is primarily a means of conveying sexual availability and/or provocativeness. Indeed, by 1991, in Schult and Schnider's study of appearance, perception and rape victims, focused on more revealing and overtly provocative clothing, including fishnet stockings, high heels and G-string underpants,[20] which not only bare lots of flesh are also garments that are part of an iconology of the prostitute (the non-respectable woman[21]). This analogy and comparison is important; it suggests that a non-respectable woman has had many sexual experiences, and therefore the legislature will view rape as merely *another* sexual encounter, and therefore sex in this situation is just an act of seduction.[22]

Unfortunately for victims and women in general, studies during the 1970s and 1980s concluded that what constituted 'seductive' clothing by men was not corroborated by women, with data indicating that young women were more likely to dress 'fashionably' rather than 'sexily'.[23] Indeed, many female respondents were unable to identify specific garments as 'sexy'.[24]

What is under discussion, then, is whether items of clothing might be considered sexually provocative, why this might be and whether acts of dressing in said clothes is a conscious or deliberate attempt to seduce? But seduction is not sexual assault, and this is a line that seems to have been marginalised or ignored by courts and sociologists alike. Nonetheless, studies conclude that women may dress to be 'fashionable' or 'attractive', rather than sexy. This is evidenced in Mazelan's 1980 report on perceptions of rape victims, which concludes that 39 per cent of the female population 'dressed in a manner likely to provoke rape',[25] which indicates the level of confusion regarding terms, and/

or highlights the controversial, circumstantial and interpretation of clothing in relation to such serious crime.[26]

Referencing Warshaw's 1988 study of 'date rape',[27] Johnson discusses how men might perceive rape as 'justified' when considering who paid for what, how much was spent and whether the woman dressed 'provocatively'.[28] Johnson's own study emphasised how a sample group of men responded to 'date rape' scenarios that highlighted circumstances, money spent and the clothing and demeanour of the victim, when they were asked to consider the extent to which they would have acted like the perpetrator. By 1995, when Johnson's research was published, clothing was less a contributing factor than the confusion surrounding what constituted rape, specifically in a 'date' situation.[29] As Stirling acknowledges, regardless of what one was wearing, context and perception of intent are fundamental to the crime: 'It appears that such transposition distorts the meaning of almost all women's clothes, rendering it provocative or objectifying no matter if it was intended or perceived in its original setting.'[30]

Perception of provocative dress and the intention of the wearer has been the subject of many socio-legal studies. In Edmonds and Cahoon's study students at Augusta College, GA, were shown two images of the same woman.[31] In both images the woman's face was obscured, encouraging students to consider only her clothing (although her gait and posture were evident). They were asked to consider which image (if any) showed any indicators that might lead to the rape or robbery of the woman depicted.[32] The emphasis here was on clothing; the woman was dressed either conservatively or 'sexy clothes'. The study concluded that respondents found the woman in 'sexy' clothing more likely to be raped and/ or robbed than the conservatively dressed one.[33] This implies that 'sexy' clothes do not merely equate with sexual availability but also with additional levels of perceived moral transgression. Therefore, we might also conclude that wavering from sartorial norms or merely dressing in a manner deemed 'inappropriate' might be considered an act of social as well as a moral deviance.

The focus here is on clothing, but it is important to note that often other attributes are treated and manipulated in the same way. For example, a woman who wears make-up as opposed to one who does not might be considered more sexually alluring and thus more responsible for her attack. An attractive woman might be considered more naturally 'seductive' or have her appearance enhanced symbolically through descriptions in court documents, i.e. 'Beauty Queen',[34] which might be considered either 'wholesome' or 'vain', depending on whether the term is being used by the prosecution or the defence.

So, ultimately, it is the strategy of the defence to re-undress the victim and reveal her sexual character through her clothing, and it is this courtroom performance that is considered most conclusive to jurors.[35] Clothes therefore become significant indicators of morality and intent,[36] which might also be considered 'victim blaming'.[37]

Why are clothes 'sexy'? Perceptions of provocative dress

In its most basic sense, clothing is worn next to the body and as such can be considered a boundary[38] between the personal and the private, – a protective surface that covers and shields the vulnerable flesh beneath from external predators. Just from this simple assumption we can start to see discourses surrounding the body and sex, the constructs of the erotic versus the social body, the clean and the dirty, the intimate and the shared, emerging as if clothing were merely a foil, a present waiting to be unwrapped. This seeming illicitness is developed further when we consider the potential of clothing as a practical and symbolic object. As a mask, clothing simultaneously reveals and conceals, thus rendering the body a site for both dressing and undressing, and ultimately a site of the gaze, an object of striptease.[39]

Fashion, a product of modernity, of Debord's 'Spectacle',[40] in which the consumption and display of new consumer goods, trends and styles epitomise and characterise the zeitgeist and one's place in it, offers the opportunity for consumers, and especially women, to position themselves as part of that spectacle, to parade, to show off and to be consumed by participants and watchers alike. In Walter Benjamin's unfinished *Arcades Project* (written between 1927 and 1940, but first published in 1999), this practice is described as 'illusory', a means by which women are commodified, and much like that of the prostitute women become both subject and object, the seller and the wares.[41] So what is evident here is that fashion commodifies and, by association, objectifies women. This constant, pervasive dialogue between the fashion system, from its clothing and accessories, to magazine spreads and advertising through to extended industries such as film, and later television, seeks to encourage women to enhance their appearance in order, if one is to take a post-Marxist approach, to purchase the elements of life that capitalism has seemingly taken from them, i.e. love, friendship, happiness. So, as Benjamin asserts, the natural is replaced with the artificial, and the image and its presentation becomes a primary means of self-expression and empowerment. As fashion trends continuously change, the race to keep up and ultimately escape the decay and ageing of the natural body becomes the end rather than the means.

For Benjamin, the illusion of youth and beauty are central to the success and presentation of fashion, but his argument could well be extended to include sexual attractiveness – or, as Lipovetsky notes, 'the poetics of seduction',[42] as 'youth' and particularly pre-maternal women are considered culturally most desirable – but also to notions of the erotic, in relation to the presentation of the dressed and undressed body. Clothing has historically had a clear association with concepts of morality and social propriety, especially with regard to the behaviour and presentation of women.[43] Ultimately based on its proclivity to simultaneously reveal and conceal the body, by the eighteenth-century clothing, was considered a sign of civilisation, a means of presenting social progression, specifically the distance between Western and non-Western peoples, so the more clothing, the more civilised the wearer.[44] Even though we now have discredited much of this colonial bias, elements linger, especially in relation to the perception of sexual availability of the dressed and undressed body, which we might also consider as the relationship between the exotic and the erotic. The colonial discourse centralises on the power of the viewer to control that which is viewed; it is a master/servant relationship based on cultural and racial difference, but it is also one that assumes the dominance of men over women, rich over poor and so on. Such an analogy establishes binaries, opposites, that are articulated through dress as simply 'like us' or 'not like us' or just as 'good' or 'bad', with the dressed body prioritised socially and culturally.

From the post-war period onwards these boundaries have been blurred, to the extent that the objectified, sexual or sexy female body is the dominant form of mainstream beauty, and this has been perpetuated by the fashion industry. For example, Colin McDowell draws attention to the ways in which fashion trends emphasise and eroticise specific body parts, i.e. midriff, waist, bottom, breasts, sometimes as a means of ridiculing the female body, as with Jean Paul Gaultier's conical breasts (1990),[45] or as a means of performing characteristics, such as 'flirtatious' or 'virtuous'.[46] Such an assertion, albeit rather simplistic, ties fashion not merely to clothing styles but to fashionable bodies too, both of which highlight the promotion of an eroticised gaze.

Of course, fashion is not solely responsible for the objectification of women, nor do women slavishly follow it. However, as a cultural construct the objectification of women is presented through the dressed/undressed body, and therefore fashion is a major player in perpetuating the female body as a site of desire, and in the construction of woman as a rather one-dimensional sexual sign.[47] Nonetheless, clothing considered provocative, i.e. tight, figure-hugging, transparent, low-cut or short, showing flesh (midriff, etc.) has, since the 1960s, coincided with concomitant fashion trends. So it is possible to say that fashion trends are both provocative and objectify women to the point where they are considered knowing and/or potential victims of sexual assault.

This might be because a) fashion embraces and/or creates the zeitgeist and is therefore constantly pushing against what might be considered 'acceptable' and b) as an industry, fashion is reliant on selling not just products but lifestyles, so the rather well-worn advertising standard that 'sex sells' becomes the pivot on which the neoliberal body project meets a Lacanian lack that is fuelled and potentially met through desire and the consumption of goods.[48]

The representation of what might be considered 'sexy' is promoted through fashion advertising, magazines and the media generally and therefore becomes central to the iconography of both fashion and the fashionable body. As fashion is the primary source of circulating, disseminating, constructing and perpetuating images of beauty, when what is 'fashionable' is 'blurred' with or barely distinct from what might be considered provocative, those messages become mixed and confused, and this can prove dangerous, as women frequently dress to be fashionable and/or attractive, and, as Lipovetsky notes, fashion is ultimately defined by what women seek in appearance: 'seduction and metamorphosis'.[49]

The problem with an emphasis on knowingly dressing in a manner that might be considered provocative is ultimately one of two halves – *who* considers *what* provocative and the intended outcome of dressing in *those* clothes. In Moor's 2010 study, investigating why women choose to dress in provocative clothes, she concluded that these questions were addressed and answered in different ways, depending on whether respondents were men or women.[50] Moor's findings demonstrate that women understand fashion as a means of being 'attractive' to themselves or others and, to choose different looks that would enhance their attractiveness, with few considering their style as an intention to seduce or to gain attention from men.[51] Conversely, male respondents overwhelmingly saw 'sexily' dressed women as tempting and seductive, with nearly half always enjoying looking at women dressed in this manner.[52] So although there is a disparity in understanding and intention, the power relationships articulated in this study are vital in understanding fashion, beauty, provocative dress and gender relations. Moor concludes,

> To women, the stimulation experienced by men in response to their sexy look is assurance of their attractiveness. They do not aim to be stared or gazed at indiscriminately, as they certainly do not intend to have their space invaded against their will. In other words, they do not mean to be treated as sex objects. However, in a social structure as oppressive to women as the present one, in which men are permitted, even encouraged, to view and treat women as objects for sexual use (Berger, 1972; MacKinnon, 1989), and in which women's sexualised appearance has been made a central component of their social value (Colagero, 2004; LeMoncheck, 1985; Muehlenkamp & Saris-Baglama, 2002), it is not surprising to find that women, being cognisant of this reality, comply with the expectation to present themselves in the sexual manner that many of them do.[53]

Responses to provocative dress are essentially built on concepts of the objectification of women, which is now considered the norm, largely because of its ubiquity and the pornification or over-sexualisation of mainstream culture. Likewise, boundaries between what is considered 'sexy' dressing and trying to be 'attractive' are blurred, as many women consider their clothing choices as 'attractive', and men consider them 'provocative'.[54] Much of this is predetermined by social power and lack of it, and a means of exerting a 'sense of self'. So the disparity evidenced between an overtly 'sexualised look' and 'attractiveness' emphasises a blurred boundary between what is popularly considered to be female 'beauty'[55] and the widespread pornification of daily life,[56] which has created a climate in which the objectification of women is ubiquitous and thus normalised.[57]

We might consider the pornification of society, as outlined by authors such as Paasonen et al.,[58] as one symptom that arises from many more sociocultural conditions, i.e. postmodernism, neoliberalism, post-feminism, the body project and so on. So, pornification is defined as the overt or hyper-sexualisation of mainstream culture, i.e. the media and fashion industries, borrows iconography from pornography, and this is deemed not merely acceptable but desirable. This occurs not just in relation to the sexualised body but also in relation to gesture, posturing and the gaze. The combination of these factors, particularly in fashion advertising (and those for 'seductive' products such as perfume and cosmetics), demonstrates sexual availability and intent (slightly open lips, heavy-lidded eyes, soft posture). The ubiquity of these images obviously increases objectification, which, if we believe Lipovetsky, has always been the intention of fashion.[59]

The ubiquity of objectification and the concept of contemporary femininity as sexually powerful is an interesting paradox that arises amidst notions of post-feminism.[60] The 'power' of sexual allure presented is indeed that of the prostitute or porn star, which may be an (albeit minor) means of financial independence, but one that largely is constructed not to 'please' oneself but to bow or conform to essentially monolithic male fantasies, on a mass scale. Nonetheless, post-feminists continue to proclaim fashion as a means of personal empowerment, indicating that dressing in a 'sexy' or sexual manner is a means in which to express sexual power and liberation. Indeed, post-feminists like Rene Denfield argue that feminist critiques of objectification and 'provocative' dress in relation to sexual assaults on US university campuses are representative of a 'New Victorianism' that stifles sexual freedom of expression and repeats sexual stereotypes, i.e. women as passive and men as sexual predators.[61] Although there seems to be a logic in the post-feminist stance, looking at the sociological studies cited here combined with the proclivity of pornification and everyday sexism in contemporary society, it seems more like hollow rhetoric. What we see is an emphasis on appearance, an impression of 'sexiness' that defies the potential of that term, one that is devoid of imagination, intellect and genuine personal empowerment.[62] So, we are witness to the ultimate gendered Catch-22 situation; women who dress for themselves are actually dressing for men and men who think women dress provocatively to please them, as indicated in the sociological studies – something women respondents deny – are actually proved right.

Conclusion

This chapter started with an overview of the 'What Were You Wearing?' installation that aimed to debunk rape mythologies, myths that lead to victim blaming. There is no doubt that this exhibition was poignant and thought provoking, and the banality of the dress displayed defied notions of the objectified body and 'sexy' dressing. Yet regardless of the material 'evidence' presented in the installation, the myth persists to the extent that it is almost a prerequisite in interrogations and in seeking culpability, hence the title of the exhibition.

It is difficult to deny that what we wear, how we wear it and how our clothes are perceived by those around us are extremely important. In sexual assault and rape trials, clothing is presented as a series of semiotic clues that point to the morality or intention of the victim, whilst simultaneously acting as a means of de-personalisation (through generalisation) and disembodiment (away from or 'undressed' in relation to the victim who's clothing is embodied and displayed in court). In these examples, clothing is a foil for the victim – a state by which the 'covering' potential of garments is transformed not only as a 'revealer' of 'truth' as evidence but also as the symbolic tropes of popular concepts of a 'natural justice'. The victim is characterised by her clothes, whilst her clothes are stripped away, and replaced with de-personalised formal clothing deemed suitable for a trial and courtroom setting. We might see clothing as paradoxical here, representing enormous amounts of circumstantial and conjectural 'evidence', implying everything whilst simultaneously meaning nothing; they are real and symbolic. Either way, there is an emphasis on 'knowingness'; on knowing what different types of clothing 'mean' in different contexts, and thus 'dressing provocatively', whether this is a rigid or fluid term or if it can be universally specified or not, is presumed to be generally understood by the population and is therefore considered a deliberate and conscious act.

Concomitantly, fashion, perhaps more than any time in history, and because of its democratisation and pervasiveness or dominance within mainstream culture, now clearly and aggressively articulates its purpose, to transform and seduce.[63] Fashionable clothing, presented as 'attractive', or offering the potential to 'transform' the body, overtly, and in response to what has been described as the pornification of society, becomes a means and method of seduction, blurring boundaries between beauty and sex. Likewise, in a culture that privileges the 'look' or the surface over everything else, women frequently associate their appearance with their social worth. In the acceptance of this heightened objectification, Benjamin's 'woman of fashion' turns full-circle; it reaffirms patriarchy and the woman as a mannequin but clothing acts not as a mask to what lies beneath but as an inscription of sexual availability or nakedness. The wrapping is the present, and thus the cycle of artificiality is complete. So as long as women understand and accept 'sexy dressing' as attractive and as currency (whether social, cultural or economic), and men consider what women wear as deliberately provocative, and as long as courts blame victims rather than punishing perpetrators, rape myths will remain central to a collective consciousness, and fashion will continue to provoke.

11

SKULLS AND CROSSBONES: AMERICA'S CONFEDERACY OF PIRATES

Anne Cecil

The whole entourage had exploded in terms of numbers, of roadies and technicians, and of hangers-on and groupies. For the first time we travelled in our own hired plane, with the lapping tongue painted on. We had become a pirate nation, moving on a huge scale under our own flag, with lawyers, clowns, attendants.

KEITH RICHARDS, *LIFE*[1]

It would be easy for the layperson to attribute the recent proliferation of pirate iconography in American fashion, particularly the skull and crossbones, to the buzz around Disney's *Pirates of the Caribbean* film franchise. In fact, the recent trend was already entrenched long before the movie hype began. Ralph Lauren's Rugby appeared in 2004, featuring the Jolly Roger as logo emblem. Many other designers and retailers from all price points and markets had been using pirate symbols long before. In fact, pirate iconology and iconography is never completely out of American fashion. While its popularity waxes and wanes in the mainstream, numerous youth subcultures wear the symbols with pride, keeping them alive until they are next co-opted and brought to the fore through mass fashion outlets.

The American obsession and fascination with pirates is deeply embedded in US culture. In a sense, Americans and pirates are interchangeable, sharing a great deal in their culture and ideologies. Using a scholarly analysis of the golden age of piracy through the works of David Cordingly, Pat Croce,

Gabriel Kuhn, John Matthews and Marcus Rediker and popular culture's constant romanticisation of pirates through a variety of media combined with an investigation of piracy today, this chapter will explore the similarities in ideologies and trace the acculturation of pirate iconography into American consumer society through the military, sports, subcultures and mainstream fashion. While subcultural theory has moved beyond the investigations of the late 1970s by the Birmingham School, I have chosen to include some of the subcultural references from Dick Hebdige's book *Subculture: The Meaning of Style* in this discussion.[2]

Introduction: Pirate symbols in American institutions

Perhaps it was America's founding by outsider malcontents, or maybe it is the portrayal of the irascible Captain Jack Sparrow so deftly played by Johnny Depp in *Pirates of the Caribbean*. Whatever the reason, America has a long history and fascination with pirates and their symbolism.

In 2011, a Google search for pirate museums in the US shows the word 'pirate' associated with 17 institutions in the US. From Maine to San Diego, the coastal states have rich recorded histories of pirates. The Atlantic seaboard was the territory of choice for the glamorised and legendary Black Beard. His black market reign ended on 2 December 1718 when Lieutenant Robert Maynard bested and beheaded him in violent hand-to-hand combat, resulting in a public display of victory by hanging the severed head from his yardarm for all to see.[3]

Pirate themes abound in other American popular culture media outlets for consumers of every age. *The Pirates of the Caribbean* franchise is hugely popular, with the brand extending from the classic Disney theme park ride, to a film trilogy and even as far as the iconic US sweets, M&Ms. Television, eager to capitalise on the trend, followed suit. On 28 March 2006, the Style channel's 'Whose Wedding is it Anyway?' featured a pirate-themed wedding on the Philadelphia tall ship-cum-restaurant, the Moshulu. ABC's 'Wife Swap' showed an episode on 18 September 2006 featuring a family who follows a code they call 'pirattitude' that focuses on questioning societal conformity. In its first season, TLC featured a $15,000+ pirate theme in their series 'Outrageous Kids Parties'. Pirates are a perennial crowd pleaser in the Mummers Parade, a renowned Philadelphia New Year's Day tradition. In the 2011 parade, the Polish American String Band offered up their rendition with a performance titled 'Shipwrecked', taking first place Captain's prize and second place in the Viewer's Choice Awards.

Similarities between pirate and American cultural ideology

As Marcus Rediker summarises in Gabriel Kuhn's *Life under the Jolly Roger: Reflections on the Golden Age of Piracy*,

> The early makers of the [pirate] tradition were what one English official in the Caribbean called 'the outcasts of all nations' – convicts, prostitutes, debtors, vagabonds, escaped slaves and indentured servants, religious radicals, and political prisoners, all of whom had migrated or been exiled to the new settlements 'beyond the line'.[4]

While on the surface it appears that the American love affair with pirates is based on their romanticised archetypes through popular culture – *The Pirate* (1822), *Treasure Island* (1883 – the book that arguably invented the modern myth of piracy and hidden treasure[5]) *Peter Pan* (1903, 1953), *The Pirates of Penzance* (1879), *Captain Blood* (1935), *Hook* (1991) and more recently *Pirates of the Caribbean* (2003) – in fact, every wave of American immigration can be described in Rediker's terms. It is this affinity with being 'outcasts' and the right to live freely that resonates and leads American ideology to share many of the same values as pirate ideology, rebellion against government in search of freedom; an established democracy where everyone is considered equal and there is justice for all; self rule created by the people for the people; unity and loyalty to your group (i.e. patriotism); pioneering new frontiers, embracing adventure and an entrepreneurial spirit, albeit based in opportunism and inclusion of peoples from multiple cultures and classes.

A brief history of piracy

Piracy is not new, nor has it been limited to Europe and the Americas. Pirates have been around as long as humans have sailed the seas. The first recorded pirate activity was noted in the seventh century BC in the Mediterranean and Aegean seas. In the fourth century, Alexander the Great tried to eradicate it, with little success. The Romans waged a more successful campaign, but they too were unable to end it completely. European history is fraught with Viking pirate attacks from the eighth to the twelfth centuries AD. With the discovery of the Americas in the fifteenth century, the riches flowed and so did the pirates. To stop the hijacking, the British government often partnered with the shrewder outlaws and created a class of privateers to shore up their naval forces, one of the key factors leading to the golden age of piracy in the seventeenth and eighteenth centuries.[6]

Piracy continues to be of great international concern today, with the most recent hotbed being off the Somali coast.

Conditions that lead to the golden age of piracy (1690–1730)

In the late 1600s and early 1700s a series of events occurred that paved the way for the golden age of piracy. In 1651, the English government passed the Navigation Acts, which stipulated that no goods could be brought into England or her colonies, for example, North America, except in British ships with British crews, levying enormous taxes. This gave rise to a huge black market to avoid taxation. In 1689, King James I made peace with Spain, ending war on the high seas, allowing the establishment of a network of shipping lanes and ports for the transport of goods predominantly by the British, Dutch, French and Spanish during the eighteenth century. Finally, in 1713 the War of Spanish Succession ended and with it the wealth enjoyed by the privateers of the day, who had been able to keep 100 per cent of their plunder. The ranks of unemployed navy men and privateers exploded. During wartime, many of the navy men had lived under harsh and unjust rule and the privateers who had enjoyed wealth from their sanctioned pillaging found their resources cut off. Both factions were disgruntled. These conditions, coupled with the large market for untaxed goods in North America, gave rise to the golden age of piracy.[7]

Articles of piracy or the US Bill of Rights?

Unhappy with poor treatment and lack of opportunity in society's sanctioned seafaring institutions, many seamen joined together with former privateers and began a life of piracy. Bands of pirates constructed a social structure based on a foundation of ancient and medieval maritime life.[8] Marcus Rediker writes,

> Pirates constructed that world in contradistinction to ways of the world they left behind, in particular to its salient figures of power, the merchant captain and the royal official, and to the system of authority those figures represented and enforced.[9]

Each crew began with a written Document of Articles that is surprisingly similar across all groups. Articles included instructions on allocation of authority, distribution of plunder and enforcement of discipline. The articles allowed the pirates to form a rough, improvised, egalitarian social order, with authority in the hands of the collective crew.[10]

Each set of articles was determined and signed by each individual crew. Each crew member was a free man with a voice in the decision-making process and the ability to move up the ship's ranks or leave the pirate life.[11] Each man had one vote. Each ship elected a captain who had complete authority in fighting, chasing and being chased. They also elected a quartermaster who championed the interests of the crew, adjudicating minor disputes and distributing food and money. In general, the plunder was distributed based on the skill level and duties of each crewman who was considered to be a risk-sharing partner, with the lowest level receiving one share.[12] Generally, the captain, quartermaster and a few others like the gunner, carpenter, sail maker and surgeon, who were integral in keeping the boat and crew going, got one and a half or two shares of the plunder.[13]

Rediker reports the governance of the ship in detail. The ship was governed by the crew in total, or by the 'council', with the crew voting on their decisions. Each ship set up a disability fund to care for those debilitated by accidents, protect skills, enhance recruitment and maintain loyalty amongst the group. Finally, the articles covered discipline, which was decided by the majority. Three major methods of discipline were employed. Fights were settled with a duel of pistols followed by swords on land. Disruptive crewmen were marooned on an island. The most egregious crimes, usually a captain who abused his power, lead to execution. Swearing an oath of honour and signing the articles cemented the crew.[14] Sound familiar? These principles form the foundation of the US Bill of Rights, the first 10 amendments of the US Constitution.

Rediker declares that during the golden age of piracy, pirates established an elaborate social code that included a system of rule, custom and symbol, a collective ethos where they banded together against common threats.[15] The most commonly known symbol of piracy is the 'pirate flag', also known as 'the Jolly Roger'.

The Jolly Roger or 'the banner of King Death'

In *Under the Black Flag*, David Cordingly states,

For more than two centuries a black flag with a white skull and crossbones emblazoned on it has been the symbol for pirates throughout the Western World. In this form it appears in all the pirate stories from Walter Scott to Robert Louis Stevenson, with artists taking their lead from the writers. The masterful pictures of Howard Pyle's *Book of Pirates* and N.C. Wyeth's illustrations to the 1911 edition of *Treasure Island* no doubt helped to fix the image in the people's minds, and it was constantly reinforced by its use on the stage and screen.[16]

With this particular image so deeply embedded in Western culture as *the* icon of piracy, it is interesting to note that the Jolly Roger is only one of many pirate flags. For many centuries Spanish cemeteries were often marked with *campo santo* or actual skulls and bones, leading to their symbolic association with the concept of death. Jenifer G. Marx notes that the image appeared on seventeenth-century English tombstones as well.[17]

David Cordingly discusses the origin and meaning of the skull in pirate iconography. Traditionally, sea captains used the symbol of the skull to mark a death at sea. Pirates co-opted this icon and other common symbolism of the day on their flags to strike mortal terror and conjure fear and dread in their prey. Working with – dancing skeletons (i.e. dancing with death), raised glasses (i.e. toasting death), weapons (i.e. slaughter to come), hourglasses and wings (i.e. time running out or flying away), each pirate combined typical symbols of skulls, crossed bones, skeletons, daggers, cutlasses, spears, bleeding hearts, hour glasses, raised glasses, wings and initials into a logo that allowed them to develop what might be considered a brand identity depending on their personal mythology.[18] Some pirates furthered their brand identity through brand extension, offering a variety of 'logo' iterations. Bartholomew Roberts, also known as Black Bart, produced one flag that showed his figure standing on the skull of a Barbadian's head and a Martinican's head to express his rage at their respective authorities trying to capture him. The flag is a visual communication that embodies the pirate code.

Marcus Rediker estimates that more than 2,500 men sailed under the skull and crossbones.[19] This symbol and the skull and cutlass became the most common of the marks; according to Marx, they became 'a potent symbol of pirate solidarity'.[20] Pirate flags became known as 'Jolly Roger' – 'the banner of King Death'. There are three schools of thought on the origin of the name. The most commonly found explanation is that Jolly Roger comes from the French 'jolie rouge', meaning 'pretty red', which had been used to describe the blood-red banners flown by privateers. The second theory bases the Jolly Roger on the Jolly, Rogue where rogue was replaced by the English Roger, a term for vagabond, beggar or vagrant. The third theory suggests that it is the flag of the Devil, also known as 'Old Roger'.[21]

Symbols were flown on red or black grounds. Two conflicting theories are offered. Croce's research suggests that the red ground indicated battle, while the black flag indicated death.[22] Conversely, Black argues that pirates used the privateers' signals where black warned against resistance and red indicated there would be no mercy.[23] Whichever is true, there is no doubt that merchant seamen during the golden age of piracy (1690–1730) did not want to see either a red or black pirate flag! The establishment of the pirate flag, much like that of the American flag, defines a break with the homeland and becomes a true of symbol transnationality.[24]

A cultural institution is first to co-opt the icon

Dick Hebdige points out Clarke et al.'s 1976 theory of subcultural adoption of objects and icons:

> The objects chosen were, either intrinsically or in their adapted forms, homologous with the focal concerns, activities, group structure and collective self-image of the subculture. They were 'objects in which (the subcultural members) could see their central values held and reflected'.[25]

It is interesting to note that the symbol of lawlessness was first adopted by the antithesis of pirates, the military. By 1759 the 17th Lancers of the British Army had co-opted the skull and crossbones as its cap badge, becoming known as the 'Death or Glory Boys'. The present-day successors, the Queen's Royal Lancers, continue its use today. US Marine Corps reconnaissance battalions also use this emblem. In 1914, submarines of the Royal Navy began flying the flag upon return from a successful combat mission where some action had taken place. In World War II this became common practice for the Royal Navy and the Royal Australian Navy, indicating bravado and stealth. Still in active use today, the Jolly Roger is the emblem of the Royal Navy Submarine Service and the US Navy Aviators.

Professional sports – swagger, solidarity and fear

While in truth cruel men and women motivated by greed, pirates were and still are legends regarded with awe and fear, two qualities that lead to success in the sporting arena.[26] Hoping to capitalise on these themes, the Pittsburgh baseball team of the National Baseball League (NBL) adopted the name 'Pirates' as early as 1891. By 1950, the Pittsburgh Pirates, and later the Oakland Raiders and Tampa Bay Buccaneers of the National Football League (NFL), adopted pirate icons as their logos. The Raiders in particular sport their image of outlaws, thugs and thieves proudly. Their players have a history of being 'dirty' (i.e. not playing fair). Fans are rabid and frenzied members of 'Raider Nation', propelling Raider skull and crossbones logo team merchandise to the top NFL team sales consistently nationwide.

Modern-day subcultures appropriate and redefine the meaning of the symbol

According to Rediker, the adoption of the flag declared the use of colour and symbol as the signifier of a gang.[27] This concept was adopted as an identifier by the infamous Crips and Bloods in Los Angeles. Numerous subcultures have and continue to appropriate the skull and crossbones icon and reposition meaning based on their own cultural ideology and identity.

Surfers, skaters, bikers, rockers, Goths, skinheads, metal heads and punks adopted the skull to symbolise dissent, angst and misunderstanding. While all these subcultures cultivated an outsider rogue identity, each group developed a meaning for the symbol within the context of their subculture's ideology. Goths romanticised the mystical dark side. Skinheads adopted Aryan intimidation practice. Biker, surf and skate culture used the symbol as a sign of cheating or defying death. Punks used the symbols to demonstrate nihilist dissent and share many similarities with pirate culture. From the concept of societal 'outcast', to an anarchist and revolutionary momentum,[28] to a similar cultural structure, punk, with its characteristic local scene enhanced with international reach, shares many of the segmentary tribal characteristics as put forth by Marshall Sahlins in Kuhn's *Life under the Jolly Roger*. Kuhn interprets Sahlins' comments, 'The tribe maintains its identity through cultural similarity rather than a continuously shared existence.' Sahlins continues,

> … Insofar as these groups are alike, they respond the same way to the world and thus develop an historic identity if not exactly a polity. … [There are] fraternal orders with chapters established in different locales – so that for the price of a secret handshake one may be able to cadge a free lunch in another place.[29]

To this day, when punk bands tour the US they look for local 'crash pads' to keep touring expenses low. When travelling the world, punks can find acceptance among their tribe on the local scene through music listings in the local entertainment media and the internet.

There are varying views as to whether pirate culture was truly multicultural. Those who believe it was argue that the outlaw culture was colour blind, while those who believe it was not argue that the pirates of colour were captured slaves who were kept on as servants. In any event, there is evidence that pirate culture included people of colour, and this closely resembles the make-up of punk culture as well. From the early connection between punk and reggae in the UK, multicultural participation was part of punk ideology from its inception. As Hugh Rankin asserts, 'Shared feelings of marginality are a solvent which can ameliorate racial … barriers.'[30]

There is no doubt that pirate culture has a bad record on gender, with evidence of only two female captains, Anne Bonny and Mary Read. To be fair, society in general had a poor record on gender at the time, so it is no surprise that pirate culture would reflect these views. While Bonny and Read had to enter pirate society disguised as men, they did achieve recognition in a male-dominated society. Punk ideology also promises gender equality, and certainly women had made some strides in society by the early 1970s – or had they? There are those who will argue both sides on this issue as well. Again, it is important to remember that punk is highly localised, and there may have been many examples of gender and multicultural inclusiveness on some local scenes, while there was less opportunity for inclusion in others. While punk women display a variety of dress, there is a segment that dresses like punk men. A recent example of this practice can be seen in the styling of Lisbeth Salander, the female protagonist as she is portrayed in the film adaptation of Stieg Larsson's *Millennium* trilogy. Further, both pirates and punks rely on the same fashion concept, that of bricolage, as signifier. Both subcultures cobble together outfits from garments begged, borrowed, stolen or purchased, often reworked or repaired. These outfits create a mash-up of colour, style and texture, assaulting the eyes of the outsider, while revealing an insider's code to their own.

Two mainstream subcultures – rock and metal co-opted the skull and crossbones and moved it into mass consumed public property by selling their skull-based mascots (in the case of metal, indicative of adolescent boys fantasies) on posters, album covers, flags, t-shirts and buttons.[31] In America, these two subcultures attract a predominantly suburban fan base with a need for conformity within their groups and the disposable income to buy into the symbolism. With the exception of the Goths and their romantic dark side, it is interesting to note that the subcultures appropriating the symbol are considered to be predominantly male.

The symbol in fashion today

Hebdige endorses Lefebvre's 1971 comment on acculturation of subcultural symbols into the mainstream via mass-market consumption: 'That which yesterday was reviled today becomes cultural consumer-goods; consumption thus engulfs what was intended to give meaning and direction.'[32]

Today the symbol has become ubiquitous, reiterated through all levels of fashion from mass to couture and all markets of both genders (Figure 11.1). Even pets are in on the trend. The skull and crossbones have come to symbolise 'pirattitude' – living your life the way you want to, with no apologies; never having to keep up with the Joneses; not settling for the mundane; having the courage to question authority; living and loving passionately, having a zest for life; seeing

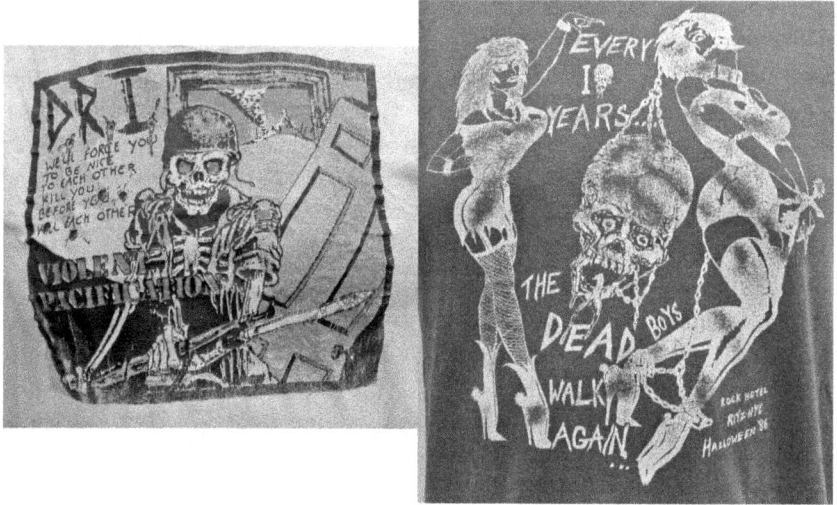

Figure 11.1 Dead Boys and DRI t-shirts from the collection of the author. Image reproduced with permission of the author.

life for all its possibilities; launching into the unknown for sheer adventure; being free and living freely.[33] Clinton V. Black confirms that sentiment, emphasising the words of Bartholomew Roberts, '… contrasting the horrors of "honest service" with the pleasure and ease and liberty and power (and, one might add, with the 'honour' and 'justice' as they understood it) of the pirate way of life: 'Who', he asked, 'would not balance creditor on this side, when all the hazard that is run for it, at worst, is only a sour look or two at choking?'[34]

Treasure Island, *Peter Pan* and *The Pirates of Penzance* continue to appear in popular culture today. Along with the *Pirates of the Caribbean* trilogy, 'Wife Swap' and the 2007 CBS series 'Pirate Master', based on 'Survivor', through popular culture we continue to romanticise and sanitise pirates into an endearing archetype.

Keeping the Jolly Roger alive

Hebdige comments on the changing meanings of symbols in subcultures: 'Objects are made to mean and mean again as "style" in subculture.'[35]

As of 25 February 2007 the (London) *Sunday Times* Style supplement proclaimed the skeleton motif as 'going down', however, Victoria's Secret and Delia's catalogues featured skull and crossbones swimwear for Summer 2007, while Alloy showed the theme on a variety of tops in Autumn 2007 catalogues. Oriental Traders catalogue consistently devotes several full pages to the popular adult and children's pirate merchandise theme. A tour of shops in Philadelphia

Figure 11.2 An assortment of merchandise 2006-present from various price points using the skull and crossbones motif owned and photographed by the author.

and Maryland (2007) showed pirate symbolism still strong across the fashion apparel and accessory markets, particularly in the junior and teen category (Figure 11.2).

While the mainstream fashion frenzy is probably on the wane, the Jolly Roger will never die. The 6 June 2007 edition of the *Philadelphia Weekly* reported the motif trending up in hip-hop fashion. Local Philadelphia-area teen Isaiah Mathis of *American Rockstar* said, 'I do the skull thing, cities, crazy letters, tie-dye art, rhinestones, chains.' The *American Rockstar* crew is part of a larger 'rock star' trend sweeping across the country, evidenced by hip-hop culture expanding into and borrowing from rock music, art and fashion. Harlem rapper Jim Jones of the Dipset crew brought a rock 'n' roll aesthetic to hip-hop fashion with his characteristic skull pendants and belt buckles, studded bracelets and metal wallet chains.

But the rock influence didn't surface in rap music until 'Party Like a Rockstar' by the Atlanta-based Shop Boyz hit the radio in April 2007. (By May the rock star anthem was the No. 1 ringtone in the country, although the Shop Boyz's debut album *Rockstar Mentality* did not even hit stores until 19 June.) 'After that bandanna-wearing skulls with crossbones are popping up all over hip-hop clothing, accessories, music videos and party fliers.'[36] Youth subcultures continue to keep the trend alive until mainstream fashion craves Jolly Roger once again.

Politics of piracy

The use of the term 'piracy' in terms of media dates from 1603 in Britain, labelling those who violated a Royal Charter given to the Stationers' Company of London in 1557, which awarded them a monopoly on publications. This charter was followed in 1709 by the Statute of Anne, which established copyright law and used 'piracy' to refer to 'unauthorized manufacture or sales of work in copyright'.[37]

With the advent of technologies allowing the individual to copy, media piracy has grown. From bootleg albums and movies to the use of copyrighted material in rap music and internet mash-ups today, Piracy is growing and industry is worried.

As Chris Land points out in his essay 'Flying the Black Flag', 'So long as people keep consuming piracy – rather than practicing it – then capitalism won't have a problem. But if people started actually engaging in piracy, Disney would be one of the first up in arms.'[38]

In April 2010, Greg Sandoval of CNET reports that the US Government Accountability Office (GAO) cannot definitively say how piracy is impacting the US. There is anecdotal evidence that show media piracy is 'a drag on the US economy, tax revenue, and in some cases potentially threatens national security and public health', but data is unreliable. The report concludes that 'the US economy *may* grow more slowly because of reduced innovation and loss of trade revenue'.[39]

As we can see, pirate sentiment lives on: from the appropriation of space through the act of squatting in unused buildings, or on the airwaves by pirate radio, to the commandeering of public resources or waste and transformation into a sustainable life style through the freegan movement, among others, to the expropriation of copyrighted materials and redistribution through open cyberspaces, the fundamental ideologies recorded in the Articles of Piracy or the US Bill of Rights are an integral part of subversive activity today.

High seas piracy rages on today

The resurgence of piracy in Somali waters seems initially attributable to the fall of the Siad Barre regime and advent of the civil war. Left with no governing body in a clan-based society to protect the vital fishing grounds of the Somali coast from illegal fishing and toxic dumping, former fisherman banded together and took to the high seas to protect their livelihood.[40]

As clan lords noted the profitability of the hijackings, they have entered the fray and now facilitate the pirate activities, splitting the proceeds with the pirates.[41] Armed with sophisticated weaponry – AKM assault rifles, RPG-7 rocket propelled grenade launchers and semi-automatic pistols – and organised into a military inspired confederation, these modern-day pirates model those of the golden age. With skill and knowledge of the seas, militia muscle and technical expertise, these outlaws claim to be protecting what is theirs.

The paradox of piracy continues. Are these pirates cruel and greedy thugs and thieves, or are they protecting their own and fighting 'the 'Man'? Are they helping their economy by spending their spoils in port, or harming their fellow man by stealing? Only time will tell. One thing is for sure, as did those who came before them, they will provide the fodder for more pirate lore to come.

12

A LOUSE IN COURT: NORWEGIAN KNITTED SWEATERS WITH 'LUS' ON BIG-TIME CRIMINALS

Ingun Grimstad Klepp

Early one morning in 2008 I was sitting in make-up for a Norwegian morning television show and felt the trained hands of the make-up artist smooth out my face with paint. It wasn't the first time I'd been there. With a population of 5 million there are not many clothing researchers to choose between in Norway, and with plenty of weather and outdoor activities, clothes are important. Questions such as how to dress children for physical activities outdoors are equally relevant every autumn and before every winter vacation and every Easter, when Norwegians go to their cabins, and the ideal is to spend as much time as possible outdoors. I have talked about the choice between wool and synthetic fibres and also about traditional Norwegian knitwear, but this time the subject was somewhat different. The Norwegian Islamist Arfan Bhatti stood, as the first person in Norway to be accused of violating a new terror clause in the Penal Code. The striking thing for the Norwegian press was that he appeared in court in a Norwegian knitted sweater, a so-called *lusekofte* [lit: lice jacket], and he wasn't the first. Before him, the accused in the biggest robbery in Norwegian history and the accused in the most discussed triple homicide had dressed in the *lusekofte* in court.

This was the day's news on the morning television show, on the radio as well as in the biggest newspapers. I myself was wearing a home-knitted *lusekofte* and had planned to strike a blow for this beautiful, colourful and characteristic garment, which is both traditional and constantly renewed. I wanted to answer their question with another question: What *should* a man accused of a serious crime wear? Shouldn't we welcome the few alternatives that actually exist for dressing men? And isn't it the lack of alternatives, rather than the use of them, the problem? But as often happens, things did not go according to plan. The questions that I was asked and that were also discussed in newspapers and on the radio were as follows: Why did Bhatti and other infamous criminals choose the *lusekofte*? Would this affect the reputation of the *lusekofte*? And would the use of *lusekofte* influence the verdict?

Thanks to the vast storing capacity of the internet there are still a number of news stories and discussions about this inappropriate use of the *lusekofte*. In addition, new jokes, cartoons and commentaries are constantly produced. These discussions provide a rare occasion to see how people think about both the *lusekofte* and about the clothes worn by criminals. 'Right' and 'wrong' clothes are otherwise things that are felt and thought, more than said and written.[1] I shall therefore use the discussions in Norwegian media to discuss criminals and their clothes. What do the media stories say about the relationship between men's clothes, and how credibility and neutrality are understood? Or more directly: What was it about the *lusekofte* that made it so shocking in the courtroom?

Wolves in sheep's clothing

In particular, three criminals have become famous for wearing the *lusekofte* in court. These will be assessed, as well as several other instances of *lusekofte* in court.

The Orderud case is one of the most thoroughly media-covered homicide cases in Norway. On Whit Saturday 1999, Mr and Mrs Orderud and their daughter were shot and killed in their home on Orderud farm. Four people were charged and convicted as accessories to the triple homicide. Per Orderud, the son and brother of the murder victims, and his wife received the longest sentences. It is not known who actually committed the murders.

During the court trial the accused became celebrities and have been ever since. Per Orderud wore the knitted sweater both in court and in interviews with the press. However, there has never been a debate about whether this was appropriate or not. To the extent that this issue has been discussed, it is in connection with the wearing of *lusekofte* by other criminals.

The NOKAS robbery was the robbery of a Norwegian Cash Service' department in Stavanger in 2004. The robbers were equipped with bulletproof vests, helmets, balaclavas, gloves and boiler-suits and were heavily armed. The exit from the city's police station was blocked by a burning truck. The counting centre was attacked with a sledgehammer, a battering ram and 113 shots were fired with automatic guns. A police chief inspector was shot and killed. The perpetrators escaped with NOK 57.4 million, which makes this not only the most brutal but also the biggest robbery in Norwegian history. One of the people convicted for the NOKAS robbery and named as the mastermind in the case was David Aleksander Toska. Like Per Orderud, he is a Norwegian citizen with a Norwegian background, but unlike Orderud, he had been previously convicted of a number of crimes. Although the crime was widely reported and debated, the incident that caused the greatest media and public attention was his appearance in court in a *lusekofte* on the first day of the NOKAS trial. There are several pictures of Toska wearing a *lusekofte*, both inside and outside the court room. He was also pictured when he tried to open a big bar of Freia milk chocolate with his teeth during a court recess.

Arfan Bhatti is a Norwegian citizen of Pakistani descent and a resident of Oslo. He was formerly convicted several times, for, among other things, threatening behaviour, blackmail and violence. He was the first Norwegian ever to be tried for violating new terror clauses in the Norwegian Penal Code in 2008. At the time he was convicted for firing shots at a synagogue in Oslo, but found not guilty on the count of planning a terrorist act. He was also sentenced for four attempted murders in connection with a shooting at a private home. Bhatti wore *lusekofte* on the first day of the trial and had an orange in his hand. This was perceived as a clear reference to Toska's chocolate. To understand this link one needs to be familiar with Norwegian culture. As mentioned, an Easter trip to the cabin is a Norwegian ritual. *Lusekofte* is a type of sweater that is often used on such trips, and among the ritual activities is sitting outside in the snow sunbathing whilst eating chocolate (from a Norwegian brand, such as Freia) and oranges. Freia's slogan, 'a little piece of Norway', is associated with situations such as these. In the discussion of Bhatti's use of *lusekofte* the reference was to Toska, as in the headlines '*lusekofte* buddies' or in claims that Bhatti 'took a Toska'.[2]

'*Lusekofter*' – Norwegian sweaters

The *lusekofte* is a woollen sweater or jacket in a knitted pattern. The name *lusekofte* (lice jacket) refers to the isolated stitches, traditionally not only white on black but also the opposite or in other colours (Figure 12.1). The older form of *lusekofte* is also called 'a Setesdal sweater' and is worn by men as part of their regional folk costume.

A characteristic of Norway is the preservation of a living, popular textile tradition more enduring than that in many other nations, and this tradition remains prolific. This rich knitting tradition is still alive and evolving. However, there is surprisingly little scientific or academic research on the topic – most of the documentation is found in pattern and coffee-table books.[3] The *kofte* is constantly evolving both at the hands of professional designers and by amateur knitters and is used both in traditional forms and in ever-new combinations.

Figure 12.1 Close-up of Norwegian knitted sweater, showing '"lus" (lice)'. Photo by
Tone Skårdal Tobiasson.

Late industrialisation and a large degree of home production, together with
conscious, collecting of local traditions,[4] revitalisation and design, preserved
knitting and knitting patterns as a living tradition in Norway. Few other craft
traditions can show a similarly unbroken line of knowledge outside of educational
institutions. A notable surge occurred in connection with the Olympic Games in
Lillehammer in 1994. Several Norwegian designers who are currently making a
name for themselves also use Norwegian knitting as their starting point. The idea
of the real and authentic Norwegian sweater turns up in very different contexts.
This is a consequence of a heterogeneous reality where no one really owns the
interpretation or definition of the Norwegian sweater.[5]

These sweaters are common in Norway. They are worn by men, women and
children alike, especially in relation to outdoor recreation and cabin trips, as well

as by spectators at winter sports competitions. Nevertheless, it is not uncommon to see the sweaters worn as work wear or as everyday wear for both women and men. The most notable use of the *lusekofte* as work wear is demonstrated by the Cabinet in their national budget discussions, i.e. as seen in a famous picture of the then prime minister of Norway, Gro Harlem Brundtland, wearing a version called a 'Marius sweater' at the budget conference in 1988. The Norwegian brand Oleana has updated the *lusekofte* as smart/casual wear for women with great success, and it didn't go unnoticed that Michele Obama bought four of these jackets when she and her husband visited Oslo in 2009. Today *lusekofter* are even more popular with Facebook groups and a lot of different events like *koftetog*, parades of people wearing *lusekofter*.

Folk costumes are more frequently worn in Norway than in other Western countries, particularly at family celebrations such as Christmas, christenings and weddings, and it is the most popular form of dress for girls at the confirmations. Both Norwegian and Sami folk costumes are regarded as formal attire. It has become increasingly common to wear folk costumes at formal royal dinners, i.e. the *lusekofte* therefore may, as part of a man's folk costume, be worn to a ball at the royal palace.

Home-knitted sweaters are typical familial gifts for both adults and children. So much part of national culture, in Norwegian souvenir and home crafts stores sweaters of differing standards are familiar goods, and although a traditional format, new patterns are continually being developed. Indeed, sweaters or mittens with Norwegian patterns are given as gifts to foreign guests both privately and professionally. The most obvious of this form of gifting is in Norway's biggest celebrity magazine *Se og Hør*, which features photographs of international celebrities dressed in jackets presented as gifts by the magazine. At the same time they are associated with something frugal and Norwegian.

The Norwegian use of these sweaters only partly corresponds to Joanne Turney's analysis of knitted sweaters in the UK.[6] As in the UK, they became particularly popular with the emergence of vacations and leisure and have been associated with an active outdoor life. Turney argues that men with knitted sweaters are portrayed as 'men at leisure' either at the workplace or sporting arena, and not engaged in competition, challenging themselves in less aggressive pastimes.[7] This is also true in Norway. The largest manufacturer of knitwear, Dale, develops a new model for every major winter sports championship, which is often displayed on the greatest sports stars, but in more relaxed situations than those in which we are used to seeing them. Further, Turney writes that the use of hand-knitted sweaters shows that a man is loved by a woman. This aspect may be less pronounced in Norway due to the general popularity of knitting combined with the fact that home craft stores and companies like Dale of Norway have made hand-knitted clothes easily available, but knitting sweaters for a boyfriend is both something girls are warned against (the relationship will then end) and

Figure 12.2 Old designs from Dale of Norway are part of the museum at the factory, which is open to the public. Photo by Tone Skårdal Tobiasson.

at the same time very common. Many Norwegian men therefore have sweaters knitted by their wives and other close relatives, and maybe even some from their ex or ex-mother-in-law further back in the wardrobe (Figure 12.2).

The *lusekofte* Bhatti wore in court was a knitted jacket of the model Vail from Dale of Norway. Toska wore a model that was more like a Setesdal sweater, also manufactured by Dale. Both sweaters were relatively new machine-knitted models, yet the traditional concept remains; they are inconspicuous and still on sale.

A key element of the media debate surrounding the *lusekofte* as worn in court centred around the place of the *lusekofte* in Norwegian culture. Several experts were interviewed and commented on the rich cultural history of the knitted jacket. '*Lusekofta* is a symbol of our Norwegian identity. It is a trademark – a folk costume. Knitting has been a part of Norway's image since we broke with the Danes', says knitwear expert Annemor Sundbø,[8] who in the same article also states that 'the *lusekofte* symbolizes victory and should radiate dependability'. Different newspapers used words and epithets like 'all Norwegian' and 'proto-Norwegian', 'one of the most important symbols of Norwegian culture' and 'the most Norwegian of all garments'. Incidentally and conversely, the fact that the *lusekofte* is frequently used as a gift for foreigners and is an important souvenir was not highlighted. However, one article did mention that in the Norwegian-Pakistani population it was 'not uncommon' to wear a knitted jacket to show respect for Norwegian friends.[9]

Revitalisation, romanticism and ruralism are important characteristics of the knitted sweater in other countries as well,[10] but in Norway this is more strongly linked with a notion of nationhood. In Norway national romanticism is embraced more enthusiastically and perceived as less problematic, both because of historical circumstance (a small and poor country, governed by others for 400 years) and because the nation is celebrated through a children's parade rather than through military parades or political manifestations.[11]

Clothes in court

The clothes use of judges and lawyers in Norway is strictly regulated and pursuant to law. As in most other countries, lawyers and judges wear a black gown, but not a white wig, as they do in the UK.[12] The law lists a number of sartorial details, ranging from fabric provisions – the gown should be made of 'black woollen cloth with wide sleeves and reach to the middle of the shin'[13] – to decoration and detailing. Some of the details indicate rank, as is often found on uniforms. Supreme court judges should, for instance, have a red velvet trimming, whereas judges in the court of appeals and the Director of Public Prosecutions should have robes with a black velvet trimming, and lawyers and prosecutors should have black silk trimming. The court clerk's gown should have a narrow collar without trimming,[14] but with regard to the clothes of other participants the court's own webpage just says 'ordinary nice clothes'.[15] What constitutes 'ordinary, nice clothes' is not specified, and as we have already seen, in some contexts the *lusekofte* is indeed regarded as nice – even as formal dress.

To my knowledge, there has been little debate about clothes worn in court. The clothes of female victims in rape cases have been highlighted, but focusing on the clothes worn outside of the courtroom.[16] There has also been a debate about the use of the hijab in the courtroom, which has extended into other contexts. In addition to the discussion regarding the *lusekofte*, there has been a debate about another *kofte* in Norway, another traditional garment, and its use and proposed ban in the court environment. This is the traditional Sami costume for both women and men and consists of an embroidered jacket in a woven fabric, sometimes leather, with a belt. Jackets and hats are decorated with ribbons, lace, pewter thread embroideries, mica and leather. Decorative ribbons are sometimes sewn to the bottom of the bodice and the sleeves. The decoration can show local affiliation.

Neutrality was the principal argument for the proposal of this new provision. However, much of the response argued against the proposal, claiming a ban would violate international conventions on the rights of indigenous peoples and be at odds with Norwegian policy, where respect for Sami culture is emphasised. During the debate, it emerged that the *kofte* is not uncommon in court cases in Finnmark (the area in the north of Norway where the presence of Sami culture is strongest), where it is even worn by judges. This practice is in line with the use of the Sami *kofte* at official meetings and in institutional life in general. The *kofte* is the most commonly worn garment in the Sami parliament, the highest publically elected body for Sami issues. The proposal for a ban was not passed, and today lay judges, court ushers and others who work for the courts cannot be denied the wearing of garments that are regarded as religious or political, whether they are Sami, *kofte* or hijabs. The *lusekofte* was not mentioned in this discussion, which primarily concerned the relationship between Sami clothes and modern Western men's clothes.

The wearing of the *lusekofte* in court has also been discussed before. In a custody hearing in 2003 a police prosecutor appeared in a *lusekofte*. According to an online newspaper the judge is quoted as saying, 'It is disrespectful towards the accused and the court not to dress correctly. It is like showing up in a track suit at a wedding or swimming trunks at a funeral. You just don't.'[17] The wearer defended himself in the online newspaper: 'My *kofte* was like a piece of finery, a beautiful specimen from the Home Crafts store',[18] explaining the use of the *kofte* was a coincidence, because the custody hearing was held at short notice, but the policeman has not repeated this sartorial faux pas, saying, 'The court room is a serious place, so I fully respect that there has to be a strict dress code.'[19] The statement is diplomatic, he wanted to show respect for the rules, but he still feels that his *kofte* was 'a piece of finery' and therefore was in agreement with the requirement to wear 'nice clothes' in court.

Since 'nice clothes' are in no way clearly defined; to what degree defence attorneys are responsible for, or interfere in the way their clients dress, is also significant. Most assume that defendants choose their own clothes, but in a commentary, one journalist claims that Arfan Bhatti's *kofte* must have been the defence attorney's idea. Under the headline 'Circus director John Chr. Elden', he argues that the '*lusekofte* trick' unfortunately is 'a credibility blunder and causes significant harm to Arfan Bhatti's image'.[20] The article is composed of quotes from various players that all address the lawyers' responsibility for the way their clients dress. On the one hand Elden says, 'I don't interfere with what the client wears', while another defence attorney is quoted as saying, 'We emphasise that our clients don't embarrass themselves by the way they dress. Neither too formal, nor the opposite, because it is all about credibility.' The leader of the Norwegian Bar Association's Criminal Law committee gives 'courses in the choice of clothes' for new lawyers and says that 'clients quite often ask about what they should wear. The advice we give is to dress nicely. We advise against overdone clothing because it draws attention away from what the trial is about.'

The article concludes that Elden should have strongly dissuaded the use of *lusekofte*, whether it was ironic or not. He should, rather, have advised his client to 'change into a nice shirt, a tie and a slightly conservative sweater'.[21]

The argument here is that the court is an environment where nice clothes, somewhere along the lines of a shirt and tie and a conservative sweater, are appropriate. 'One should – to the best of one's ability – be appropriately dressed for any occasion' is a main rule in the Norwegian standard work on etiquette.[22] Dressing appropriately for the situation and environment remains a strong norm even today and is frequently discussed in connection with clothes for sports and outdoor recreation.[23] However, the choice of clothes is more often discussed as a matter of taste and 'identity', than as a question of location and behavioural expectations. Both in the limited material available regarding suitable dress for lay people in court and outlined in the abovementioned article, there appears to be an emphasis on dressing appropriately for the occasion. The clothes should be 'nice' and thus show respect for the serious and solemn aspect of the court.

The *lusekofte* trick

The debate that followed in the wake of Toska's choice to wear a *lusekofte* in court centred around the question of why this choice had been made and the subsequent fallout. Several articles described this action as performative, using metaphors from the stage. 'The court is a stage where it is possible to show oneself to the nation and the judges. And particularly to one's own' and '[a]s a prop Toska had a milk chocolate, a little piece of Norway'.[24] However, the aim of the court is not to entertain, but to arrive at truth and justice. By examining witnesses the lawyers attempt to draw a picture of who the accused is, what has happened and the part the accused played in these events. The goal of the court, in Erving Goffman's terms, is to acquire knowledge about what has happened off-stage, to reveal the true self, behind the mask.[25] In such a situation all details become important, and dress is one of the few elements in addition to language that contributes to showing who the accused is and thereby also how what is said should be interpreted. As *Aftenposten*, Norway's biggest newspaper, wrote two days after this event, 'Statements that Bhatti thinks are credible in relation to the burden of proof against him do not hold. And a *lusekofte* does not help.'[26]

I think that increasingly courtrooms are stages and centres in which the accused can perform in order to seduce the jury. This is particularly true in the case of countries in which trials are televised. In addition, the increased popularity of crime and court shows on television encourages a public awareness of the relationship between playing a role and providing a convincing defence. Frequently, the concepts of truth and justice are understood as fluid terms, rather than 'fact', which further facilitates the potential to 'act' rather than 'be'. Under these circumstances, clothing becomes a costume, something that will make the performance more convincing.

The questions posed to me that morning were what did the accused and the defence team want to achieve by using a *lusekofte*, and what effect did it have? These questions appeared and reappeared in newspapers and blogs. The fundamental question regarding this clothing decision was who were the audience? As on all stages, there is not necessarily any correspondence between who the director thinks will be the audience and who actually sees the play. Moreover, it is not at all certain that everyone will see it in the same way.

One stylist is sure that 'the outfits are carefully planned', but points out that the accused want to appear 'credible and down-to-earth, so they are trying to fool us'.[27] The purpose was to appear like an average Norwegian. Others thought that the garment was meant to make the defendants look harmless and 'signal that the accused is 'one of us',[28] demonstrating 'Norwegian identity and belonging'.[29] The word 'us' in all of these quotes indicates that the Norwegian public as well as the court were the intended recipients. The extent to which it had any positive effect has been discussed, too. One public relations expert claimed that the 'Toskabunad [viz. Norwegian national costume]' was a successful tactic. The *lusekofte* makes us think of serious criminals as not different from 'most people'.[30] However, others thought that it was not wise for Bhatti to choose the same costume as Toska. 'The knitted sweater could divert attention away from what the case was really about. But perhaps the sweater is what made him get off as lightly as he did?'[31] Whether the 20-year prison sentence is 'light' is, of course, another matter.

One researcher on violence was more concerned about other criminals as observers. Like most others she believes that the choice of clothes was strategic.

> Normally, people in these groups are not concerned with clothes and symbols. By putting on a knitted garment they show belonging to Norwegian society, but also to each other. … What they wear does not mean anything in relation to the trial, but it means something for their image. Bhatti is accused of terrorism, which means an attack on Norway. At the same time he shows up in court with one of the most important symbols of Norwegian culture. That is hardly coincidental.[32]

A Norwegian-Pakistani lawyer took a similar stance in a conference on the relationship between the press and the criminal fraternity. He talked about an exposed youth with a fundamental distrust of established society who lack good role models. 'A terrorism suspect wearing a *lusekofte* may be a more powerful influence, and in this connection pose a bigger threat, than a *lusekofte* wearer convicted in a mugging and murder case.'[33] Again we see that the important observers are potential criminals, but without this being presented as a conscious choice by Bhatti.

Recent clothes research emphasises that clothes affect not only the way others see us but also how we see ourselves or how we are. Clothes do something to us. Anthropologist Janet Andrewes has argued that clothes have the ability to transform the body,[34] and Daniel Miller uses the same argument in his discussion of clothes as 'lived garments'.[35] This means that people have access to ideas that are associated with the shape of the clothes. The body does something to the clothes, and the clothes do something to the body.[36] This implies an understanding of clothes as something very different from a superficial exterior.[37] Instead, it questions the Western idea of a true inner self in opposition to an external facade. None of the articles reflect this more modern view on the effect of clothes. A commentary in one of the tabloids comes closest:

> The cold light of the court makes the clear colours in Bhatti's *lusekofte*, a garment which criminals after David Toska seem to have reserved for court occasions, stand out. The garment's good-humoured homeliness is probably intended to reflect the role Bhatti has assumed in court. He appears with a significant degree of openness and politeness. Bhatti builds credibility.[38]

It is possible that Bhatti consciously or unconsciously chose the *lusekofte* not just to be seen in it but also because he wanted to become, to be or to bring out in himself particular characteristics such as 'openness' and 'politeness'. In the article this is referred to as a 'role', again confirming Goffman's theory. However, the effect of clothes can be understood as more than a role, namely, as something with a profound influence on who we are. As mentioned above, such a view is conditioned on our willingness to dissolve the clear dichotomy between the inside and the outside, which is so important for the understanding of the person in modern Western thinking. In light of the capacity of the material for ambiguous messages and double meanings there is no reason to believe that the message is unambiguous or only intended for a single person or group. Rather it is likely that Bhatti wanted to salute Toska while at the same time to choose clothes that show 'respect for the court' and, if possible, highlight certain aspects of himself.

In the media discussions it is evident that whether the *lusekofte* was 'appropriate' for the 'occasion' that a trial is, was not only to do with the occasion as such, but also with who wore the garment. It was Bhatti's use of *lusekofte* that spurred the debate, and not the other accused. One article summarised what the *lusekofte* sweaters signal in court as follows:

> intrinsic calm, steadiness, homeliness, Norwegianness and national unity. A reputation we all like. Per Orderud 'used the symbol for all it was worth, and

got away with it.' *Then one of Norway's* worst robbers turned up. David Toska got more attention for his use of *lusekofte* than Orderud, because there was something surprising about a man in balaclava appearing in the public sphere with this garment.

He admittedly got away with it because he is ethnically Norwegian. But Toska's use of the lusekofte changed the symbolism and many probably thought of it as the 'thug sweater'.

The last in the criminal lusekofte pack is an urban Muslim bomber with Pakistani roots suspected of terrorism. Bhatti entered smiling before the flash lights of the press, well prepared by his lawyer, John Christian Elden. In his left hand shone an orange like the Easter sun, and in his 'back pocket' he carried the Quran, that the prosecution so efficiently had given him access to.[39]

The same elements reappear in other articles and blogs. The three accused have some characteristics that make them more or less suited to wear a *lusekofte*. Per Orderud is suited because he is ethnically Norwegian, healthy to the core and has hereditary right to a farm. David Toska is, if not suited, then at least not directly offensive because he, too, is ethnically Norwegian, but unsuited because he is a man 'in a balaclava'. Arfan Bhatti, on the contrary, is unsuited. He is urban, Muslim, a terrorism suspect – and not ethnically Norwegian.[40] We see, in other words, that their degree of Norwegianness is essential and, furthermore, that this Norwegianness is measured by looks, religion, background and urbanity as well as previous clothes use.

Norway likes to see itself as a democratic and egalitarian society with little racism. The fact that the reactions to the three *lusekofte* comrades were so different is a discouraging finding. For years Norwegians have been proud of our *lusekofte* sweaters and have gladly given them to visitors and exported them to different countries without questioning the recipient's skin colour or religion. The large amount of attention Bhatti received is possibly a sign that the 'war on terror' has increased racist tendencies in Norway, but it could also be interpreted as an example of an abandoned ideology surviving in material culture and the norms associated with the use of clothes and other objects.[41]

Credible and neutral men

Several blogs commented that the accused should not choose 'contrived clothes' or be 'too dressed up or dressed down', and have commented on how 'ordinary, nice clothes'[42] should be understood: a nice shirt, a tie and a somewhat conservative sweater. This way of dressing is characterised not only by details such as colours and types of garments, but it is also directly associated with a certain political orientation (conservative). Furthermore, this way of dressing can be characterised as a kind of dissolved suit.[43] The suit is central to the emergence of modern society, with the triumph of rationality over feudalism.[44] The attire was sombre, austere and not distinctive – so that people could focus on the task at hand.[45] Modesty had become a claim to power, founded on European commodities and textile industry.[46] These people are of course not just anybody, but men. This 'nonuniform Uniform'[47] makes men part of a hegemonic culture which emerges as 'permanent' and 'neutral', outside of history and beyond particular interest.[48] The suit is one of the foremost expressions of hegemonic masculinity,[49] which has great social authority and which is therefore not easy to challenge (Figure 12.3).[50]

The Sami *kofte* challenges this hegemonic masculinity. As we have seen, the neutrality argument was the most important, an argument that is used precisely in order to defend hegemonic power. That the prohibition did not go through says something about the strength that lies in the counter-power: 'the rights of indigenous peoples' in Norway. In discussions of the *lusekofte*, too, the term 'natural' is used, although somewhat implicitly, namely, as the opposite of

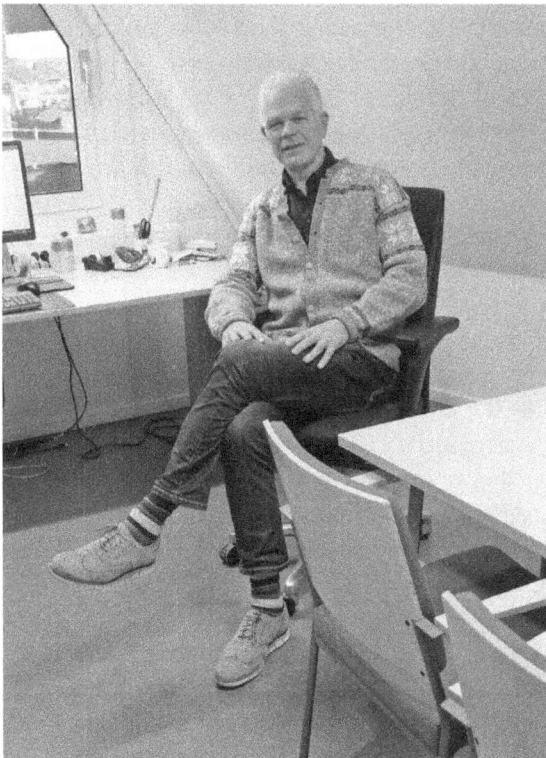

Figure 12.3 Head of Research Arne Dulsrud in a Lusekofte at work at SIFO, Oslo Metropolitan University, 2018. Photo by Tone Skårdal Tobiasson.

artificial, but the way of dressing recommended as the 'natural' choice is not the suit, but a form of dissolved suit.[51] Such dissolved suits, for example, in the form of a shirt and jacket over more casual trousers, or shirt and jacket without a tie are used in more casual settings and as a protest against strict dress codes.[52] In order to speak from the platform of the Norwegian Storting you must wear a suit jacket. The other suit elements can be left out, however. The suit jacket is necessary to exert power (I guess you need trousers!). That the jacket here is left out and replaced by a sweater in the suggested appropriate dress for the accused is easily interpreted as a sign that the accused should renounce the part of the suit that most clearly expresses power and masculinity. The use of the other suit elements, then, points not only to respect for the court but also for the hegemonic masculine power structure in general. Substitution of the suit jacket for a conservative sweater may be interpreted in line with Joanne Turney's understanding of the cardigan: 'a garment which is neither formal nor casual, suited perhaps to those unable to fully conform or participate in either area', and 'associated with impotency and an inability to feel in control of the situation one finds oneself in',[53] and thereby undoubtedly the right garment for the repentant sinner. A suit with a jacket is not mentioned. That would probably be perceived as too powerful an outfit for the accused and spur more associations to the mafia than to a repentant sinner or an innocent accused.

As we saw in the discussion of the use of the Sami *kofte*, it is not given that everyone perceives the hegemonic masculinity as neutral. This means, among other things, that different people will feel more or less at home in such an outfit. In other words, 'a conservative style' will be perceived as 'normal' for some and as 'artificial' for others. This does not only affect the way the wearer feels but also affect the way they are seen by others, in the same way as the *lusekofte* was provocative in court only when the wearer was not 'Norwegian'. The same outfit causes different reactions depending on who wears it. They are seen differently – and thereby affect the wearer's credibility. Clothes – like other material culture – are never neutral.

Why the three accused chose to wear *lusekofte* we will never know, but the discussion about their choice has given us the opportunity to consider the ways in which people think about men and clothes, credibility and neutrality. These are topics that deserve much more attention. All concern about the future reputation of the *lusekofte* was, however, completely unfounded. Since that morning in 2008 the popularity of the *lusekofte* has grown rapidly, together with an increased interest in wool, knitting and Norwegian patterns. In the winter of 2009/2010 it could be found everywhere from Primark to Dolce & Gabbana's catwalk show, and while the Norwegian media were concerned with limiting its use, be it in terms of occasion or wearer, the *lusekofte* has appeared in constantly new guises, materials and on new wearers.

13

OUT OF THE TRENCHES AND INTO *VOGUE*: UN-BELTING THE TRENCH COAT

Marilyn Cohen

The trench coat, perhaps more than any other fashionable item of clothing, literally carries with it fictions that the wearer wraps around him- or herself at the moment the coat is put on – or embodied. Whether Humphrey Bogart in *Casablanca* (1942) or Holly Golightly in *Breakfast at Tiffany's* (1961), in film, literature or advertising, the storyline in which the trench enters is usually on the dark side, related to war, espionage, murder, confused identities or just plain bad weather. Associations to the trench-coated character call forth such popular icons as Peter Sellers as Inspector Clousseau in the *Pink Panther* series followed by Steve Martin in the same role, Dick Tracy in comics, Eliot Ness and 'the Untouchables' both on television and in the movies, the cartoon character Inspector Gadget and the television detective Columbo, played by Peter Falk. These are just some among many. Yet the trench is also a ubiquitous part of the fashionable wardrobe for women (and men), bringing to mind memorably alluring and dramatic images of Marlene Dietrich and Greta Garbo. A 2003 book by Nancy MacDonell Smith, *The Classic Ten*, includes the trench alongside the little black dress, pearls and lipstick as a fashion classic, and *Vogue* and other fashion magazines periodically re-present the trench as newly 'stylish' in spreads entitled 'Entrenched' or 'Brief Encounter', continually referencing movie narratives[1]. Even Barbie has a trench in her wardrobe.

By now the trench has been reimagined in every conceivable form, not just as a coat but as an evening dress, bathing suit and rather metonymic shoe. Aquascutum, Burberry, YSL and Prada, along with myriad other fashion houses, continually re-design the trench while always maintaining its status as a classic

Figure 13.1 Faustine Steinmentz S/S 2018 collection at London Fashion Week, September 2017. Photo by Victor VIRGILE/Gamma-Rapho via Getty Images.

(Figure 13.1). The trench coat has been done in leopard, red patent leather, black leather (*The Matrix,* 1999), suede (*Live and Let Die,* 1973), polka dots and pink in support of breast cancer. It has been lengthened and shortened, slit, ruched and ruffled, and its characteristic and originally functional elements – belts, flaps, D-rings, buttons, cuff and pockets – have been almost comically rearranged and reassembled with what might itself be considered a criminal assault on its formal integrity. These many incarnations suggest that the trench, like the colour black, as John Harvey wrote in *Men in Black*, is about more than externals but has to do with relations between people and society and the ways in which people display their dark interiors.[2] Indeed, the coat has gone from being military equipment and the sign of the detective or the reporter to the accoutrement of the flasher. As such, the trench coat is truly about the 'spectacular'; it controls, covers and then reveals. It is about inside and outside, concealment, display and surprise – and demonstrates that fashion is not just a system but a series of practices related to the body, performance, masquerade and modernity. The trench coat forces one to question whether fashion is a fiction or whether the realities of life simply require fictional attire.

How does a coat go from being military equipment to the outerwear of the flasher – from the uniform to the transgressive – and stay a fashion classic? In an attempt to solve this mystery, this writer has walked down noir-ish streets trying to lure the trench out of the shadows but has only been able to shine a torch on labryrinthine plots that implicate the trench. I invite the reader down some of those paths with assurance that there are no actual dangers but only unsolved mysteries. Indeed, what one finds, aside from a few rather shifty-looking characters, are solely the shifting signifiers and signifieds of the trench. To begin then, this chapter will look briefly at the historical moment of the trench's production. It will next examine how the trench as material culture made its way into literary and visual fiction – and how those fictions continue to be recycled and consumed today. Finally, I hope to 'expose' the flasher – both male and female – lurking beneath or within the fashionable trench.

To paraphrase Detective Friday of television's *Dragnet* fame beginning in the 1950s, I will begin with the 'facts'.[3] The trench coat originated during World War I. Disputed as to its origins by either Burberry or Aquascutum, it appears that Thomas Burberry made the original trench worn primarily by officers of the upper class as an alternative to the heavy serge greatcoat. The trench warfare that characterised World War I necessitated coats able to withstand the damp as well as to carry equipment. Made of gabardine fabric invented by Burberry from yarn treated to be waterproof prior to weaving, the trench had storm flaps at the front and back to redirect water away from the body of the coat and its wearer. A raglan sleeve made it easy to put on and take off. The epaulets secured rifles, binoculars, whistles and gloves, and the D-rings on the belt could hold grenades. The coat also had a detachable lining, double breasting for increased warmth, and multiple pockets with which to carry maps, provisions and ammunition. Many of these elements figure in the classic trench coat as vestiges of military conflagration and preparedness. Since only officers and Warrant Officers Class I in the British army were permitted to wear it,[4] which was purchased by the officer himself and could be made by any tailor, the trench coat, besides marking the wearer as military and an adherent to codes of patriotism, standardisation and conformity, also indicated an elegant or upper-class status.

The trench coat then climbed out of the trenches with those fortunate enough to survive the war and walked into civilian life. In 1919, in an American short story, a young woman says that she 'wouldn't wear no trench coat around the Forty-Second St & Broadway trenches, because it would be insulting to the army'.[5] But by 1921, in the British *Blackwood's Magazine*, a periodical published from 1817 to 1980, a notation read 'Irish newspapers tried to throw the blame on the forces of the crown' by saying that the men wore trench coats but 'never adding that practically every young man in Ireland nowadays wears a so-called trench-coat'.[6] Thus, by the early 1920s the trench was seen all over the streets in both Britain and the US and was no longer strictly the garb of the officer, yet still carried with it the military and 'macho' authority attributable to fighting men in wartime. In fact, Hemingway in the early 1920s suggested that a 'slacker' who hadn't served in the war could find himself a military trench coat in a surplus store and deceptively integrate himself into the cadre of returning veterans – a performative identity even then attached to the wearer simply by donning the coat.[7]

By 1931 a play staged on Broadway in New York City, entitled *Design for Murder* and starring Tallulah Bankhead, was described as 'a fast moving highly tensed whodunit' and had the 'ruggedly handsome' detective dressed in a trench, indicating that the military-style coat had become the outerwear of a detective,[8] and while I could not verify any use of the trench coat in the original version of Dashiell Hammett's *Maltese Falcon* – and the cover of the first edition of the book shows no detective in a trench – in Raymond Chandler's novels, the detective Philip Marlowe wears a trench coat, at least by 1939 in the novel *The Big Sleep*.[9] Later publications of the *Maltese Falcon*, as well as numerous other mysteries, feature the trench, judging from the covers of paperback editions of crime or mystery novels published from the 1930s on, and in the 1940s, movies based on these stories, including many a film noir, were advertised through poster images depicting trench-coated characters. These glamorous men and women used the trench to cloak, shield and hide narratively while at the same time the coat helped to construct them as dangerously outside and other by virtue of their star persona, ironically and spectacularly hidden by the coat. By the post-war period, as an advertisement using an image of Detective Friday demonstrates, a spiffy trench gave the wearer the aura of a captain, but now a suburban captain of industry. The copy here reads 'careful designing gives this officer's type trench coat the feeling of military swagger' and highlights its 'full military collar, trench flap and epaulets'. Nevertheless, even if General Patton and Prime Minister Churchill both wore trench coats during World War II, it appears that the trench-wearing character more often than not became a signifier of murder and mayhem. The coat became a formulaic bearer of masculine stereotypes – its epaulets, lapels, flaps and belt all extensions of maleness – like guns, as can be seen in the cover of the 1935 paperback novel *Murder from the East* by Carroll John Daly. The trench was the coat of intrigue, embodying potential violence and phallic know-how – even in France – as can be seen in the poster for *The Samurai* (1967) featuring Alain Delon wearing one. The woman wearing the trench thus became transgressive by putting one on.

If the trench had originally been worn by an upper-class British military officer, in hardboiled American detective fiction, the trench was worn by a lower-middle-class man in a murky urban milieu. As John Cawelti has written in his analysis of detective fiction, in contrast to the classic British detective in the manner of Sherlock Holmes, who solves the crime methodologically and scientifically and repairs a temporary break in the social structure, the hardboiled American detective, such as Hammett's Sam Spade or Chandler's Marlowe, may find the murderer, but the social world within which he moves remains chaotic and grim.[10] The trench coat as written into this scheme becomes the uniform of a truth seeker needing protection from corrosive elements of humanity. The coat isolates and protects him permitting him to operate independently – alone and somewhat undifferentiated from the masses. The coat as a bearer of military past also may speak to a nostalgia for order and patriotism – as it does in the film *Casablanca.* Mediated by fiction, the trench coat in these stories has changed class, substituting a personal code for a military one. (Indeed, it is noteworthy that by 1931 a trench coat costing $2.98 was available to everyone for consumption through the Sears, Roebuck catalogue.) These American crime stories assert a cynical view of man's place in society, and it is somewhat ironic that the detective wearing the trench essentially remains covered as he seeks to uncover.

Other than the detective, it is, of course, the journalist, another truth seeker, most associated with the trench as uniform or signifier – a direct result of reporters in World War I wearing it at the front. Today many blogs reference the trench coat, as do many news anchors, and the phrase 'being in the trenches' metaphorically signifies 'real' experience. Yet when used on a dust jacket cover or in a movie poster, the man in the trench coat can often remain a shadowy, foggy or otherwise ambiguous figure. At times driven close to shirking his own code of honour, the trench-coated character can sometimes be either the detective *or* the murderer. In Alfred Hitchcock's *Dial M for Murder* (1954), for example, the sameness of the trench coat worn by two different men serves to confuse the true identity of the murderer with the one mistakenly accused of the crime. The trench coat, therefore, symbolically manifests a series of contradictions. It obscures and hides identity while at the same time embodying a search for authenticity. The coat continually relates this dichotomy of concealment and display to grander themes of good and evil – its pockets, flaps and buttons suggestive of things unseen and unknowable, as well as potentially dangerous. A functional way to conceal weapons, for example, the coats were most unfortunately worn by the so-called 'Trench Coat Mafia', those teenagers responsible for the horrific killings at Columbine High School in Colorado in 1999.[11]

Fictions continue to be spun around the coat in fashion editorials. In a series of five full-page photos shot by Deborah Turbeville for *Interview* magazine in 2000, models or mannequins in trench coats are set opposite classic movie images of trench-coated stars. An image of Robert Mitchum, for example, in the movie *Out of the Past* (1947) is juxtaposed with a model dressed in a Moschino polka-dotted trench and wearing Vivienne Westwood gloves. The classic *Breakfast at Tiffany's* image of Holly and Paul trench-coated in the rain appears next to a model in a Ralph Lauren trench. The text for the series reads, 'This season's biggest fashion cover-up is also one of Hollywood's biggest fashion allies! Few other garments suggest so much by showing so little. And fewer still seem able to grant their wearer so much mystery.' Allies refers to the war, and the nomenclature of mystery is obvious. The text beckons the fashion-conscious reader to buy and wear the coat and take on glamorous identities. In this manner, it reiterates Anne Hollander's thesis that fashionable dress draws on pictorial or painterly images of visual desire.[12] Turbeville's photographs situate the models in seedy offices and bars capitalising on noir-ish venues and spectacles to invest (or re-invest) the coat with narrative or fictive allure. In the February 2010 *Vogue* editorial 'Brief Encounter', Sean Combs and Natalia Vodnianova also play parts in a fictionalised movie, text and image specifically borrowed from Bogart and Bergman in *Casablanca.* The use of fog and the trench thrown over the suitcase in one of the photos accentuate this association.[13] In yet another *Vogue* fashion editorial on the trench coat, models sitting alone on a director's chair against a simple white backdrop wear expensive versions of the coat. However, less costly styles appear on models outside in the street, with boyfriends and trench coats linked together to invest the everyday with romantic mystery.[14] A contemporary blog, 'Detective Agency Fashion', likewise features the trench with copy that reads, 'Add a little mystery to your winter wardrobe.' Real people featured on these blogs wearing the coat also reify it with fictional identities: Tal Sharon, a filmmaker, for example, said of his trench, 'I got it at H&M six months ago, for $150. It has the "thirties Mafia meets modern European meets every day serial killer" look I'm after.'[15] In 2009, Angela Ahrendts, the CEO of Burberry, started an online site for people to submit photos of themselves wearing a trench with their own storylines. Another similar site is the Fedora Lounge.[16] All of these blogs and editorials associate the fashionable trench with stories redolent of espionage or crime, even if the crime in many cases is simply one of 'stolen' fictional identity.

Semiotics, however, requires that distinctions be made among signifiers. In film images the trench coat becomes an expressive piece of material culture. That is, the trench coat as worn in film is able to convey information by means of its very materiality brought near to the spectator through stills and close-ups. The multiple designs of the trench, for example, can shift through representation in relation to where or who is wearing the coat or in relation to the very constitution of the coat itself. Is the coat belted neatly or is it tied or knotted? Is the fabric fresh, pressed or wrinkled? Is it white, khaki or black? The trench speaks visually not only through its elements but also by how those elements are portrayed in relation to the body. In the Robert Mitchum image from *Out of the Past* (Figure 13.2), for example, the actor wears the coat heavily wrapped around his body, draped almost toga-like – making the body underneath palpable. Mitchum's maleness seeps into the dense texture of the gabardine coat and into the tensely twisted knot of the belt to convey a visceral history of a life lived hard. His agency carries over into the coat. In contrast, Peter Sellers as the bungling Inspector Clousseau wears an overly large and too clean, white trench humorously devoid of manliness through its scale in relation to Clousseau's body, and by Clousseau's inability to make any personal mark on it, as Mitchum has (Figure 13.3). Also in contrast to Mitchum, Clousseau often gets trapped inside

Figure 13.2 Robert Mitchum and Jane Greer in *Out of the Past* (1947). Photo by Sunset Boulevard/Corbis via Getty Images.

Figure 13.3 Peter Sellers, *The Pink Panther* (1975). Photo by Stanley Bielecki Movie Collection/Getty Images.

his clothing and literally loses his trousers and his trench coat to the phantom thief he chases. The humour comes from the contrast of what we know the trench to be and what Clousseau is not. The same can be said of the Woody Allen character in *Play it Again, Sam* (1972), a comically neurotic man who tries to channel his hero Bogart by superficially emulating his style of dress – the trench coat. He may wear the trench, but he hardly truly 'embodies' it.

Peter Falk as Columbo in the television series of the same name is often cited as a model of a trench-coated detective.[17] Yet Columbo wears a raincoat with no belt. Does this count as a trench? Is the trench simply a lined or unlined khaki raincoat? In the *Trench Book*, published by Aquascutum, there are many pictures of people in khaki raincoats with no belts, including one of Cary Grant.[18] If the trench has to have a belt, and many do define it this way, then, perhaps, it is the very absence of the belt on Columbo's coat that delineates his character. Columbo is a detective whose deceptively dishevelled manner and wrinkled coat hide not a physical weapon but a razor-sharp mind. Perhaps Columbo does not need the belt (consider the meanings of that word). Interestingly, Columbo rarely closes his coat, which enhances his apparent guilelessness while gathering information to solve a case. He also hardly ever takes his coat off – meaning he never settles comfortably into the milieu that he investigates. The raincoat, of which the trench is a variant, even when transparent, is a barrier, a barrier between person and place or space, symbolic of someone in transit or in process. It is surely this for Holly Golightly, who, desperately afraid of settling down and uncertain of her identity, wraps herself in a Givenchy trench and wears oversized dark sunglasses to complete the disguise. (When Holly finally does acknowledge her love for Paul at the end of the film, the two appear in the rain in a duet of matching trench coats that express their 'couplehood' (Figure 13.4).)

If fashion serves to conceal and reveal the body simultaneously, the trench coat conceals fashion behind a seeming functionality, but the multiplicity of its buttons and flaps conversely expands imaginaries of transition and display that may be related to how the trench takes on its unique sexual dimension for both men and women. Often it is the trench worn by the male flasher or woman in expectation or provocation of sexual experience. As Nancy McDonell Smith writes, the fun of the trench is that it can be covering everything or nothing.[19] One fashion label, called 'What Lies Beneath', even entered the lingerie market offering underwear for different personalities but including a trench coat in its otherwise limited product line to capitalise on this use of the coat. (It is described by copy as a 'new line of intimates, loungewear, and trench coats [*wink, wink*]').[20] The transparent trench by Galliano makes this even more obvious. Katherine Frank, who writes about stripping, both as an accomplished theoretician and as a stripper herself, describes costume as adding the erotic component to stripping. She quotes Katherine Liepe-Levinson, a performance theorist, who states that costume, in fact, serves as an environment or frame for the stripper.

Figure 13.4 Audrey Hepburn and George Peppard wearing trench coats in *Breakfast at Tiffany's* (1961). Photo by Paramount Pictures/Sunset Boulevard/Corbis via Getty Images.)

Levinson writes, 'Costumes are environments for bodies, and like the interior design of theatres, they not only frame those bodies, but also engage the wearers and viewers in environmental reciprocities with cultural symbols of gender and desire.' Frank also cites Mario Perniola, who postulates that eroticism takes its power from transit, the movement towards the unveiling, or the transition between clothing and nudity.[21]

The trench, with its variety of closings and openings, augments the narrative potency of the coat, particularly given the contrast of the originally masculine coat to the female body. Perhaps the implicit notion here is that the woman as seducer needs the aggressively masculine coat to sanction the 'criminal' behaviour of actively seeking out sex. If seeing and perception are two different forms of cognition, as Peggy Phelan writes,[22] then a trench coat requires the spectator to read and think and wonder about the various possibilities related to flaps, belts and pockets – what is inside and what is outside, but while the trench-coated naked woman will generally reveal herself in a private setting, the male flasher shows himself in a public one. The flasher needs to validate himself as a man by displaying himself to a stranger. The trench coat as representative of widely advertised codes of masculinity, stemming from its combination of military and detective tropes, might serve to reinforce the very imaginings that set in motion the compulsive drive to 'flash'. That is, the coat itself represents the masculinity that the flasher desires to put on and show. In each case, the user of the trench – whether male or female – literally makes the coat into a kind of personal performance space, an environment within which to act or play-out sexual identity. As Efrat Tseelon notes, and as seems especially relevant here, instead of disguising identity, masking or hiding the body (in this case via the trench coat) it can enhance the projection or thrill of sexuality.[23] If the trench coat opens to reveal not a layer of clothing but instead the surprise of nakedness – and the public display of the nude body is more often than not construed as criminal – then the fashionable trench coat truly comports with Tolstoy's view of fashion as a revelation of nakedness.[24]

That the trench coat is about performance is especially evident in the number of flasher costumes on the market for the Halloween holiday in the US that affirm and acculturate this kind of sexual drama. Such dramas more quietly play out for women by advertising the trench as a 'look' that will bring the gaze onto the feminine wearer. By buying the coat, the consumer purchases a mysterious life, a history, as it were, attached to a once highly functional garment, but the various versions of the coats in materials that are not in fact weather-proof compromise its functionality and make it into an inauthentic garment whose styling or performativity overrides meaningful value and asserts instead a commodification of experience. A trench coat constructed from leather or suede must necessarily alter the meanings of the coat in daily life as its utility is subverted by fabrics that cannot and should not be worn in the rain. Similarly, polka dots, pink or red patent leather when applied to the trench challenge the origins of the coat – replacing male agency with the feminine potential for transformation. The coat becomes a multivalent material object conforming to broader ideas regarding gender.

Beverly Gordon suggested that were a pair of Guess jeans found years from now, their worn quality, rips and tears, might read to future historians as belonging to young women who worked long hard hours of physical labour wearing the same pair of jeans repeatedly. Actually 14- or 15-year-old girls wear the jeans in an attempt to clad themselves in the more romantic lives of others.[25] The same holds true for the trench. Like Guess jeans, the trench coat requires an intertextual reading alongside literature, advertising and film, which have 'coated' the coat with mini-narratives of fictional and functional display. The contemporary trench read through its fictions continues to reference the soldier, the detective and the reporter, but the coat itself has become a series of elements whose cultural elasticity speaks to Caroline Evans' speculations on fashion, modernity and the self. For Evans, fashion makes visible the 'ambiguity, anxiety and gender instability of modern life' by transforming 'the body and the psyche to cope with worldly environments'.[26] In these terms, the trench began as an artefact of modernity functioning as protection from meteorological elements and morphed into a psychological barrier. (It is certainly no accident that its fashionable resurrection in the US occurred alongside wars in Iraq and Afghanistan.)

The deconstruction of the trench in the second half of the twentieth century and into the twenty-first, its creative reconstruction of its constituent elements, almost akin to a Picasso portrait of the 1930s that wildly repositions facial features and body parts, makes it an icon of postmodernity, a polysemic form within that the individual can individuate him- or herself. Its once functional modernity has been replaced by its imaginary. Just as a uniform can serve as a model of standardisation and conformity, against which one transgresses the rules of society, the trench, once part of military equipment, next the coat and code of the detective, has become a signifier of cultural dichotomy. Jennifer Craik has written that for women a uniform articulates ambivalent attitudes regarding modern femininity. She writes, 'In the postmodern world, the symbolic baggage of the uniform may lie more in its excessive, parodic, erotic and comedic elements than in its denotation of order, discipline, authority, and control.'[27] The many iterations of the trench coat perfectly signify this range of associations, making fashion out of fiction and fiction out of fashion – marking a permeability between real life and narrative in which fashion exposes the condition of modern life as an unsolved mystery.

14

FROM *REVOLTING* TO *REVOLTING:* MASCULINITY, THE POLITICS AND BODY POLITIC OF THE TRACKSUIT

Joanne Turney

This chapter investigates the contemporary phenomena of the re-appropriation of sportswear (specifically the tracksuit) into everyday/non-sporting dress. Following recent media moral panics regarding social disobedience, deviant behaviour, lack of civic responsibility and consequent links to masculinity in crisis, issues surrounding sartorial coding have never been so central to the political agenda (i.e. 'hoodie' is an object, but it is also a person, deemed outside of normative culture and society). From ASBO youths to casual loungers, acrylic sportswear has become a staple of the male wardrobe, particularly for those not engaged in sporting pursuits. This chapter, much like the tracksuit, is composed of two distinct but interdependent areas of enquiry that aim to consider sport-less sportswear, its popularity and why these synthetic garments pose such a threat to the status quo. These are the subversion of normative dress codes and contemporary performances of masculinity in a 'leisure' society.

Here, the juxtaposition of the words 'track' and 'suit' will present a critique of the construction of masculine ideals through dress, whilst the performance of dominant and formal modes of masculine behaviour (such as sport and competition) will be comparatively discussed with reference to informal and antisocial activities. The two-piece tracksuit is therefore presented as indicative of new binary codes that dictate popular performance modes of masculinity, i.e. competition/consumption, competitor/spectator, active/passive, smart/casual and so on. Likewise, the term 'revolt' will be used and considered as a site of resistance (as in Imogen Tyler's *Revolting Subjects*) as an indicator of social protest and of social abjection.[1]

By analysing this prolific and seemingly innocuous sporting garb as both object and myth, the discussion positions the tracksuit as a sign of transitory masculinities and consequently indicative of social instability, and possible social threat. The tracksuit heralds the death of patriarchy. As an item of sportswear, the tracksuit is a pre-performance garment; it warms the wearer, keeping muscles flexible and the wearer largely hidden, and only through its removal are the intentions of the wearer as competitor visible. It is a garment of restlessness, of preparation, of thinking, of focus and ultimately one that, when unzipped, literally releases the beast. In everyday life, the tracksuit has similar properties; it hides the wearer and by association, intent. But what and who are in competition? What will be released when the body (potentially) emerges? The tracksuit, when worn on the street, will be considered in these terms: as the garb of the socially resting competitor; the temporary outsider for whom normative codes of behaviour and performance are viewed suspiciously from the side-lines.

An introduction to the tracksuit: In 'sporty' style

Initially a sporting garment popularised by athletes in the 1960s, the tracksuit developed into a wardrobe staple for men and women from the 1970s onwards. Like other garments, the tracksuit too has been subject to fashion and style changes, i.e. cotton towelling in the 1970s, the techno shell suit and the velour lounge suit in the 1980s and the first 'designer' tracksuit courtesy of Juicy Couture in the 1990s.[2] The transformation of the tracksuit from sportswear to a fashion item was a transition that responded to the zeitgeist, an example of a 'fitness chic' instigated in the 1970s and developed into a full-blown gym culture in the 1990s. Yet the tracksuit is not merely the clothing of the active, of fitness fanatics, but it is also the favourite garb of those 'at leisure', wearers wanting to feel comfortable, informal, cosy. Somewhere in between these opposing groups of wearers, rests something seemingly more suspect and potentially threatening; the teenager, the hoodie, the 'layabout' or 'yob', the seeker of trouble and the person who is most likely to be 'up to no good'.

It is the aim of this chapter to consider the value of the tracksuit in each of these incarnations, whilst also considering the ways in which the tracksuit can be understood as a garment that most readily represents and speaks of changes in, and attitudes to masculinity from the 1970s onwards. The cultural emphasis is primarily on dress in the UK, but as the period is indicative of globalisation, deindustrialisation and the homogenisation or 'flattening' of culture through the widespread circulation and manipulation of images, domination of multinational corporations and communications technologies, it is inevitable that additional 'outside' references will influence or contribute to the responses and appropriations of the garment.

It is fair to say that by the late 1970s, the tracksuit had become a sign of disenfranchised masculinity. Such identification came initially from the circulation of iconic imagery from the 1968 Mexico Olympic Games, in which African American athletes, wearing tracksuits, gave the Black Power salute on the winner's podium. Globally circulated, the significance of the Black Power salute in these circumstances heralded a social sea-change. This gesture was seen to be the culmination of dissatisfaction in a post-civil rights America, punctuated by race riots and anti-Vietnam demonstrations, which, spreading to Mexico City (host to the games), had witnessed the shooting of protesters by the authorities. Change was coming, and it seemed no one would be able to stop it. Gary Younge recollects,

> The sight of two black athletes in open rebellion on the international stage sent a message to both America and the world. At home, this brazen disdain for the tropes of American patriotism – flag and anthem – shifted dissidence from the periphery of American life to primetime television in a single gesture. ... Globally, it was understood as an act of solidarity with all those fighting for greater equality, justice and human rights.[3]

A sentiment that was evidenced symbolically by Oliver Brown in an interview with Tommie Smith (one of the athletes) 44 years later that

> what he [Smith] and Carlos demanded to be understood was the suffering of black America; as such, their ostensibly simple act of revolt concealed a complex web of symbolism. Where Smith's raised right hand stood for black power, Carlos's left signified black unity. The black scarf that Smith wore denoted black pride, while his black socks represented black poverty in a then corrosively racist American society.[4]

It was this iconography that was returned to in 1998 for the launch of Sean Combs' (aka Puff Daddy) appearance on an advertising hoarding in New York City's Times Square wearing his 'Sean John' signature velour tracksuit; his body encased in black, his arm raised in a power salute. Priced at $120, the tracksuit bore witness to its evolution stylistically and symbolically, but not necessarily its humble financial beginnings.[5]

The circulation of this symbolism had resonance in the UK and, combined with Bob Marley's red, gold and green tracksuit, translations of Black ethnicity became both mainstream and fashionable in the 1970s.[6] The tracksuit was not merely something that sociocultural instigators had worn and thus appropriated but was far more symbolic of escape from social constraint per se. For example, the central themes of sport and entertainment synthesise as indicators of a Black British male identity that aspires to emancipation; music and sport were ways in which Black men had negotiated some semblance of freedom and celebrity, and therefore visible (rather than 'invisible' or disenfranchised) recognition within mainstream British culture and society.[7] This firmly situated the tracksuit as the clothing of the competitor, both athletic and social, and thus was imbued with rebellion. In this context, one might consider the tracksuit the emblem of not merely 'Black Power' (although this was the primary motivation) but the disenfranchised per se; the competitor may be hidden beneath the nylon, but he is still there, waiting to fight, to compete and perhaps to gain an element of recognition through actually 'being seen'.

By the mid-1980s, Run DMC had sealed the fate of the tracksuit (like many other hip-hop artists and fans), by wearing the old skool Adidas two-piece reminiscent of those worn for the 1968 'salute'. Preferring the clothing worn on the street rather than couture – i.e. Kangol, Adidas, Reebok and so on – the hip-hop adoption of the tracksuit became a sign of ownership, power, anti- or alternative fashion. Yet simultaneously, the tracksuit was becoming increasingly popular within mainstream fashion, and also with those considered 'outside' fashion, the middle-classes and the elderly. This seems completely contradictory; a garment that is rebellious, marginal and political, and is somewhat race specific, suddenly gains popularity with groups of people diametrically opposite? One might start to explain this phenomenon as being a result of the cult of leisure developed in the 1980s that focussed on fitness and the body as a project, in addition to changing representations of masculinity during the period.

The development of a fitness culture originated in the US in the late 1970s with the publication of Jim Fixx's autobiographical and self-help title, *The Complete Book of Running*,[8] which encouraged thousands of predominantly White, middle-class men to take up jogging. Fixx's mantra was simple: active people live longer,[9] and consequently he inspired many (including the retired and those with heart conditions) to run to increase their life expectancy. When jogging, one needs suitable attire and the tracksuit is the perfect item; it warms muscles and is easily removed if one becomes too hot. It protects one from the elements, but it also indicates personal responsibility; it speaks of someone who is in control of his (her) destiny and has the power, in Fixx's words at least, to extend life. Such an analogy firmly positions the wearer in a God-like role, pitching man against the world, the elements and the inevitable. In a tracksuit, man is both man and superman, ego and super-ego, performing a Foucaultian battle that will ultimately result in the mastery of the mind over the weakness of the flesh.[10]

The nurturing of a cult of fitness was not limited to outdoor pursuits, as it also fostered a gym culture that promoted the development of physical strength through weight training. Here, we see the 'body project' in action; the body is something that needs to be healthy, honed, muscular and continually worked on in order to maintain its strength and (phallic) power, but one which also needs visual monitoring, posturing and, to a certain extent, recognition. This is a body that needs to be looked at, consumed and compared with the vast number of images of six-pack torsos displayed in advertising and magazines for men during the period.[11] This more visible male body (or what Gill et al call 'hypervisibility')[12] has been understood as a response to a) a marked increase in consumerism aimed at men that coincided with gender politics and legislation aimed at non-discrimination[13] and b) a concomitant cultural obligation to inhabit and demonstrate masculinity through a competitive individualism promoted not only through the ideologies of right-wing governments globally (and more specifically, Thatcherism in the UK)[14] but also through the celebrification of specific male sports stars (prowess, endorsements, magazine editorials on personal life, etc.), specifically tennis stars, Bjorn Borg, John McEnroe and Jimmy Connors, individual sportsmen rather than team players.[15] Both elements embrace the zeitgeist of buzz-words and phrases that position the body as both a project and site of consumption, i.e. 'dress for success', 'feel the burn', 'use it or lose it' and most significantly in the construction of mind over matter – 'no pain, no gain'. These were, as Gary Whannel notes,

> The themes of Thatcherism – individual self-reliance, hard work, enterprise and self-promotion were echoed in fitness chic. The activities of the new competitive individualism placed an emphasis on the work ethic. The slogans of the gym 'no pain, no gain', 'if it ain't hurting, it ain't working' and 'feel that burn' paralleled the political rhetoric of Thatcherism. The narcissistic focus on appearance and 'self' emergent in the 1970s … moved centre stage.[16]

The focus on the individual was paramount and the emphasis on personal responsibility for health, lifestyle, appearance and even destiny, created an industry that catered to these new responsible consumers; it was called 'leisure'. Although the term 'leisure' might, to some minds, imply sitting around and not working, the converse was actualised, as activities became more scheduled, professionalised and technologised, as if fitness was merely another articulation of work.

The purpose of the tracksuit was changing; it was now a sign of intent, whilst retaining an air of power and recognised excellence or celebrity. It was the clothing to be 'seen in'; worn on the way to and from the gym, pool, court, aerobics room and so on, it demonstrated to those outside of these sporting arena that the wearer 'meant business'. The tracksuit wearer was 'in control' of their body and by association their mind and the world that they inhabited. With such an emphasis on the garment facilitating the wearer to inhabit the zeitgeist, the adoption of the tracksuit as a fashion item was merely moments away.

The fashion for sportswear in the 1980s, particularly in the US was, according to Ingrid Loschek, the product of two diverse and new sporting activities; the predominantly White, female and middle-class pastime of aerobics and the working-class, Black and predominantly male-dominated break-dancing.[17] Clothing for both activities, she notes, was similar, and brands developed to suit these diverse markets and thus accommodate similarly disparate consumers. She states, '... sportswear stood for youth and youthfulness, for fitness, power and an active lifestyle; it was a symbol of status or differentiation and, above all, ease of wear, in other words, of the comfortable.'[18] So what is evidenced here is the symbolic potential of the garment, or the 'myth' that Barthes discusses,[19] in which sporting prowess and the sporting body are equated with physical power, but when combined with historical significance of the garment, it becomes a symbol of social power; the active becomes activist. This is further solidified, when one considers the comfort of the garment – clothes one feels at ease with – and thus an 'at ease with' the ideology of the garment is realised, even if one is neither engaging in sporting activities nor is physically fit. This is what Bourdieu describes as 'symbolic capital', suggesting that if the body 'looks' as if it is fit or 'sporty', whether it actually is, is irrelevant.[20]

Fashion is rarely about comfort, yet the relationship between clothing and comfort was at the forefront of design innovation, with sports technology and styling a fundamental element of fashion during the period. For example, Courrèges noted in 1979,

> So the clothes made for sport must be embodied and made into part of the rest of life. We must introduce a more relaxed, at-ease style to everyday clothes, even eveningwear. The ennoblement of sporting clothes is achieved not simply by making a tracksuit in silk or wool but by studying the tracksuit and incorporating the elements that make it so comfortably wearable in clothes which are stylish and flattering.[21]

This was partially the aim of Juicy Couture, a Los Angeles company that launched in 2001 and was ubiquitous globally by 2003. Juicy made tracksuits 'sexy' (rather than 'flattering' as Courrèges had hoped), considering the relationship between comfort and glamour, much of which was reliant on accessorisation (strappy high heels, the latest designer handbag, small dog) or a celebrity clientele (Brittney Spears, Jennifer Lopez, Madonna, in the UK, Katie Price). The tracksuit was not baggy and concealing like its male counterpart, rather it was fit to the body, with short-waisted jackets and thigh hugging trousers, almost like a second skin.

> The Juicy tracksuit changed the way women dressed. It was a design of its time on a par with Chanel's little black dress and Yves Saint Laurent's *Le Smoking* in the way that it captured the zeitgeist – the celebrity takeover of fashion, the casualization of culture and women's yoga – and Pilates-toned lifestyles. ... The tracksuit was an attainable status symbol, a new urban uniform for first class and coach class that came on the scene at a time when the fashion and magazine publishing industries were discovering celebrity sells ....[22]

An emphasis on clothing comfort, accessibility and recognition of the potential for smart/casualwear was considered the fusion of fashion with life, a sentiment embodied in the casual chic of Anne Klein, Calvin Klein, Ralph Lauren and a host of American ready-to-wear designers. Many of these incarnations featured in womenswear collections and incorporated new fibres such as Lycra, whilst such casual clothing for men embraced the scientific and was of a professional standard, combining hi-tech performance fabrics and fibres for an amateur market. The seeming blurring of boundaries between professional and amateur offers an interesting dimension to an understanding of the tracksuit: that one could potentially perform (or appear to perform) like an athlete even when one is not, and even at leisure (for the tracksuit is a leisure-suit) one can look and dress like a 'professional'. So, here is another paradox that highlights the contentious sartorial pairing of 'track' and 'suit'; sport and business, comfortable and formal, technology-driven and traditional. Yet for all the diametrically opposed semantics, 'track' and 'suit', both embrace and promote traditional notions of masculinity, i.e. power, rationality, single-mindedness, focus, direction, competition and ultimately fighting and winning. But what happens when the tracksuit is not worn by a professional driven by the competition of the sports-field? What happens when the comfortableness of the garment replaces the discipline of performance? What happens to notions of masculinity when these garments are appropriated for use in other contexts?

To this point, the history and consumption of the tracksuit has largely been one of struggle, drawing attention to power relations and elevating the dispossessed, or asserting one's business acumen in a 'leisure' and everyday arena. Its focus has been essentially a levelling of the playing field with an emphasis on a right to compete (and consume), including as if one were actually in a work environment. The tracksuit has embodied social justice whilst embracing the zeitgeist through fibre technology and democratised, comfortable dress. Yet in Britain at least, the tracksuit in the twenty-first century is a sign of antisocial activity and has become a symbol of the 'happily' dispossessed: rioters, thieves, the mass unemployed, revolting youths in revolting mass manufactured, cheap grey and uniformed tracksuits. The tracksuit is no longer the sign of the lone revolutionary; it is now a sign of an army that threatens the status quo (should media reports be believed).

In a study of neoliberalism in Britain, Imogen Tyler considers how minority groups and communities have been engaged in acts of revolt, and how these acts have been mediated, reported and responded to by the controlling majority as exemplars of disgust and horror.[23] In her argument she considers the ways in which neoliberalism, which *presents* a democracy of classlessness, creates a space that vilifies groups to the point of creating social abjection,[24] establishing a class that is beneath class.[25] Therefore the abject group crosses a boundary – a social and emotional boundary – that distances them, by consensus, as outside of and other to, the mainstream and therefore revolting to it. This group must exhibit sustainable characteristics or behaviours (or have these characteristics bestowed upon it, through, say, stereotyping, and thus be associated with them) that are repellent to the majority, i.e. contamination, disease, immorality, criminality and so on.[26]

As disgust is built on consensus, it must take a form that will make it recognisable. Or, one must encounter the object of disgust in order to be disgusted, and that object must rationalise and legitimise feelings of disgust beyond the distinction of that which is 'not me'. With this in mind, it is possible to suggest that the most significant indicator of group identity is through dress and behaviour, or the performance of the self through clothing.[27] As Diana Crane observes, 'Clothes as artefacts "create" behaviour through their capacity to impose social identities and empower people to assert latent social identities.'[28] Therefore, one might suggest that although clothing per se cannot determine behaviour, socially stigmatised clothing can offer the potential to distort normative and accepted patterns of behaviour, and likewise certain items of clothing can brand the wearer as 'Other'.[29] In relation to the tracksuit, we might consider 'disgust' at wearers as a symptom of wider sociopolitical and gender discourses emerging in the 1980s.

Although the predominant model in dress history is to consider the popularity of the tracksuit within male fashion as an extension of US rap and Black hip-hop style, its perpetuation in the UK was decidedly White and working class. It's popularity developed at a time when deindustrialisation[30] was at its height and masculinity was undergoing what the media called a 'crisis', the combination of which destabilised traditional notions of working-class masculinity. It would be easy at this juncture to consider the tracksuits' history from here on as an extension of youth subcultural dress, but it is far more than this, primarily because pretty much everyone can wear a tracksuit. (These similarities have been addressed in my work on hoodies in this volume and elsewhere.) If everyone has access to the same form of dress, does it become homogeneous or global, and how might this be understood as rebellious or revolting?[31]

If womenswear is considered a controlling force through its perceived discomfort, i.e. restriction of movement, tight fit, lacing (as it has been historically and by a variety of authors), which have been seen as correlating to social control, role and position, then, if we are to continue this binary, it should be absent from the male wardrobe. Historically this has not been the case, as menswear has also involved lacing and uncomfortable fashion garments, but with the advent of tailoring and the bespoke use of clothing to disguise undesirable bodily flaws, comfort seems to have been subsumed into class-based forms of control or hierarchy, such as 'smartness', by which comfort and formality can coexist. This implies that social control through clothing is not merely gender based, but it also emphasises class relations as 'smart' comfort comes at a cost; it's neat, fitted, good quality and probably comes from Savile Row. This has been most obviously evidenced in menswear from the early twentieth century onwards, where changes in manufacture and retail developed a mass market that democratised clothing, but even though a clerk was able to dress like a CEO, the details, quality and levels of 'smartness' or sartorial coding remained apparent. Class and clothing, or rather the inhabiting of clothing or the performance of the self through dress, demonstrated details and behaviours that had the potential to betray the wearer's background. This is Bourdieu's cultural capital in action;[32] how one consumes and wears clothing matters. This was particularly evident in the tracksuit's adoption by sports spectators rather than competitors in Britain during the 1980s, and it is from this sociocultural and historical moment that the tracksuit became not only an indicator of disenfranchised masculinity but also a sign of a transitional masculinity that is renewed through crisis, one which might be described as 'at rest'.[33]

Earlier in this book, I have considered the ways in which sportswear was used by subcultural groups (the 'Casuals') to communicate issues of sociocultural disenfranchisement through the performance of specific types of masculinity. The conclusion positioned specific elements of sportswear as expressions of re-appropriated bricolage, which, through wearing, became as indicative of a carnivalesque performance, through which power hierarchies were negotiated.

> 'Pit-hardened' young males, with no pit or shipyard within which to vent their machismo, sublimate their traditional industrial toughness into the carnivalesque. ... Indeed, it could be argued that the carnivalisation of popular culture provides a vital emotional prop for coping with rapid change.[34]

Therefore, the appropriation of luxury branded sportswear (Pringle, Fila, Lacoste) aimed at an older middle-class consumer (golf, tennis, sailing), by working-class youths, challenged notions, and the loss of blue-collar masculinity through objectification and consumerism, whilst also maintaining and transforming notions of power and control. Initially power can be read through the 'power' or cultural capital of the brand, which firmly situates control with the marketplace. Yet, reference to the establishment of traditional forms of working-class masculinity – discipline, drive, physical dominance and a 'hardness' – remained, exhibited through expressions of violence. The 'hard' man was now dressed in 'soft' clothes, emphasising the ability for different types of masculinities to coexist rather than one supplanting another.[35] This discourse is relevant to discussions of the tracksuit because not only do they emerge from the same genre of clothing and the same social class but they reflect attitudes to deindustrialisation and what effectively became to be seen as a new underclass: the non-working class. This means that although subcultural analysis may well befit discussion of football 'hooligans', it is not necessarily appropriate for groups who merely respond to outside forces that change quickly and impact life as a direct result. Concepts of 'waiting' or 'hanging around' whilst wearing sportswear indicate the axis at which non-action (hanging around, wearing the tracksuit) and action (sport, taking off the tracksuit) meet. The on/off friction (clothes and action) imply a potential readiness, the timing and nature of which is unknown, and thus creates a climate of anxiety that longs for the reveal or climax. It is this uncomfortable praxis, the anticipation, that establishes the tracksuit as the clothing of those behaving 'suspiciously', but conversely, it expresses a social invisibility, a period of waiting, of not performing, of sitting at the margins. The tracksuit wearer, under these circumstances, can be understood as a resting competitor; someone unable or unwilling to compete and therefore suspiciously rejecting the behavioural tropes of masculinity.

As a guise, the tracksuit is both symbolic and ideal; it references the uniform of the male competitor, the business suit (jacket and trousers). Unlike the business suit, which deliberately conceals the body and emphasises the cerebral rather than physical attributes of masculinity, the tracksuit albeit potentially shrouding the body also offers the potential to reveal it. So, one can hide within it, yet remove it quickly, and much like a mask, the onlooker is fascinated by what lies beneath. Yet this more than a brief sating of desire, as in striptease. Its quick removal is significant, in relation to both the potential for criminality and representations of masculinity. This works in two ways, both of which are reliant on the structure and design of the garment. Firstly, the bagginess of the suit, combined with its elasticated waistband/zip jacket (and possible front hand-pouch) offers the potential to conceal goods and thus act as a foil for theft.[36] Likewise, the baggy trousers, combined with the gait with which they are worn, have frequently been associated with the concealment of weapons,[37] whilst baggy, loose fitting standardised clothing has long been associated with the clothing of US prison inmates and gang members.[38] We might therefore consider the tracksuit as a garment that lends itself to undisciplined behaviour, clothing the criminal.

In relation to notions of masculinity, a focus on the undisciplined wearer is also central to the construction of meaning. Although the garment may be considered 'comfortable' by the wearer, the elasticated waistband and general bagginess allows for the concealment of an undisciplined body; one can grow fat without recourse, as the waistband (and fabric) stretches comfortably accordingly, thus creating an 'uncomfortable' sign of masculinity, opposing its ideals. Therefore, unlike his professional athletic counterparts, the tracksuit-wearing man is not a competitor; he is without the discomfort required to remind him of his endeavours, without the hard work of physical exertion, either through manual labour or time spent in the gym. Yet perhaps comfort is indicative of being comfortable in one's own skin, or, a sign of a rejection of competition, of wilful non-participation in stereotypical masculine activities and behaviours? And this is where the crux of the argument lies: Are these seeming rejections of masculine sartorial codes and behaviours chosen or inflicted? Are these signs of a respite from the game or an exclusion from the field?

Furthermore, the garment itself can be seen as removing phallic power through its construction. Tracksuit trousers have no fly and they require no belt; they keep their position on the body through elastication at the waistband, much like underpants. The construction responds to a practical need; athletes need to be track-ready at a moment's notice in order to compete, but this is not necessarily so for the amateur. The removal of the sporting function from the garment renders it unnecessary and as such makes the wearer vulnerable to childish male pranks such as 'de-bagging', where the trousers are yanked down and a bare bottom revealed to onlookers. Such humiliation (potential or realised) creates a group hierarchy (debagger and debagged) whilst also establishing a climate of fear based on one of men's primary anxieties: fear of revealing one's genitals and public nakedness. In addition to schoolboy behaviours, one might also consider the tracksuit trouser as further infantilising, as the waistband enables one to be easily dressed by another (mother, nurse, care-giver), as indicated in clothing for children and the physically disabled. Indeed, in more general discussions of sociocultural examples of infantilising men, the focus continually returns to a perceived inability to 'grow up and take on adult responsibilities'. This might include working, doing household chores, participating in child care and moral economy (bill paying, food shopping, etc.). This argument counteracts notions of tracksuit wearers as serious 'go getters', whilst simultaneously arguing that feminism has rendered men domestically and socially 'useless', as women have taken their responsibilities, partially as a response to deindustrialisation but also in relation to education.

Infantilisation is further compounded when the tracksuit is considerably oversized, making the wearer appear diminutive, whilst an allusion to fatness creates a symbolic parallel with over-nurtured (and nourished) babies (mummy's boys) whilst re-establishing masculine norms of roundness equating with femininity and lack of discipline (greed). If we accept Connell's assertion that a primary element of hegemonic masculinity is independence, then the tracksuit's allusion to dependency, embodies the breakdown of these structures.[39]

Likewise, sexual assaults such as flashing (genital exposure) and other forms of lewd behaviour is increasingly perpetrated by young men wearing tracksuits, because they offer ease of access, and a uniformity that belies identification.[40] We might therefore consider the tracksuit wearer under these circumstances as an exemplar of failure: failure to conform, to compete and to 'be a man'. From this perspective, we might consider the tracksuit as the ultimate form of 'non-power-dressing', a stigmatised ensemble that concomitantly feminises and infantilises.

Conclusion

In the nineteenth century,

> Sports were heralded as character building, and health reformers promised that athletic activity would not only make young men physically healthier but would instil moral virtues as well. Sports were cast as a central element in the fight against feminization; sports made boys into men.[41]

Sports demonstrated achievement and fostered a cult of uber-masculinity that aimed to oppose the then overt effeminacy of the urban 'fop', whilst instilling an overarching homophobia that outlined the characteristics of machismo. Therefore, sport and sporting attire has, over the past two centuries at least, been fundamentally associated with the ideologies and tropes of masculinity.

This chapter has aimed to consider the tracksuit in relation to class and gender, as a sign of either fitting in or standing out. It seems pertinent here to further classify the garment into the following opposing categories: sporting versus non-sporting activity, masculinity versus femininity and insider versus outsider dress. A decidedly masculine garment, representative of sport and competition has, through wearing and performance, has become a sign of 'broken Britain' and conversely, a broken masculinity, or one that remains in stasis.

These categories are significant as they draw attention to the performance of wearing. This is to say that the tracksuit wearer is a competitor, but one that can only be identified by their own peer group, or one that is instantly recognisable as the 'Other' (as demonstrated in Harry Enfield's 1990s comedy sketches featuring the shell-suit clad 'Scousers' and the velveteen tracksuit-wearing Waynetta in 'the Slobs', Sasha Baron Cohen's racially 'Othered' 'Ali G', or the tracksuited Vicky Pollard in Matt Lucas and David Walliams's *Little Britain*). Truth is indeed stranger than fiction, and, more sinisterly, the tracksuit is instantly recognisable as the clothing of the bling-laden, jewel coloured nylon suits of the serial sex-abuser, DJ and television presenter, Jimmy Saville, or the body-hugging pastel Juicy Couture tracksuit of the glamour model, Jordan (aka Katie Price). So, whilst the tracksuit is considered a universal garment, suitable for everyone, what is evidenced in these incarnations is difference; these people are 'not me' nor are they 'like me' and therefore they are '*revolting*', whether they are '*revolt*ing' or not.

NOTES

Introduction

1 Examples include, but are not limited to, Fred Davis, *Fashion, Culture, and Identity* (Chicago, IL: University of Chicago Press, 1992); Malcolm Barnard, *Fashion as Communication* (Abingdon: Routledge, 1996); Diana Crane, *Fashion and Its Social Agendas* (Chicago, IL: University of Chicago Press, 2000); Rebecca Arnold, *Fashion, Desire and Anxiety* (London: I.B. Tauris, 2001); Alison Goodrum, *Fashion and Identity* (Oxford: Berg, 2008); and Ingrid Loschek, *When Clothes Become Fashion* (Oxford: Berg, 2009).

2 Examples include Emma Tarlo, *Clothing Matters: Dress and Identity in India* (Chicago, IL: University of Chicago Press, 1996); Victoria A. Goddard (ed.), *Gender, Agency and Change: Anthropological Perspectives* (London: Routledge, 2000); Susanne Kuchler and Daniel Miller (eds), *Clothing as Material Culture* (Oxford: Berg, 2005).

3 The most notable example of this critical approach is John C. Flügel, *The Psychology of Clothes* [1930] (New York: AMS Press, 1976), which is reviewed by Roland Barthes in *The Fashion System* (Oakland, CA: University of California Press, 1983). Both of these texts influenced the more contemporary perspective taken in Susan B. Kaiser in *The Social Psychology of Clothing: Symbolic Appearances in Context* (London: Fairchild Publications, 1997).

4 This does find historical form in Aileen Ribeiro, *Dress and Morality* (Oxford: Berg, 2003).

5 Dick Hebdige, *Subculture: The Meaning of Style* (London: Taylor and Francis, 1979); Stanley Cohen, *Folk Devils and Moral Panics*, 3rd edn (London: Routledge, 2002).

6 Stuart Lanier and Mark M. Lanier, *The Essential Criminology Reader* (Boulder, CO: Westview Press, 2006).

7 Geoffrey Pearson, *Hooligan: A History of Respectable Fears* (Basingstoke: Macmillan, 1983); George Gerbner, 'Cultural indicators: The case of violence in television drama', *Annals of the American Academy of Political and Social Science* 338/1 (2007), pp. 69–81.

8 Paul Williams and Julie Dickinson, 'Fear of crime: Read all about it?: The relationship between newspaper crime reporting and fear of crime', *The British Journal of Criminology* 33/1 (Winter 1993), pp. 33–56.

  9 Sonia Livingstone, 'On the continuing problem of media effects research', in James
     Curran and Michael Gurevich (eds), *Mass Media and Society* (London: Arnold,
     1996), pp. 165–92.

 10 This is by no means wholly subjective or indeed objective and audience response
     to such reportage has both cultural and experiential dimensions that affect the
     interpretation of such imagery. See Regina G. Lawrence, *The Politics of Force:
     Media and the Construction of Police Brutality* (Berkeley, CA: University of California
     Press, 2000).

 11 Renata Salecl, *On Anxiety* (London: The Psychology Press, 2004).

 12 Richard V. Ericson, Patricia M. Baranek and Janet B. L. Chan, *Representing Order:
     Crime, Law, and Justice in the News Media* (Toronto: University of Toronto Press,
     1991).

 13 Roland Barthes, *Mythologies*, trans. Annette Lavers (London: Paladin, 1973).

 14 For example, the BBC4 foreign language import of Danish TV's *The Killing* attracted
     a regular audience of 500,000 in 2011, unprecedented for a subtitled drama in the
     UK (see Vicky Frost, 'The Killing, a slow-moving drama with subtitles, is a hit for
     BBC', *The Guardian*, 4 March 2011. Available at https://www.theguardian.com/
     tv-and-radio/2011/mar/04/the-killing-bbc-danish-crime-thriller (accessed 19 May
     2017), whilst home-grown dramas such as *Silent Witness* attract 6 million plus
     viewers weekly.

 15 This is by no means a contemporary fascination. See Philip Rawlings, *Drunks,
     Whores and Idle Apprentices: Criminal Biographies of the Eighteenth Century*
     (London: Routledge, 1998), which offers an analysis of an intense public interest
     not merely in other people's lives, but in the lives of those who live outside of the
     parameters of respectability. Here, as in the majority of contemporary 'life in crime'
     auto/biographies, the 'deviant' becomes a 'lovable rogue', and regardless of
     criminal involvement, the subject simultaneously, and paradoxically, exists as both
     like and unlike the reader. Such moral anomalies, when narrated as in these texts,
     question accepted norms of behaviour, somewhat blurring boundaries into a margin
     which can be crossed and uncrossed at any given juncture.

 16 John Dugdale, 'The most borrowed library books of 2010', *The Guardian*, 19
     February 2011. Available at https://www.theguardian.com/books/2011/feb/18/
     library-most-borrowed-books (accessed 19 May 2017).

 17 This science can be seen as a product of the Enlightenment, originating in
     eighteenth-century Switzerland and most notably developed by the nineteenth-
     century criminologist, Cesare Lombroso in his book *Criminal Man* [1876], trans.
     Mary Gibson (Durham, NC: Duke University Press, 2006).

 18 John Harvey, *Men in Black* (Chicago, IL: University of Chicago Press, 1995).

 19 M. Kimberley MacLin and Vivian Herrera, 'The criminal stereotype', *North American
     Journal of Psychology* 8/2 (June/July 2006), pp. 197–208.

 20 'Bid to impose asbo for wearing low-slung trousers dropped', *The Guardian*, 4 May
     2010. Available at https://www.theguardian.com/society/2010/may/04/asbo-low-
     slung-trousers-dropped (accessed 5 July 2010).

 21 Walter Benjamin, *The Arcades Project* [1982] (Cambridge, MA: Harvard University
     Press, 1999).

22 Caroline Evans, *Fashion at the Edge: Spectacle, Modernity and Deathliness* (New Haven, CT: Yale University Press, 2003).

Chapter 1

1 Richard Dyer, *The Matter of Images: Essays on Representations* (London: Routledge, 1993), p. 142.

2 *Scarface*, 1932, dir. Howard Hawks and Richard Rosson, cost. uncredited.

3 *The Public Enemy*, 1931, dir. William A. Wellman, cost. Earl Luick; *Little Caesar*, 1931, dir. Mervyn LeRoy, cost. Earl Luick.

4 Stella Bruzzi, *Undressing Cinema: Clothing and Identity in the Movies* (London: Routledge, 1997), p. 69.

5 Thorstein Veblen, *The Theory of the Leisure Class* (New York: Macmillan, 1899) quoted in Malcolm Barnard, *Fashion Theory: A Reader* (London: Routledge, 2007), p. 341.

6 *The Great Gatsby*, 1974, dir. Jack Clayton, cost. Theoni V. Aldredge.

7 *Saturday Night Fever*, 1977, dir. John Badham, cost. Patrizia von Brandenstein.

8 *Midnight Cowboy*, 1969, dir. John Schlesinger, cost. Ann Roth.

9 *The Man in the White Suit*, 1951, dir. Alexander Mackendrick, cost. Anthony Mendleson.

10 Bruzzi, *Undressing Cinema*, p. 72.

11 *Each Dawn I Die*, 1939, dir. William Keighley, cost. Howard Shoup (gowns); *Dr No*, 1962, dir. Terence Young, cost. Tessa Prendergast.

12 *Scarface*, 1983, dir. Brian de Palma, cost. Patricia Norris. I am referring to the enormous influence de Palma's *Scarface* has had on contemporary rap stars, who have not only referenced the film lyrically and used its imagery for album covers and so on, but in certain cases have also modelled their on- and off-stage personae and dress sense on Al Pacino's depiction of Camonte in the film.

13 *The Untouchables*, dir. Brian de Palma, 1987, cost. Giorgio Armani and Dan Lester; *The Boys from Brazil*, dir. Franklin J. Schaffner, 1978; *The Intruder*, dir. Roger Corman, 1961; *The Boys from Brazil*, 1978, dir. Franklin J. Schaffner, cost. Anthony Mendleson; *The Intruder*, 1961, dir. Roger Corman, cost. Dorothy Watson.

14 Jean Baudrillard, *Simulations*, trans. Paul Foss, Paul Patton and Philip Beitchman (New York: Semiotext(e), 1983), p. 37.

15 John Gage, *Colour and Culture* (London: Thames & Hudson, 1993), p. 60.

16 Ibid.

17 Dialogue from *The Intruder*.

18 Mark Wigley, *White Walls, Designer Dresses* (Cambridge, MA: MIT Press, 2001), p. 177.

19 Gage, *Colour and Culture*, p. 60.

20 Ulrich Lehmann, 'The language of the PurSuit: Cary Grant's clothes in Alfred Hitchcock's "North by Northwest"', *Fashion Theory* 4/4 (2000), pp. 467–86.

21 John Harvey, 'Showing and hiding: Equivocation in the relations of body and dress', *Fashion Theory* 11/1 (2007), pp. 65–94.

22 Dialogue from *The Intruder*.

23 Guy Debord, *The Society of the Spectacle*, trans. Donald Nicholson-Smith (Detroit, MI: Red & Black, 1973).

Chapter 2

1 David Davis, cited in *The Telegraph*, 8 October 2007, in response to the urban streetwear company Criminal Damage, launching a 'faceless' hoodie.

2 Kevin Braddock, 'The power of the hoodie', *The Guardian*, 9 August 2011. Available at https://www.theguardian.com/uk/2011/aug/09/power-of-the-hoodie (accessed 11 August 2011).

3 Richard Garner ('Hoodies, louts, scum: how media demonises teenagers', *The Independent*, 13 March 2009) commented on a survey commissioned by Women in Journalism that cites the portrayal of teenage boys as 'yobs' and criminals, i.e. in regional and national newspapers 4,374 out of 8,629 stories that referenced teenage boys focused on crime and criminality.

4 *BBC News*, 2005.

5 See Michael Shaw, 'From hooligans to hoodies', *TES*, 8 October 2010. Available at https://www.tes.com/news/hooligans-hoodies (accessed 11 August 2011), which references the history of badly behaved youths as seen in the columns of the *TES* from 1915 onwards and outlines the similarity in terms of concern, if not approach or historicity.

6 Braddock, 'The power of the hoodie'.

7 Aileen Ribeiro, *Dress and Morality* (London: Bloomsbury Academic, 1986), p. 12.

8 Quentin Bell, *On Human Finery* (London: Hogarth Press, 1947) quoted in Ribeiro, *Dress and Morality*, p. 12.

9 Greg Philo, quoted in Jane Graham, 'Hoodies strike fear in British cinema', 5 November 2009. Available at https://www.theguardian.com/film/2009/nov/05/british-hoodie-films (accessed 20 February 2010).

10 India Knight, 'Let them wear hoodies', *The Sunday Times*, 15 May 2002. Available at https://www.thetimes.co.uk/article/india-knight-let-them-wear-hoodies-6vznmrml0lv (accessed 15 April 2006).

11 *The Telegraph*, 'London riots: Eric Pickles blames looting on "criminal sub-culture"', 9 August 2011. Available at https://www.telegraph.co.uk/news/uknews/crime/8691598/London-riots-Eric-Pickles-blames-looting-on-criminal-sub-culture.html (accessed 11 August 2011).

12 Julia Kristeva, quoted in Kelly Oliver (ed.), *The Portable Kristeva* (New York: Columbia University Press, 2002), p. 229.

13 Jennifer Craik, *The Face of Fashion: Cultural Studies in Fashion* (London: Routledge, 1994), p. 1.

14 Graham, 'Hoodies strike fear in British cinema'.

15 Mohammed Abbas and Kate Holton, 'London rioters point to poverty and prejudice', *Reuters*, 9 August 2011. Available at www.reuters.com/article/2011/08/09/britain-riot-contrast-idUSL6E7J91RM20110809 (accessed 11 August 2011).

Chapter 3

1 Mike Daniel, 'Rap about saggin' pants upsets gay groups', *McClatchy-Tribune Business News*, 2 November 2007, Proquest. Available at URL? (accessed 12 December 2010).

2 Discussion with mothers of the Midlothian Chapter of Jack and Jill of America Inc. in Richmond, VA.

3 Serena Kim, 'Style council', *Vibe* 9/9 (2001), pp. 206–10.

4 Hatfield, 'Hip hop gets the bounce', *Boston Globe* (30 November 1993), Section 3, p. 61.

5 Kim, 'Style council'.

6 Based on companies that sell prison uniforms. For example, The Cuff Shop, The Cornerstone Detention and the PX Direct.

7 Holly Alford, 'The zoot suit: Its history and influence', *Fashion Theory* 8/2 (2004), pp. 225–36.

8 Ibid.

9 See *Urban Dictionary*, website http://www.urbandictionary.com/

10 Anthony Westbury, 'Saggy pants symbolize what's gone wrong in black community, kids say', TCPalm, 21 October 2010. Available at http://archive.tcpalm.com/news/columnists/anthony-westbury-saggy-pants-symbolize-whats-gone-wrong-in-black-community-kids-say-ep-389105840-345689782.html/ (accessed 15 May 2011).

11 Many blog sites state that teens are saggin' for this reason, for example, the blog site 'Now that's what I'm talkin about' by Theo Johnson. He asked if sagging pants were fashion or disrespectful.

12 Associated Press, 'Florida judge rules saggy pant law unconstitutional after teen spends night in jail', *Fox News* [online], 17 September 2008. Available at http://www.foxnews.com/story/02933,424123,00.html (accessed 10 November 2010).

13 Onika K. Williams, 'The suppression of a saggin' expression: Exploring the "saggy pants" style within a First Amendment context', *Indiana Law Journal* 85/3 (2010), pp. 1188–96.

14 *Orlando Sentinel*, 'Baggy pants: Baggy pants trip up teen suspected in robberies', *Orlando Sentinel*, 26 January 2007. Available at http://articles.orlandosentinel.com/2007-01-26/news/MUSNEWS26_6_1_baggy-pants-covington-caught (accessed 13 May 2011).

15 Clarence Chavis, 'Men are looking like a fool with your pants on the ground', Part 2, *SF Men's Issues Examiner*, 9 February 2010. Available at http://www.examiner.com/men-s-issues-in-san-francisco/men-you-are-looking-like-a-fool-with-your-pants-on-the-ground-part-two?render=print (accessed 12 January 2011).

16 MC Lyte, 'Paper Thin', *Lyte as a Rock*, Track 6 (First Priority Music/Atlantic Records, 1988).

17 The Outdoor World, 'Ben Davis work pants', *The Outdoor World* [online], 2011. Available at http://www.theoutdoorworld.com/bendavispants.cfm (accessed 7 January 2011).

18 Matt Amaral, 'Latino boys in the red white and blue', *Teach 4 Real*, 2007. Available at http://www.teach4real.com/2010/07/07/latino-boys-in-the-red-white-and-blue/ (accessed 30 January 2011).

19 Slang for tight underwear.

20 Calvin Klein History [online], 2011. Available at http://www.buycalvinkleinunderwear. com/calvin_klein.com (accessed 30 January 2011).

21 Interviewed 5 youths at the Manchester, VA YMCA, at the skateboard park.

22 TransWorld SKATEboarding, 'Roots, rock, reggae, skateboarding', July 2003. Available at http://skateboarding.transworld.net/1000012446/photos/roots-rock-reggae-skateboarding/ (accessed 13 May 2010).

23 Lee D. Baker, 'Saggin' and braggin'', in Alisse Waterston and Maria D. Vesperi (eds), *Anthropology Off the Shelf: Anthropologists on Writing* (Chichester: Wiley-Blackwell, 2009), pp. 46–59, p. 42.

24 Joshua Smith, 'The legend of baggy pants', *Metro Spirit*, 19. Available at http://www.metrospirit.com/index.php?cat=1211101074307265&ShowArticle_ID=1102200508 (accessed 3 June 2010).

25 Pierre Wright, interview, 3 February 2011.

26 Interview with 10 youths, five White and five Black.

27 Darlene F. East, 'Baggy, baggier, baggiest! Young males are "glad bags": from "Fauntleroy" to rap', *NCAT Journalism Magazine*, 2002. Available at http://worldlymind.org/baggy.htm (accessed 12 January 2011).

28 Saggerboys.com, 2011. Available at http://www.saggerboys.com/ (accessed 7 January 2011).

29 Kyung Lah, 'Olympic snowboarder's "street" style offends Japanese', *CNN*, 18 February 2010. Available at http://www.cnn.com/2010/SPORT/02/18/japan.kokubo.olympics/index.html (accessed 18 February 2010).

30 Smith, 'The legend of baggy pants'.

31 Clyde Haberman, 'Can Obama help kill baggy pants look?', *New York Times*, 13 November 2008. Available at https://www.nytimes.com/2008/11/14/nyregion/14nyc.html (accessed 10 November 2010).

32 Rapheal Heaggans, *The 21st Century Hip Hop Minstrel Show: Are We Continuing the Black Face Tradition?* (San Diego, CA: University Readers, 2009).

33 R. M. Schneiderman, 'Ad campaign asks Queens bus riders to pull up their pants', *Wall Street Journal*, 17 May 2010. Available at http://blogs.wsj.com/metropolis/2010/05/17/ad-campaign-asks-queens-bus-rider-to-pull-of-their-pants/ (accessed 12 December 2010).

34 Laura Graff, 'March will protest sagging', *Winston Salem Journal*, 8 October 2010. Available at http://www2.journalnow.com/news/2010/oct/08/march-will-protest-sagging-ar-442768/ (accessed 14 December 1993; not available outside US).

35 Smith, 'The legend of baggy pants'.

36 Ibid.

37 Niko Koppel, 'Are your jeans sagging? Go directly to jail', *New York Times*, 30 August 2007. Available at http://www.nytimes.com/2007/08/30/fashion/30baggy.html (accessed 14 December 2010).

38 Slang term used to describe pants worn below the waist.

39 Brian O'Connell, 'Tighten your belt, or at least wear one', *The Irish Times* [online], 11 May 2010. Available at http://www.irishtimes.com/newspaper/features/2010/0511/1224270124758.html (accessed 12 December 2011).

40 Koppel, 'Are your jeans sagging?'

41 Marc Lamont Hill, 'Sagging pants: Hip hop trend or prison culture?' *MarcLamontHill* [online], 21 April 2010. Available at http://www.marclamonthill.com/sagging-pants-fashion-trend-or-prison-culture-7651 (accessed 21 April 2011).

42 Tannette Johnson-Elie, '*Milwaukee Journal Sentinel* Tannette Johnson-Elie column', *Knight Ridder/Tribune Business News*, 16 February 2005. Available at http://www.accessmylibrary.com/coms2/summary_0286-8288840_ITM (accessed 12 December 2010).

43 Ibid.

44 Williams, 'The suppression of a saggin' expression'.

45 Daniel, 'Rap about saggin' pants upsets gay groups'.

46 Blogging on sites such as anonymousinmate.com and others where prisoners can answer questions.

47 Hill, 'Sagging pants'.

48 Daniel, 'Rap about saggin' pants upsets gay groups'.

49 Hector Florin, 'A saggy-pants furor in Riviera Beach', *Time*, 1 October 2008. Available at http://www.time.com/time/world/article/0,8599,1846205,00.html#ixzz1Mf1sG0NO (accessed 10 November 2010).

50 Eric Montgomery, 'Is gangsta rap irrelevant?' *Riverside, CA* [online], 22 July 2010. Available at http://www.examiner.ca.riverside/is-gangsta-rap-irrelevent (accessed 8 May 2011).

51 Interview conducted with five White youths and five Black youths who sagg'.

Chapter 4

1 Mark Michaelson and Steven Kasher in *Least Wanted: A Century of American Mugshots*, 1st edn (New York: Steven Kasher Gallery, 2006).

2 LVX and the names of all casting professionals in this chapter are pseudonyms. My fieldwork at LVX was part of a larger ethnographic research project I conducted over four years (2003–7), which also included participant observation at a high-end women's modelling agency, a mid-range men and women's modelling agency, editorial offices of two fashion magazines and a photo production agency, all in New York City. This research was funded in part by the Wenner-Gren Foundation for Anthropological Research (Grant #7493), the Ford Foundation and the Graduate School of the Arts and Sciences at New York University.

3 Cf. Daniel A. Segal, 'Can you tell a Jew when you see one? Or thoughts on meeting Barbra/Barbie at the museum', *Judaism* (Spring 1999), pp. 234–41.

4 Kelley Gates, 'Identifying the 9/11 "faces of terror"', *Cultural Studies* 20/4–5 (2006), pp. 417–40; Greg Noble, 'The face of evil: Demonising the Arab other in contemporary Australia', *Cultural Studies Review* 14/2 (2008), pp. 14–33.

5 Paul Frosh, *The Image Factory: Consumer Culture, Photography and the Visual Content Industry* (New York: Berg, 2006), pp. 92–3.

6 John Tagg, *The Burden of Representation: Essays on Photographies and Histories* (Minneapolis, MN: University of Minnesota Press, 1993), p. 4.

7 Charles Goodwin, 'Professional vision', *American Anthropologist* 96/3 (1994), pp. 606–33.

8 Ibid., p. 626.

9 Allan Sekula, 'The body and the archive', *October* 39 (1986), pp. 3–64, p. 10.

10 Ibid., p. 18.

11 Jonathan M. Finn, *Capturing the Criminal Image: From Mug Shot to Surveillance Society* (Minneapolis, MN: University of Minnesota Press, 2009), p. 29.

12 Deborah Poole, 'An Excess of Description: Ethnography, Race, and Visual Technologies', *Annual Review of Anthropology* 34 (2005), pp. 159–79.

13 Finn, *Capturing the Criminal Image*; Gates, 'Identifying the 9/11 "faces of terror"'; Rachel Hall, 'Of Ziploc bags and black holes: The aesthetics of transparency in the War on Terror', in Shoshana Magnet and Kelly Gates (eds), *The New Media of Surveillance* (New York: Routledge, 2009), pp. 41–68; Mark Maguire, 'The birth of biometric security', *Anthropology Today* 25/2 (2009), pp. 9–14.

14 Noble, 'The face of evil', p. 15; cf. Peter Benson, 'El Campo: Faciality and structural violence in farm labor camps', *Cultural Anthropology* 23/4 (2008), pp. 589–629).

15 Noble, 'The face of evil', p. 29.

16 Ibid.

17 Susan Sontag, 'An argument about beauty', *Daedalus* 131/4 (2002), pp. 21–6, p. 25.

18 Anne Cheng, 'Wounded beauty: An exploratory essay on race, feminism, and the aesthetic question', *Tulsa Studies in Women's Literature* 19/2 (2000), pp. 191–217, p. 196.

19 Ibid., 195.

20 Claire Dwyer and Philip Crang, 'Fashioning ethnicities: The commercial spaces of multiculture', *Ethnicities* 2/3 (2002), pp. 410–30, p. 412.

21 Stephanie Sadre-Orafai, 'Fashion's other images', in Æsa Sigurjónsdóttir, Michael Langkjær and Joanne Turney (eds), *Images in Time* (Bath: Wunderkammer, 2011), pp. 123–30.

22 Kevin Lynch, *The Image of the City* (Cambridge, MA: MIT, 1960).

23 Ann Kingsolver, 'Contested livelihoods: "Placing" one another in "Cedar", Kentucky', *Anthropological Quarterly* 65/3 (1992), pp. 128–36.

24 Kathleen Stewart, *A Space on the Side of the Road: Cultural Politics of an 'Other' America* (Princeton, NJ: Princeton University Press, 1996), p. 201, emphasis in original.

Chapter 5

1 As with other sociological keywords launched in popular journalistic articles, such as *shinjinrui* or 'new breed' coined by Chikushi Tetsuya in 1985, the earliest published article on *kogyaru* set out to discover and define a 'post body-con generation', but had only a vague notion of a *kogyaru* beyond this. At this time she was not connected to loose socks, school uniforms or sexual deviance, but rather with stripping away the artifice, uncomfortable high heels and body-shaping underwear of grown-up working *gyaru* in their 20s, to pursue a more 'casual, natural, and healthy look' (*Spa!*, 'Kogyaru no yūwake', 9 June 1993, p. 11).

2 Since the 1980s *gyaru* has operated as an opposite to the more ideal *shōjo* (girl) in contemporary language, which tends to label women from a largely male perspective – *shōjo* implying obedient and innocent, and *gyaru* insinuating sexual, pushy, self-aware and dressed to impress one another and not appeal to male tastes (Sharon Kinsella, 'Black faces, witches, and racism against girls', in Laura Miller and Jan Bardsley (eds), *Bad Girls of Japan* (New York: Palgrave Macmillan, 2005), pp. 143–58, pp. 145–7).

3 This was a comic parody of actual 'morality committees' (*rinri iinkai*) that meet to discuss the moral health and cultural environment of minors in each local government jurisdiction every month or two – depending on the timetable of each prefecture. The men on this 'morality committee' panel included journalist Yoshii Fujiki, a 'Doctor Nakashima' and Suzuki Hirohisa, and *otaku* talent Taku Hachiro. Amusingly it transpired during a short documentary interlude within the show, in which veteran female journalist Kikuchi Yōko is seen asking girls walking into Shibuya Center-Gai 'what are *kogyaru?*,' that in her sample only one woman had heard of the term.

4 Yukiko Hayami, 'Toragyaru osorubeki enjo kōsai: Joshikōsei saisentan rupo', *AERA* 9/16 (15 April 1996), p. 64.

5 For more detail on the history and main styles of the customised school uniform in modern Japan see Sharon Kinsella, 'What's behind the fetishism of Japanese school uniforms?', *Fashion Theory* 6/2 (May 2002), pp. 215–37.

6 Kinsella, 'Black faces, witches, and racism against girls'.

7 Theresa Winge discusses the 'transition phase' of Lolitas (Theresa Winge, 'Undressing and dressing loli: A search for the identity of the Japanese Lolita', *Mechademia* 3 (2008), pp. 47–63, pp. 56–7).

8 Brian J. McVeigh, *Wearing Ideology* (London: Berg, 2000), pp. 70–5. This too was not a new problem: suspicions about fake or 'wannabe' schoolgirls donning the schoolgirls identifying 'purple-brown skirt' (*ebicha shikibu*) and dating male students in Ikebukuro Park surfaced in the first years of the twentieth century.

9 An interesting article about '*nanchatte*' accompanied by a photograph of five high-school girls attending the same high school but each wearing a different self-assembled uniform, appeared in the *Asahi Shinbun* on 15 March 2003.

10 *H*, 'Watashitachi no orutanatibu weii', April 2003.

11 Marion Hume, 'Tokyo glamorama', *Harpers Bazaar*, 1 October 2000, pp. 311–5 and p. 338.

12 Ogino Yoshiyuki, interview, 12 November 1997.

13 Arai Hiroshi, interview, 5 November 1998.

14 Eric Lott, *Love and Theft: Blackface Minstresly and the American Working Class* (London: Oxford University Press, 1993), p. 113.

15 Anthropologist Ikuya Satō discovered in the 1980s that 'this close, almost inseparable, relationship between the mass media and *bōsōzoku* activity may give one the impression that the activity is fabricated to a considerable extent by the mass media to exploit the desire of youths in motorcycle gangs for self-display. One may also consider that motorcycle gangs are merely imitating the schemes of action suggested in the media reports' (Ikuya Satō, *Kamikaze Biker: Parody and Anomy in Affluent Japan* (Chicago, IL: University of Chicago Press, 1991), p. 73).

16 Ibid., p. 3.

17 Asian Women's Foundation (AWF), *1997 Survey*, March 1998, p. 82.

18 Ogino Yoshiyuki, interview, 12 November 1997.

19 *Cawaii!*, 'Kaigai burando namaiki gōman', May 1996, pp. 20–1.

20 Mariana Valverde, 'The love of finery: Fashion in nineteenth-century social discourse', *Victorian Studies* 32/2 (Winter 1989), pp. 169–88, p. 183.

21 Richard Hoggart, *The Uses of Literature* (Harmondsworth: Penguin Books, 1957), p. 148.

22 Masaki Hirota, 'Notes on the "process of creating women"', in Wakita Haruko, Anne Bouchy and Ueno Chizuko (eds), *Gender and Japanese History*, vol. 2 (Osaka: Osaka University Press, 1999), pp. 197–219, p. 217.

23 Cited in Harry Harootunian, *Overcome by Modernity: History, Culture and Commodity in Interwar Japan* (Princeton, NJ: Princeton University Press, 2000), p. 179.

24 *Cawaii!*, July 1997, pp. 15–6.

25 *Tokyo Street News*, December 2002, pp. 34–41.

26 Ogino, interview, 12 November 1997.

27 Between 1992 and 2002 the number of girls going on to university doubled. In 1992 it was 16.1 per cent and by 2002 this figure had increased to 33.8 per cent. Source: Ministry of Education, Culture, Sports, Science and Technology.

28 Photographer Ohnuma Shōji makes mention of a girl stranded in the city centre at night, after the last train had departed, ruefully describing herself as *lunpenppoi* or 'like a beggar' (Shōji Ohnuma, *Minzoku [Tribe]* (Tokyo: Kawade Shobō Shinsha, 2001)).

29 See Laura Miller, 'Graffiti photos: Expressive art in Japanese girls' culture', *Harvard Asia Quarterly* 3 (Summer 2003), pp. 31–42.

30 Hayami, 'Toragyaru osorubeki enjo kōsai', pp. 62–5, p. 62.

31 In March 2003 I asked six fashionable young women waiting to meet their friends in cafes in Shibuya to read through this list of about 40 so-called *kogyaru* terms. All of

the women I asked to be my respondents were in their early 20s and all had been high-school girls in the period between 1995 and 2002. While they recalled *kogyaru* speech and style with amusement as something that reminded them of their schooldays, none of them agreed to ever having heard most of these terms before or in their high schools.

32 Kōji Maruta, 'Giji-ibento to shite no enjo kōsai' [Compensated dating as a pseudo event], *Osaka jogakuin tankidaigaku kiyō*, dai 30 (2000), pp. 209–22, p. 210. Whatever its origins, *kogyaru go* is reminiscent of the masculine and witty café waitress lingo of the 1920s (Miriam Silverberg, 'The modern girl as militant', in Gail Lee Bernstein (ed.), *Recreating Japanese Women 1600–1945* (Berkeley, CA: University of California Press, 1999), pp. 239–66, p. 21) and through this also bears a connection with the linguistic bricolage that the art historian Andō Kōsei suggests was the foundation of *satokotoba* – the dialect spoken in the premodern Yoshiwara brothel district (ibid., p. 20).

33 *Popteen Magazine*, 12 (1993), p. 175.

34 Details of the fascinating and strategic launch of *kogyaru* magazines by erstwhile specialist publishers of pornography producing Lolita-complex material for men are included in a forthcoming book by the author, 2012.

35 In autumn 1997 and summer 1998 I distributed a four-page self-completion questionnaire survey titled 'Wakai hitotachi: media to pop-culture ni tsuite no kansō' (Young people's impressions of the media and pop culture), to 36 respondents from a range of locations around central Tokyo and Saitama prefecture. There were nine male, 24 female and three gender-undisclosed respondents between the ages of 15 and 22 years old. All respondents had been middle- or high-school students or were just about to graduate from high school at the peak of media coverage on *kogyaru* and compensated dating in 1996 and 1997, and most had been the high-school peers or participants of *kogyaru* style. All of the surveys were completed anonymously but respondents received some encouragement and a verbal overview of my research in advance.

36 Of these 36 high-school children and freshman university students, most had heard about 'compensated dating' from the media. In response to the question: 'Do you remember when you first heard the term "compensated dating"? How did you hear about it?', nine out of 12 male and gender-undisclosed respondents said they could not recall where they first heard the term; two out of the 12 said they could remember and that they first heard the term on television, and one male respondent said he witnessed a compensated date in Chiba prefecture and 'knew what it was'. Among female respondents, four out of 24 could not remember where they first heard of it; one out of 24 first heard the term from a friend and 19 out of 24 said they first heard about it from a drama, the news or the media. While only one out of the total of 36 respondents recalled first hearing about compensated dating from a friend, the majority, comprising a higher proportion of the female than male respondents, indicated that they first heard of it through watching television.

37 Hashimoto, interview, 30 November 1997.

38 Shinji Miyadai, *Seikimatsu no sahō: Owarinaki nichijō o ikiru chie* [*Millenial Etiquette: The Art of Living a Never-ending Everyday Life*] (Tokyo: Recruit, 1997), pp. 260–3.

39 John W. Dower, *Embracing Defeat: Japan in the Wake of World War II* (New York: W.W. Norton and Company The New Press 1999).

40 Ibid., p. 148.

41 Ibid., p. 155.

42 Silverberg, 'The modern girl as militant', pp. 241–6.

43 Cited in Barbara Satō, *The New Japanese Woman: Modernity, Media and Women in Interwar Japan* (Durham, NC: Duke University Press, 2003), p. 65.

44 Quoted in Mariko Asano Tamanoi, *Under the Shadow of Nationalism: Politics and Poetics of Rural Japanese Women* (Honolulu: University of Hawaii Press, 1998), p. 222.

45 Cited ibid., p. 70.

46 Ohnuma, *Minzoku*.

47 Quoted in Shannon Bell, *Reading, Writing, and Rewriting the Prostitute Body* (Bloomington, IN: Indiana University Press, 1994), pp. 48–9.

Chapter 6

1 50 Cent, 'P.I.M.P', *Get Rich or Die Tryin'*, Aftermath Entertainment/Shady Records/ Interscope Records, Track 11, 2003.

2 According to International Federation of the Phonographic Industry (IFPI), 'Recording Industry in Numbers 2010', 28 April 2010. Available at http://www. snepmusique.com/wp-content/uploads/2014/01/rin2010.pdf (accessed 2 February 2015), p. 5, in 2009 global recorded music sales generated US$17 billion – despite an overall decline in music revenues resulting in part from piracy and a global economic depression – and hip-hop accounts for approximately 10 per cent of that (Ta-Nehisi Coates, 'Hip-hop's down beat', *Time*, 17 August 2007. Available at http://www.time.com/time/magazine/article/0,9171,1653639,00.html (accessed 6 January 2010)).

3 'Mainstream' is here taken to refer to the form(s) of hip-hop presented via MTV and other mass-media, non-specialist outlets.

4 Which is not to suggest that the viewer actively sets out to deny the humanity of the woman cast in the 'ho' role, but the repudiation of her individuality is a defining aspect of the persona and part of what makes her so beguiling, so the focus herein will be on the 'ho's' sociocultural symbolic function, rather than the agency of the individuals found framed in this manner.

5 The phrase 'bros before hoes' presents a pithy précis of the problematic and gendered divisions caused by the type of relationship that such empty encounters create, with women positioned as usurpers who threaten the fraternal bond that exists between equals.

6 Barbara L. Fredrickson and Kristen Harrison, 'Throwing like a girl: Self-objectification predicts adolescent girls' motor performance', *Journal of Sport and Social Issues* 29/1 (2005), pp. 79–101.

7 Susie Orbach, *Bodie* (London: Profile Books, 2009), p. 116.

8 The 'ho's' youth is of significance here in offsetting the power implicit in the expensive accessories that she sports: it is taken as read that there is no way for a young woman to achieve material success without utilising her body to secure some type of influential male sponsor, and part of what makes age 'unappealing' in women is that it starts to disrupt the ownership of these symbols of power.

 9 Frederic Rouzaud, *The Economist*, special issue, 8 May 2006.

10 John Harlow, 'Bubbly bursts as bling crowd desert Cristal over "racism"', *Sunday Times*, 9 July 2006. Available at https://www.thetimes.co.uk/. Available at https://www.thetimes.co.uk/article/bubbly-bursts-as-bling-crowd-desert-cristal-over-racism-cwxnmg60brm (accessed 6 January 2010).

11 Marta Casadei, 'New Burberry models', *Vogue Italia*, 4 February 2011. Available at http://www.vogue.it/en/magazine/daily-news/2011/02/burberry-spring-summer-2011-adv (accessed 1 March 2011).

12 Laura Mulvey, 'Visual pleasure and narrative cinema' [1975], in Leo Braudy and Marshall Cohen (eds), *Film Theory and Criticism,* 5th edn (New York: Oxford University Press, 1999), pp. 833–44, p. 844.

13 Ludacris, 'Ho', *Incognegro*, Disturbing the Peace, Track 12, 1999.

14 50 Cent, 'P.I.M.P'.

15 Ibid.

16 Ibid.

17 Packaged Facts, 'The Young Urban consumer: How hip-hop culture affects the lifestyle and buying decisions of 12- to 34-year olds', 1 May 2008. Available at http://www.marketresearch.com/product/display.asp?productid=1692747 (accessed 7 January 2010).

18 Reg Bailey, 'Letting children be children: Report of an independent review of the commercialisation and sexualisation of childhood', Department for Education, June 2011. Available at https://assets.publishing.service.gov.uk/government/uploads/attachment_data/file/175418/Bailey_Review.pdf (accessed 5 January 2010), p. 32.

19 Ibid., p. 41.

20 Ibid.

21 British Board of Film Classification, cited ibid., p. 34.

22 Amnesty International UK, 'UK: New poll finds a third of people believe women who flirt partially responsible for being raped', press release, 2005. Available at https://www.amnesty.org.uk/press-releases/uk-new-poll-finds-third-people-believe-women-who-flirt-partially-responsible-being (accessed 3 January 2010).

23 Lesley Thomas, 'The sobering subject of consent', *The Telegraph*, 28 March 2007. Available at http://www.telegraph.co.uk/comment/personal-view/3638785/The-sobering-subject-of-consent.html (accessed 9 January 2010).

Chapter 7

 1 See Mikhail Bakhtin, *Rabalais and His World* (Bloomington, IN: Indiana University Press 1984) for an overview and discussion of the carnivalesque.

 2 The popularity of 'football hooligan' films as a specific genre in recent British film history can be indicated by the volume of movies made within a 10 year period.

Examples include, but are not limited to, *The Football Factory* (dir. Nick Love 2004); *Green Street* (dir. Lexi Alexander 2005) and *Green Street 2: Stand your Ground* (dir. Lexi Alexander 2009); *The Rise of the Foot Soldier* (dir. Julian Gilbey 2007); *Awaydays* (dir. Pat Holden 2008); *Cass* (dir Jon S. Baird 2008); *The Firm* (dir. Nick Love 2009), a remake of the film with the same name, starring Gary Oldman (dir. Alan Clarke 1989); *The Rise and Fall of a White Collar Hooligan* (trilogy, dir. Paul Tanter, 2012, 2013, 2014); *The Hooligan Factory* (dir. Nick Nevern 2014). Additionally, several films use football hooliganism as part of the mise-en-scene and narrative, including *St George's Day* (dir. Frank Harper 2012) and *Top Dog* (dir. Martin Kemp 2014). The majority of these films were based on hooligan memoirs and novels aimed at a young male audience.

3   For example, Stone Island, a favourite brand of football casuals in the 1980s, found favour in 2017 when it was adopted by rappers Drake and Travis Scott. Likewise, other 'old skool' sportswear brands have been re-popularised as an indicator of the 'authentic' in an increasingly trend-led menswear market, and thus as a sign of the consumer as connoisseur.

4   Francis Gilbert, *Yob Nation: The Truth About Britain's Yob Culture* (London: Portrait Press, 2006), p. 108.

5   Steve Redhead notes that the 2005 publications of Britain's hooligan gangs, sold out within a year and were republished, whilst the Christmas 2007 publication of an account of Leeds United fans had sold out by the new year, 2008: Steve Redhead, 'Terrace terrors and glamorous hooligans', Mobile Accelerated Nonpostmodern Culture (MANC) 8, 2009. Redhead also coined the term 'hit and tell', which encapsulates these nostalgic morality tales, penned by hooligans.

6   Lunt, Peter Kenneth and Sonia Livingstone, *Mass Consumption and Personal Identity: Everyday Economic Experience* (Buckingham: Open University Press, 1992), p. 7.

7   Andrew Millie, *Securing Respect: Behavioural Expectations and Anti-social Behaviour in the UK* (Bristol: Policy Press, 2009), p. 48.

8   Adrian Harvey, *Football: The First 100 Years* (London: Routledge, 2005), p. 95.

9   Patrick J. Murphy, John Williams and Eric Dunning, *Football on Trial: Spectator Violence and Development in the Football World* (London: Routledge, 1990), p. 39; this has been contradicted by Stephen Wagg, *The Football World: A Contemporary Social History* (London: Harvester Press, 1984), p. 198, who outlines the ways in which the relations between club, management and fans have always been instigated by the middle class.

10 Brad Beaven, *Leisure, Citizenship and Working-Class Men in Britain, 1850-1945* (Manchester: Manchester University Press, 2005), p. 74.

11 As a fan noted, 'We are Aberdeen. We "stand free". We love our club and we love our country. We love our clothes and we love the buzz of coming to places like this and having a mental day out.' Dan Rivers, *Congratulations, You Have Just Met the Casuals* (London: John Blake Publishing Ltd., 2007), p. 96.

12 Indeed, football spectatorship, as well as the participation in sporting activity, was considered to have a civilising effect on the working classes, improving levels of drunkenness and other forms of antisocial behaviour. See, for example, Eitzen, D.

Stanley, *Sport in Contemporary Society: An Anthology* (Oxford: Oxford University Press, 2014), p. 261.

13 Gary Armstrong, *Football Hooligans: Knowing the Score* (Oxford: Berg, 1998), p. 8.

14 Ian Taylor, cited in Richard Giulianotti, *Football: A Sociology of the Global Game* (Oxford: Blackwell, 1999), p. 40.

15 Nancy Armstrong and Leonard Tennenhouse (eds), *The Violence of Representation: Literature and the History of Violence* (Abingdon: Routledge, 1989), p. 46; Bakhtin, *Rabelais and His World*, pp. 303–50.

16 Jean Lipman-Blumen quoted in Simon Winlow, *Badfellas: Crime, Tradition and New Masculinities* (Oxford: Berg, 2001), p. 39.

17 Pumfrey, quoted in Jennifer Craik, *The Face of Fashion* (London: Routledge, 1994), p. 191.

18 Garry Whannel, *Media Sports Stars: Masculinities and Moralities* (London: Routledge, 2002), pp. 64–5.

19 Michel Foucault, *Discipline and Punish: The Birth of the Prison* (New York: Random House Publishing, 1975).

20 Donald F. Sabo, Jr and Ross Runfola, *Jock: Sports and Male Identity* (Englewood Cliffs, NJ: Prentice Hall Inc., 1980), p. 7.

21 Antony Easthope, *What a Man's Gotta Do: The Masculine Myth in Popular Culture* (London: Paladin Grafton Books, 1986), p. 52.

22 Jay Allen, *Bloody Casuals: Diary of a Football Hooligan* (Ellon: Framedram Publishers, 2004), p. 22.

23 Winlow, *Badfellas*, p. 51.

24 Ian Hough, *Perry Boys: The Casual Gangs of Manchester and Salford* (Wrea Green: Milo Books, 2007), p. 268.

25 Caroline Gall, *Zulus: Black, White and Blue: The Story of the Zulu Warriors Football Firm* (London: Milo Books, 2005), p. 3.

26 Ibid.

27 Stella Bruzzi, *Undressing Cinema: Clothing and Identity in the Movies* (Abingdon: Routledge, 1997), p. 72.

28 Gall, *Zulus*, p. 71.

29 'Most days were the same: we used to mess around, try and pull any girl that would have us, talk about clothes, walk around St. David's shopping centre ten times in a day, anything to pass the time and not spend money as most of us were on a maximum of £30 per week', Kaged, respondent Abraham, ibid., p. 254.

30 Gall, *Zulus*, p. 53.

31 Gilbert, *Yob Nation*, p. 82.

32 Whannel suggests that the converse of the muscular male body is that of the male waif. Frequently, tracksuits are used within popular culture texts to denote unemployment and a lifestyle characterized by a wanton hedonism that at its worst could be described as antisocial and self-destructive. An example of this is the film adaptation of Irvine Welsh's Trainspotting (dir. Danny Boyle) 1996. Whannel, *Media Sports Stars*, p. 74.

33 Beatrix Campbell and Adam L. Dawson, 'Indecent exposures: Men, masculinity and violence', in Mark Perryman (ed.), *Hooligan Wars: Causes and Effects of Football Violence* (Edinburgh: Mainstream, 2001), pp. 62–76, pp. 70–7.

34 Jay Allan, *Bloody Casuals: Diary of a Football Hooligan* (Ellon: Framedram Publishers, 2004), p. 18.

35 Rogan Taylor, Director of Liverpool University's Football Research Unit, quoted ibid., p. 74; see also Martin Knight, *Common People* (Edinburgh: Mainstream Publishing, 2000), pp. 177–8.

36 Dick Hobbs quoted in Winlow, *Badfellas*, p. 86.

37 Hough, *Perry Boys*, pp. 146–53.

38 It is important to note that not all soccer casuals were from working-class or inner-city backgrounds. See David Waddington, *Contemporary Issues in Public Disorder* (London: Routledge, 1992), pp. 117–39.

39 Elizabeth Wilson, *Adorned in Dreams: Fashion and Modernity* (London: Virago, 1985), p. 8.

40 See Hough's description of the Adidas Black Shadow training shoe; Hough, *Perry Boys*, pp. 131–5. Hough attaches iconic status to the shoe in terms of style and rarity. See also his discussion of Adidas Tennis Comfort shoe: ibid., pp. 164–5.

41 Paolo Hewitt and Mark Baxter, *The Fashion of Football* (Edinburgh: Mainstream Publishing, 2006), pp. 190–1.

42 Stan Smith's were the first all leather training shoes and gained a huge popularity in Liverpool in 1979. See Hough, *Perry Boys*, pp. 54–5.

43 Tim Edwards, *Men in the Mirror: Men's Fashion, Masculinity, and Consumer Society* (London: Continuum International Publishing Group Ltd., 1997), p. 130.

44 Rivers, *Congratulations*, p. 73. Chelsea APF (Anti Personnel Firm) were also known as the 'Pringle Boys' as a nod to their favoured brand of knitwear. See Allan, *Bloody Casuals*, p. 84.

45 Lorne Brown and Nick Harvey, *A Casual Look: A Photo-diary of Football Fans, 1980s–2001* (Brighton: Football Culture UK, 2002).

46 Waddington, *Contemporary Issues in Public Disorder*, p. 120; see also Neil Spencer, 'Menswear in the 1980s', in Juliet Ash and Elizabeth Wilson (eds), *Chic Thrills* (London: Pandora, 1992), pp. 40–8, p. 47.

47 Phil Thornton, *Casuals: Football, Fighting and Fashion* (London: Milo Books, 2003), pp. 130–1.

48 Wagg, *The Football World*, p. 204.

49 Examples include Stanley Cohen, *Folk Devils and Moral Panics*, 3rd edn (London: Routledge, 2002) and Dick Hebdige, *Subculture: The Meaning of Style* (London: Taylor and Francis, 1979).

50 See Hewitt and Baxter, *The Fashion of Football*, p. 177. They state that notions of secrecy and elitism borrowed from mod culture filtered into the style of the soccer casuals: also Hough, *Perry Boys*, pp. 38–41.

51 Cohen, *Folk Devils and Moral Panics*, pp. 146–202.

52 'Welsh Dresser', quoted in Hewitt and Baxter, *The Fashion of Football*, p. 184.

53 Sophie Woodward, *Why Women Wear What They Wear* (Oxford: Berg, 2007), p. 67.

54 John Bale, *Sport, Space and the City* (London: Routledge, 1993), p. 43.

55 Waddington, *Contemporary Issues in Public Disorder*, p. 136.

56 Murphy, Williams and Dunning, *Football on Trial*, 39.

57 Pierre Bourdieu, cited in Frank Mort, *Cultures of Consumption: Masculinities and Social Space in Late Twentieth Century Britain* (London: Routledge, 1996), p. 15.

58 A term used in the McCann Erikson market report 'Manstudy', 1984, referenced ibid., pp. 15–16

59 The new man is essentially an advertising concept that aims to embrace contemporary and changing attitudes to masculinity, encompassing all of the elements of the 'old' man (fatherhood, provision, sporting prowess, competition, strength and so on) whilst exhibiting a connection with what one might describe as a 'feminine' side, traits of nurturing, caring, narcissism and the display of a sexualised body. Although the 1960s had afforded fashionable men a return to a behaviour and dress style indicative and reminiscent of the eighteenth-century dandy, and youth groups and subcultures had adopted forms of sartorial narcissism previously unseen in the twentieth century, it wasn't until the mid-1970s that an overtly sexualised masculinity became mainstream. Such developments were evident in popular cinema, as in *American Gigolo* (1980), in which Richard Gere's character displays a narcissism previously unseen, and in *Saturday Night Fever* (1977) where the opening scene captures a young John Travolta strutting whilst presenting himself as a fashionable and sexual being. These characters were aware of their sexuality, their sexual power and their appearance, which very much contributed to their identity.

60 Joanne Entwistle, *The Fashioned Body* (London: Polity Press, 2000), p. 174; *Hard Looks: Masculinities, Spectatorship and Contemporary Consumption* (New York: Palgrave Macmillan, 1996), pp. 167–8; Craik, *The Face of Fashion*, p. 190.

61 Hewitt and Baxter, *The Fashion of Football*, p. 200.

62 Michael Willmott and William Nelson, *Complicated Lives: Sophisticated Consumers, Intricate Lifestyles, Simple Solutions: The Malaise of Modernity* (London: Wiley, 2003), pp. 66–72.

63 Thornton, *Casuals*, p. 70.

64 Rob Shields, *Places on the Margin: Alternative Geographies of Modernity* (London: Psychology Press, 1992), p. 100.

65 Bethan Benwell, *Masculinity and Men's Lifestyle Magazines* (Oxford: Wiley-Blackwell, 2003), pp. 60–2.

66 Bill Osgerby, *Youth in Britain since 1945* (Oxford: Wiley-Blackwell, 1998), p. 64.

67 Hough, *Perry Boys*, p. 268.

68 Martin King and Martin Knight, *Hoolifan: 30 Years of Hurt* (Edinburgh: Mainstream Publishing, 1999), p. 57.

69 Richard Martin and Harold Koda, *Jocks and Nerds: Men's Style in the Twentieth Century* (New York: Rizzoli, 1989), p. 26.

Chapter 8

1   Gilles Lipovetsky, *The Empire of Fashion: Dressing Modern Democracy*, trans. Catherine Porter (Princeton, NJ: Princeton University Press, 1994).

2   Malcolm Barnard, *Fashion as Communication* (Abingdon: Routledge, 1996).

3   Katalin Medvedev, 'Socialism, dress and resistance', in Donald Clay Johnson and Helen Bradley Foster (eds), *Dress Sense: The Emotional and Sensory Experience of Clothes* (Oxford: Berg, 2007), pp. 23–35 and 'Ripping up the uniform approach: Hungarian women piece together a new communist fashion', in Regina Lee Blaszczyk (ed.), *Producing Fashion: Commerce, Culture, and Consumers* (Philadelphia, PA: University of Pennsylvania Press, 2008), pp. 389–418; Ildikó Simonovics and Tibor Valuch (eds), *Öltöztessük fel az Országot! Divat és Öltözködés a Szocializmusban* (*Let's Dress the Country! Fashion and Clothing in Socialism*) (Budapest: Argumentum, 2009); Djurdja Bartlett, *Fashion East: The Spectre that Haunted Socialism* (London: MIT Press, 2010), p. 10.

4   Personal communication with GY, 19 July 2003.

5   Personal communication with NY, 6 March 2005.

6   Lajos Mesterházi, *Férfikor* (*The Age of Men*) (Budapest: Kossuth, 1967).

7   Medvedev, 'Socialism, dress and resistance'.

8   James Laver, *A Concise History of Costume* (London: Thames & Hudson, 1979).

9   Tibor Valuch, *Magyarország Társadalomtörténete a XX. Század Második Felében* (*The Social History of Hungary in the Second Half of the 20th Century*) (Budapest: Osiris Kiadó. 2001) and *A Lódentól a Miniszoknyáig* (*From the Loden Coat to the Miniskirt*) (Budapest: Corvina Kiadó/1956-os Intézet, 2004).

10 See Item No. 540.61 in the Open Society Archives, Budapest, Hungary.

11 Personal communication with TE, 26 January 2005.

12 See Item No. 1520/66 in the Open Society Archives, Budapest, Hungary.

13 Valuch, *A Lódentól a Miniszoknyáig*.

14 Personal communication with N, 9 February 2005.

15 K. Burucs, 'Újrakezdés', *História* 5/3 (1983), pp. 26–8.

16 Ibid.

17 Jenő Gárdonyi, 'Kemény ítélet vár az elkövetőkre', *Esti Hírlap*, non-dated in the archival sources.

18 Personal communication with KK, 11 July 2002.

19 According to Marx, there is no such thing as 'socialist state'. Marx said socialism is the first stage of communism, which is classless, and hence has no further need for a repressive state. In 1951, Trotskyists in the 4th International called states like Hungary 'deformed workers states' after Trotsky's description of the USSR as a 'degenerated workers state'. Others have referred to the system in Hungary as 'state capitalism', 'bureaucratic collectivism' or 'post-capitalist' and so on. The regime itself coined the term 'socialist state'.

20 This indicated that the (export) economy was being oriented towards the consumer needs of the West, not Hungary, and, in fact, Hungary was partly becoming a low-wage colony for Western consumers.

21 Michel Foucault, *Discipline and Punish: The Birth of the Prison*, trans. Alan Sheridan (London: Allen Lane, 1977).

22 Personal communication with E, 6 March 2004.

Chapter 9

1 The modernisation of Swedish law has occurred progressively, from the decriminalisation of homosexual acts in 1944 until the current discussion on removing the requirement for sterilisation in connection to sex-change operations.

2 Judith Butler, 'Critically queer', *GLQ: A Journal of Lesbian and Gay Studies* 1/1 (1993), pp. 17–32, p. 18.

3 Bruno Latour, *Reassembling the Social: An Introduction to Actor-Network-Theory* (Oxford: Oxford University Press, 2007), p. 35.

4 Judith Halberstam, *In a Queer Time and Place: Transgender Bodies, Subcultural Lives* (New York: New York University Press, 2005), p. 121.

5 Maurice Merleau-Ponty, 'The experience of the body and classical psychology' [2002], in Mariam Fraser and Monica Greco (eds), *The Body: A Reader* (London: Routledge, 2005), p. 53.

6 Elizabeth Grosz, *Volatile Bodies: Toward a New Corporeal Feminism* (Bloomington, IN: Indiana University Press, 1994), p. 11.

7 Gail Weiss, *Body Images: Embodiment as Corporeality* (New York: Routledge, 1999), p. 9.

8 Sara Ahmed, *Queer Phenomenology: Orientations, Objects, Others* (Durham, NC: Duke University Press, 2006), pp. 2–3.

9 Throughout this article I will use the informants' actual names, or the names they use themselves in their everyday life.

10 At the time, Klara was active in a social liberal part.

11 Erving Goffman, *Relations in Public: Microstudies of the Public Order* (New York: Transaction Publishers, 2010), p. 51.

12 Ahmed, *Queer Phenomenology*, p. 20.

13 Bruno Latour, 'The slight surprise of action: Facts, fetishes, factishes', in *Pandora's Hope: Essays on the Reality of Science Studies* (Cambridge, MA: Harvard University Press, 1999), ch. 9.

14 For a closer reading on the issue, compare Judith Butler's *Gender Trouble: Feminism and the Subversion of Identity* (New York: Routledge, 1999), pp. 9–11 with Latour's *Reassembling the Social*, p. 34.

15 Halberstam, *In a Queer Time and Place*, p. 154.

16 Latour, *Reassembling the Social*, p. 80.

17 Grosz, *Volatile Bodies*, p. 80.

Chapter 10

1 Avigail Moor, 'She dresses to attract, he perceives seduction: A gender gap in attribution of intent to women's revealing style of dress and its relation to blaming the victims of sexual violence', *Journal of International Women's Studies* 11/4 (May 2010), pp. 115–27, p. 116.

2 Rape, Abuse and Incest National Network (RAINN), 'Campus sexual violence: Statistics', n.d. Available at https://www.rainn.org/statistics/campus-sexual-violence (accessed 1 December 2017).

3 Ibid.

4 'What Were You Wearing?' installation, Jen Brockman and Mary Wyandt Hiebert, 2017.

5 Amy Grubb and Emily Turner, 'Attribution of blame in rape cases: A review of the impact of rape myth acceptance, gender role conformity and substance use on victim blaming', *Aggression and Violent Behaviour* 17/5 (2012), pp. 443–52, p. 443.

6 Grubb and Turner note that that the reporting of rape cases could be as low in the UK as 6 per cent, with a more realistic figure of 200,000 rapes occurring in the UK per annum, at the time of their study (ibid., p. 444).

7 Malcolm Barnard, *Fashion as Communication*, 2nd edn (Abingdon: Routledge, 2002); Fred Davis, *Fashion, Culture and Identity* (Chicago, IL: University of Chicago Press, 1994).

8 Umberto Eco, *A Theory of Semiotics* (Bloomington, IN: Indiana University Press, 1976).

9 Alinor C. Sterling, 'Undressing the victim: The intersection of evidentiary and semiotic meanings of women's clothing in rape trials', *Yale Journal of Law and Feminism* 7/1 (1995), pp. 87–132. See details of the William Kennedy Smith trial in which the defence's case rested on the lack of damage to the victim's bra. It was argued that if the victim's account of the rape was accurate, then the bra would be damaged, thus presenting the victim as untruthful and incredible (ibid., p. 113).

10 This is important if the victim is proved to have been lying about what she was wearing at the time of the rape. This is called 'impeaching evidence'. See ibid., p. 106.

11 Melvin Lerner and Dale T. Miller, 'Just world research and the attribution process: Looking back and ahead', *Psychological Bulletin* 85/5 (1978), pp. 1030–51.

12 Madeleine van der Bruggen and Amy Grubb, 'A review of the literature relating to rape victim blaming: An analysis of the impact of observer and victim characteristics on attribution of blame in rape cases', *Aggression and Violent Behaviour* 19/5 (2014), pp. 523–31, p. 524.

13 Sterling, 'Undressing the victim', p. 120.

14 Ibid., p. 1; Ed M. Edmonds and Delwin Cahoon, 'Female clothes preference related to male sexual interest', *Bulletin of the Psychonomic Society* 22/3 (1984), p. 14.

15 Sterling, 'Undressing the victim', p. 112.

16 Roger Terry and Suzanne Doerge, 'Dress, posture and setting as additive factors in subjective probability of rape', *Perceptual and Motor Skills* 48/3 (1979), pp. 903–6.

17 Eugene Mathes and Sherry Kempher, 'Clothing as non-verbal communicator of sexual attitudes and behaviour', *Perceptual and Motor Skills* 43/2 (1976), pp. 495–8; Terry and Doerge, 'Dress, posture and setting'.

18 James Scroggs, 'Penalties for rape as a function of victim provocativeness, damage and resistance', *Journal of Applied Social Psychology* 6/4 (1976), pp. 360–8.

19 Suresh Kanekar and Maharukh Kolsawalla, 'Factors affecting responsibility attributed to rape victims', *Journal of Social Psychology* 113/2 (1981), pp. 285–6.

20 Deborah G. Schult and Lawrence J. Schneider, 'The role of sexual provocativeness, rape history, and observer gender in perceptions of blame in sexual assault', *Journal of Interpersonal Violence* 6/1 (1991), pp. 94–101; cf. Mark A. Whatley, 'Victim characteristics influencing attributions of responsibility to rape victims: A meta-analysis', *Aggression and Violent Behaviour* 1/2 (1996), pp. 81–95, p. 85.

21 Ibid., p. 90.

22 Ibid.

23 F. Cunningham and D. Weis, 'Perceptions of sexy clothing by college females', Association of College Professors of Textiles and Clothing Proceedings: Combined Central, Eastern and Western Regional Meetings, Monument, CO (1985); cf. Lacinda Lewis and Kim K. P. Johnson, 'Effect of dress, cosmetics, sex of subject, and casual inference on attribution of victim responsibility', *Clothing and Textiles Research Journal* 8/1 (Fall 1989), pp. 22–7, p. 23.

24 Edmonds and Cahoon, 'Female clothes preference related to male sexual interest', cf. Lewis and Johnson, 'Effect of dress, cosmetics, sex of subject', p. 23.

25 Patti Mazelan, 'Stereotypes and perceptions of the victims of rape', *Victimology: An International Journal* 5/2 (1980), pp. 121–32; Lewis and Johnson, 'Effect of dress, cosmetics, sex of subject', p. 23.

26 Lewis and Johnson ('Effect of dress, cosmetics, sex of subject') outline a variety of academic studies surrounding rape victims and their dress, appearance and gesture/ deportment. These include Terry and Doerge, 'Dress, posture and setting', which concluded that 'seductive dress' was more likely to incite sexual assault, Scroggs, 'Penalties for rape', who suggested that judges were more likely to award shorter sentences for rapists where women were seen to be dressing provocatively, and Kanekar and Kolsawalla, 'Factors affecting responsibility attributed to rape victims' and Mathes and Kempher, 'Clothing as non-verbal communicator', who focused on specific items of clothing and the perceived morality of the victim (1989, p. 23).

27 Robin Warshaw, *I Never Called it Rape: The Ms Report on Recognizing, Fighting, and Surviving Date and Acquaintance Rape* (New York: Harper & Row, 1988).

28 Kim K. P. Johnson, 'Attributions about date rape: Impact of clothing, sex, money spent, date type, and perceived similarity', *Family and Consumer Sciences Research Journal* 23/3 (March 1995), pp. 292–310, p. 293. Johnson found that whether the perpetrator was considered to blame was less reliant on money spent than on the clothing of the victim (ibid., p. 306).

29 Ibid., p. 308.

30 Sterling, 'Undressing the victim', p. 104.

31 Ed M. Edmonds and Delwin Cahoon, 'Attitudes concerning crimes related to clothing worn by female victims', *Bulletin of the Psychonomic Society* 24/6 (1986), pp. 444–6.

32 Ibid., p. 444.

33 Ibid., p. 445.

34 Karen Dion, Ellen Berscheid and Elaine Walster, 'What is beautiful is good', *Journal of Personality and Social Psychology* 24/2 (1972), pp. 285–90; Marsha B. Jacobson, 'Effects of victim's and defendant's physical attractiveness on subject's judgements in a rape case', *Sex Roles* 7/3 (1981), pp. 247–55; Marsha B. Jacobson and Paula M. Popovich, 'Victim attractiveness and perceptions of responsibility in an ambiguous rape case', *Psychology of Women Quarterly* 8/1 (1983), pp. 100–4; Kevin D. McCaul, Lois G. Veltum, Vivian Boyechko and Jacqueline J. Crawford, 'Understanding Attributions of victim blame for rape: Sex, violence and foreseeability', *Journal of Applied Social Psychology* 20/1 (1990), pp. 1–26, cf. Whatley, 'Victim characteristics influencing attributions of responsibility to rape victims', p. 90. Whatley provides a comprehensive overview of all of the literature on this subject from the 1970s to the 1990s.

35 Sterling, 'Undressing the victim', p. 115.

36 Ibid., pp. 112–13. Sterling suggests that these approaches are not necessarily about evidence per se. Because these clothes are taken out of context (the rape scene to the courtroom, and the embodied to the disembodied) they misrepresent the meaning and wearing of clothing in this particular context, in an attempt to shame the victim (ibid., p. 120).

37 Whatley, 'Victim characteristics influencing attributions of responsibility to rape victims', p. 82.

38 Alexandra Warwick and Dani Cavallaro, *Fashioning the Frame: Boundaries, Dress and the Body* (Oxford: Berg, 1998), p. 22.

39 Ibid., p. 128.

40 Guy Debord, *The Society of the Spectacle,* trans. Donald Nicholson-Smith (Detroit, MI: Red & Black, 1970).

41 Walter Benjamin, *The Arcades Project* [1982] (Cambridge, MA: Harvard University Press, 1999), p. 10, cf. Caroline Evans, *Fashion at the Edge: Spectacle, Modernity and Deathliness* (New Haven, CT: Yale University Press, 2003), p. 114.

42 Gilles Lipovetsky, *The Empire of Fashion: Dressing Modern Democracy*, trans. Catherine Porter (Princeton, NJ: Princeton University Press, 1994), p. 51.

43 Aileen Ribeiro, *Dress and Morality* (Oxford: Berg, 2003).

44 John C. Flugel, *The Psychology of Clothes* (London: Hogarth Press, 1930); Lipovetsky, *The Empire of Fashion*, p. 51. Lipovetsky notes that fashion, or dress at least, was a sign of the civilising influence of love, as demonstrated in European courts since the Renaissance. Fashion, through its nuances, extended the poetics of courtship and tenderness towards women and offered a more civilised approach to life beyond the battlefield.

45 Colin McDowell, *The Anatomy of Fashion: Why We Dress the Way We Do* (London: Phaidon, 2013).

46 Lipovetsky, *The Empire of Fashion*, p. 112.

47 John Berger, *Ways of Seeing* (London: Fontana, 1972); Moor, 'She dresses to attract', p. 116.

48 Warwick and Cavallaro, *Fashioning the Frame*, p. 25; Lipovetsky, *The Empire of Fashion*, p. 112.

49 Ibid.

50 Moor, 'She dresses to attract'.

51 Ibid., pp. 120–1.

52 Ibid., p. 121.

53 Ibid., p. 123.

54 Ibid., pp. 123–4.

55 Ibid.

56 Susanna Paasonen, Kaarina Nikunen and Laura Saarenmaa, *Pornification: Sex and Sexuality in Media Culture* (Oxford: Berg, 2008); Attwood, Feona, *Mainstreaming Sex: The Sexualisation of Western Culture* (London: I.B. Tauris, 2014).

57 Ariel Levy, *Female Chauvinist Pigs: Women and the Rise of Raunch Culture* (New York: Simon & Schuster, 2006).

58 Paasonen, Nikunen and Saarenmaa, *Pornification*.

59 Lipovetsky, *The Empire of Fashion*, p. 112.

60 Imelda Whelehan, *Overloaded: Popular Culture and the Future of Feminism* (London: The Women's Press, 2000), p. 29.

61 Rene Denfield, *The New Victorians: A Young Woman's Challenge to the Old Feminist Order* (New York: Warner Books, 1996) quoted in Whelehan, *Overloaded*, p. 29.

62 Levy, *Female Chauvinist Pigs*, p. 198.

63 Lipovetsky, *The Empire of Fashion*, p. 112.

Chapter 11

1 London: Weidenfeld and Nicholson, 2010.

2 Dick Hebdige, *Subculture: The Meaning of Style* (London: Taylor and Francis, 1979).

3 John Matthews, *Pirates* (New York: Atheneum Books for Young Readers, 2006).

4 Gabriel Kuhn, *Life under the Jolly Roger: Reflections on Golden Age Piracy* (Oakland: PM Press, 2010), p. 52.

5 Matthews, *Pirates*.

6 Ibid.

7 Pat Croce, *Pirate Soul: A Swashbuckling Journey through the Golden Age of Pirates* (Philadelphia, PA: Running Press, 2006), p. 2.

8 Marcus Rediker, *Villains of All Nations* (London: Beacon Press), p. 286.

9 Ibid., p. 267.

10 Ibid., p. 261.

11 Croce, *Pirate Soul*.

12 Rediker, *Villains of All Nations*, pp. 262–4.

13 Croce, *Pirate Soul*.

14 Rediker, *Villains of All Nations*, pp. 263–8.

15 Ibid., pp. 276, 281.

16   David Cordingly, *Under the Black Flag: The Romance and the Reality of Life Among the Pirates* (New York: Random House, 2006), p. 115.

17   Ibid., p. 106.

18   Ibid., p. 116.

19   Rediker, *Villains of All Nations*, pp. 278.

20   Ibid., p. 106.

21   Krzysztof Wilczynski, 'Jolly Roger', 18 March 2007. Available at http://www.pirateinfo.com/detail/detail.php?article_id=59 (no longer available).

22   Ibid., p. 14.

23   Ibid., p. 21.

24   Kuhn, *Life under the Jolly Roger*, p. 59.

25   John Clarke, Stuart Hall, Tony Jefferson and Brian Roberts, 'Subcultures, cultures and class', in Stuart Hall and Tony Jefferson (eds), *Resistance Through Rituals: Youth Subcultures in Post-war Britain* [1975] (London: Routledge, 1976), pp. 9–74, cited in Hebdige, *Subculture*, p. 114.

26   Matthews, *Pirates*.

27   Rediker, *Villains of All Nations*, p. 278.

28   Kuhn, *Life under the Jolly Roger*, p. 118.

29   Marshall D. Sahlins, *Tribesmen* (Englewood Cliffs, NJ: Prentice Hall, 1968) quoted in Kuhn, *Life under the Jolly Roger*, pp. 45–6.

30   Hugh F. Rankin, *The Golden Age of Piracy* (New York: Holt, Rinehart and Winston, 1969) quoted in Kuhn, *Life under the Jolly Roger*, p. 570.

31   Arash Vahdati, 'Skull symbol', 23 June 2010 [online] Available at http://www.kolahstudio.com/Underground/index.php?s=skull+crossbones&submit=GO (accessed 10 November 2010).

32   Henri Lefebvre, *Everyday Life in the Modern World* (New York: Harper and Row, 1971), cited in Hebdige, *Subculture*, p. 92.

33   Tori Baur, 'Pirates invade ABC Television's "Wife Swap" in season opener', 5 September 2006. Available at http://www.keepthecode.com/2006/09/pirate-invade-abc-television-wifeswap.html (accessed 17 February 2007).

34   Ibid., p. 25.

35   Hebdige, *Subculture*, p. 3.

36   Kate Kilpatrick, 'White riot', 6 June 2007. Available at http://www.philadelphiaweekly.com/view.php?id=14772&highlight=White (accessed 21 July 2007; not available outside US).

37   Darrell Panethiere, 'The persistence of piracy: The consequences for creativity, for culture, and for sustainable development', Global Alliance for Cultural Diversity, UNESCO (2005). Available at http://unesdoc.unesco.org/images/0014/001455/145517e.pdf (accessed 15 July 2007).

38   Chris Land, 'Flying the black flag: Revolt, revolution and the social organisation of piracy in the "golden age"', *Management and Organizational History* 2/2 (2007), pp. 169–92, quoted in Khun, 2010; pp. 179–80.

39 Greg Sandoval, 'Feds raise questions about big media's piracy claims', *cnet*, 12 April 2010. Available at http://news.cnet.com/8301-31001_3-20002304-261.htm (accessed 25 July 2008).

40 Johann Hari, 'You are being lied to about pirates', *The Independent*, 5 January 2009.

41 Ishaan Tharoor, 'How Somalia's fishermen became pirates', *Time*, 18 April 2009.

Chapter 12

1 Ingun Grimstad Klepp, *Klær, kropp og velvære. Hva vil det si å føle seg velkledd*?. *In Modets metamorfoser. Den klädda kroppens identiteter och förvandlingar* (Stockholm: Carlsson Bokförlag, 2009).

2 *VG*, 1 April 2008, p. 6.

3 I. G. Klepp and T. S. Tobiasson (in press) *Norsk strikkehistorie* (Hugesund: Vormedal forlag, 2018).

4 Annichen Sibbern Bohn, *Norwegian Knitting Designs* (Olso: Grøndahl, 1929).

5 Ibid.

6 Joanne Turney, *The Culture of Knitting* (Oxford: Berg, 2009).

7 Ibid., p. 31.

8 *VG*, 1 April 2008, p. 6.

9 'Strikk i strid: Lusa er ikke lenger på gangen', *Dagbladet*, 6 April 2008. Available at https://www.dagbladet.no/nyheter/strikk-i-strid/66459258 (accessed 28 July 2018).

10 Turney, *The Culture of Knitting*, p. 35.

11 Barbro Blehr, *En norsk besvärjelse: 17 maj-firande vid 1900-talets slut* (Nora: Bokförlaget Nya Doxa 2000).

12 Colleen Gau, 'Conventional work dress', in Joanne Eicher and Phyllis Tortora (eds), *Berg Encyclopedia of World Dress and Fashion*, vol. 10: *Global Perspective* (Oxford: Berg, 2010), pp. 85–96, p. 85.

13 Lovdata, 'Regler om bruk av rettskapper m.v. ved domstolen', 1 August 1995. Available at http://www.lovdata.no/for/sf/jd/td-19950623-0577-0.html#3 (accessed winter 2011).

14 Ibid.

15 Norges domstoler. Available at http://www.domstol.no/no/Nar-jeg-skal-i-retten/Oppforsel-i-retten/ (accessed Winter 2011).

16 Sharron J. Lennon, Kim K. P. Johnson and Theresa Lennon Schulz et al. 'Forging linkages between dress and law in the U.S., Part I: Rape and Sexual Harassment', *Clothing and Textiles Research Journal* 17/3 (June 1999), pp. 144–56.

17 Jarle Aabø, 'Sirkusdirektør John Chr. Elden' (Circus director John Chr. Elden), April 2008. Available at http://e24.no/kommentar/spaltister/aaboe/article2341188.ece (accessed Winter 2011).

18 Ibid. 'The Home Crafts Store' here refers to Den Norske Husflidsforening's outlets. The Home Crafts Store is North Europe's biggest outlet for home crafts, mainly

textiles and wood-ware. The association was founded in 1891 and has been at the centre of Norwegian home crafts since. That something is bought at the Home Crafts Store guarantees that the object is of quality and part of the Norwegian Home Crafts tradition.

19 Ibid.

20 Ibid.

21 Ibid.

22 Waldemar Brøgger, *Skikk og bruk* (Oslo: Cappelen, 1960).

23 Ingun Grimstad Klepp and Silje Elisabeth Skuland, *The Rationalisation of Consumption - Reasons for Purchasing Outdoor Recreational Outfits*, in Maria Vaccarella and Jacque Lynn Foltyn, (eds), *Fashion-Wise* (Oxford: Inter-Disciplinary Press, 2013), pp. 43–52.

24 The slogan used in commercials for Freia milk chocolate is 'a little piece of Norway'. *Dagbladet*, 'Strikk-i-strid', Available at https://www.dagbladet.no/nyheter/strikk-i-strid/66459258 (accessed 28 July 2018).

25 Erving Goffman, *The Presentation of Self in Everyday Life*, Monograph No. 2 (Edinburgh: University of Edinburgh Social Sciences Research Centre, 1958).

26 *Aftenposten*, 29 April 2008, p. 6.

27 Christian Ramberg, 'Toskas lusekofte Ikke tilfeldig', *Lyden av Norge*, 21 August 2005. Available at http://www.p4.no/story.aspx?id=169693 (accessed winter 2011).

28 Iskwews Hjørne på www, iskwew.com 'Hva Skjedde Med Lusekofta?' 31 March 2008. Available at http://iskwew.com/blogg/2008/03/31/hva-skjedde-med-lusekofta/ (accessed Winter 2011).

29 *P4* 1 April 2008, p. 1. Available at https://emea01.safelinks.protection.outlook.com/?url=https%3A%2F%2Fwww.p4.no%2Fnyheter%2Fble-lusekofte-kamerater-i-fengsel%2Fartikkel%2F267180%2F&data=01%7C01%7CJ.A.Turney%40sot on.ac.uk%7Cfc4e3f261c8644dad3af08d6a0b4178b%7C4a5378f929f44d3ebe896 69d03ada9d8%7C1&sdata=hq%2BaAvIcbZBuSy6fIcTnzOrPJLHDkDSdQZFo dj3KPjc%3D&reserved=0

30 Heidi Schei Lilleås, 'Bhatti tok on Toska', Nettavisen, 2008. Available at http://www.nettavisen.no/innenriks/article1720564.ece (accessed winter 2011).

31 https://emea01.safelinks.protection.outlook.com/?url=https%3A%2F%2Fwww.hjertebank.no%2F%3Foffset%3D1260803664000&data=01%7C01%7CJ.A.Tu rney%40soton.ac.uk%7Cfc4e3f261c8644dad3af08d6a0b4178b%7C4a5378f929f4 4d3ebe89669d03ada9d8%7C1&sdata=dA3ayllqEmeGoLJ2fWbeWAVGDv1Fy exvkAed7iRc9mI%3D&reserved=0

32 Ibid.

33 Rollemodell i tiltaleboksen? *In Varden*, 17 April 2008. Available at http://www.varden.no/meninger/leder/rollemodell-i-tiltaleboksen-1.865485 (Accessed 28 July 2018).

34 Janet Andrewes, *Bodywork: Dress as Cultural Tool* (Leiden: Brill, 2005).

35 Daniel Miller, 'Introduction', in Susanne Küchler and Daniel Miller (eds), *Clothing as Material Culture* (Oxford: Berg, 2005), pp. 1–12.

36 Andrewes, *Bodywork*.

37 Miller, 'Introduction', pp. 1–12.

38 Jon Olav Egeland, *Dagbladet*, 1 April 2008, p. 8.

39 Jarle Grivi Brenna and Ingunn Andersen, 2008 - Strikkegenseren var Bhattis forslag. In *VG*, 31 March 2008 18:10 Oppdatert: 31 March 2008. Available at 18:37 https://www.vg.no/nyheter/innenriks/i/GoE4B/strikkegenseren-var-bhattis-forslag (accessed 28 July 2018).

40 Aabø, 'Sirkusdirektør John Chr. Elden'; Lilleås, 'Bhatti tok on Toska'.

41 Ingun Grimstad Klepp, 'Patched, louse-ridden, tattered: Clean and dirty clothes', *Textile: The Journal of Cloth & Culture* 5 (2007), pp. 254-75.

42 Ddomstol.no. https://www.domstol.no/no/Sivil-sak/Oppforsel-i-retten/ (accessed 28 July 2018) and it goes without saying that a man in a *lusekofte* cannot be a rabid antisemite. http://hablog.us.splinder.com/post/708573 (accessed winter 2011).

43 Tone Hellesund, 'Dressen - det mandligste av alt"', in Liv Hilde Boe & Anne Sofie Hjemdahl (eds), *Kropp og Klær* (Oslo: Norsk Folkemuseum 2000), p. 138.

44 Anne Hollander, *Sex and Suits* (Sparkford: Claridge Press, 1994).

45 Ruth P. Rubinstein, *Dress Codes* (Oxford: Westview Press, 2001), p. 45.

46 Susanne Küchler and Daniel Miller (eds), *Clothing as Material Culture* (Oxford: Berg, 2005), p. 49; Hollander, Anne, *Seeing Through Clothes* (New York: Avon), p. 445.

47 Rubinstein, *Dress Codes*, p. 86.

48 Dick Hebdige, *Subculture: The Meaning of Style* (London: Taylor and Francis, 1979), p. 16.

49 Raewyn Conell, *Masculinities* (Cambridge: Polity Press 2001), p. 26.

50 Ibid., p. 156.

51 Kristine Pettersen, *Dress med press – En studie av mannlig klesbruk i stortingssalen*. SIFO rapport 7-2004, http://www.hioa.no/Om-HiOA/Senter-for-velferds-og-arbeidslivsforskning/SIFO/Publikasjoner-fra-SIFO/Dress-med-press-En-studie-av-mannlig-klesbruk-i-stortingssalen, 2004, p. 81.

52 Ibid., p. 113.

53 Turney, *The Culture of Knitting*, p. 35.

Chapter 13

1 Nancy MacDonell Smith, *The Classic Ten: The True Story of the Little Black Dress and Nine Other Fashion Statements* (London: Penguin Books, 2003). The fashion spread 'Entrenched', photographed by Michael Thompson, appeared in American *Vogue* in February 2000, beginning on p. 276. 'Brief Encounter', photographed by Annie Leibovitz and featuring P. Diddy with Natalia Vodianova, another of many fashion spreads devoted to the trench, appeared in American *Vogue* in February 2010, beginning on p. 158. The text connected the editorial to the 1941 film classic *Casablanca*: 'In the closing shot, she wears a trench coat – icon of tearful cinematic goodbyes since Bogie said, "Here's looking at you kid", to Ingrid Bergman in *Casablanca*.' It features a trench designed by Nina Ricci and available for $2,750.00 at Nordstrom department stores. Fashion editorials referencing the trench in other magazines are too numerous to reference here. Magazine illustrations of the trench or military fashion for women go back at least as far as

January 1918 in American *Vogue*, which illustrates the 'trench' vest directly related to military dress of World War I.

2 John Harvey, *Men in Black* (Chicago, IL: University of Chicago Press, 1995), p. 10.

3 A popular series on American television that originated on radio, *Dragnet* starred Jack Webb as Sgt Friday, who often wore a trench coat. The series ran on television from 16 December 1951 to 23 August 1959 and from 12 January 1967 to 16 April 1970. 'All we want are *the facts*, ma'am' was the phrase popularised on the show. Sgt Friday, a 'seeker of truth', often wore a trench coat while he investigated a crime.

4 There are many descriptions of the evolution of the trench coat, but all agree that British officers originally wore the coat. Jane Tynan has written that British officers were responsible for the cut and class of their uniform while rank and file were given uniforms. She writes extensively on the evolution of the trench coat in World War I and the mechanisation of the soldier through the uniform based on Foucault. Jane Tynan, '"Tailoring in the trenches": The making of First World War British Army uniform', in Jessica Meyer (ed.), *British Popular Culture and the First World War* (Boston, MA: Leiden, 2008), pp. 71–94. Nick Foulkes, in a more popular account of the trench writes, 'It was also important that as well as keeping warm and dry, the officers of His Majesty's Armed Forces were smartly turned out and the trench coat looked great. It may sound fatuous, but the British army at that time maintained many nineteenth century attitudes; among them the cult of the aristocratic "officer class", one of the duties of which was elegance.' Nick Foulkes, *The Trench Book* (New York: Assouline, 2007), p. 79. In World War II those American soldiers wearing the trench coat were also officers because the coat was not available in great quantity.

5 Nina Wilcox Putnam, *Believe You Me!* (New York: George H. Doran Company, 1919). John Dos Passos describes an officer in goggles and 'mud-splattered trench coat' in *Three Soldiers*, published in 1921, and Edna Ferber describes a civilian man wearing 'spats, and a check suit, and what is known as a trench coat …' in *The Girls*, also published in 1921.

6 *Blackwood's Magazine*, vol. 209, 1921. Civilian journalists covering World War I at the front appropriated the trench coat, and it was co-opted by future generations of news reporters. Paul Loukides and Linda K. Fuller, *Beyond the Stars III: The Material World in American Popular Film*, *Beyond the Stars III: The Material World in American Popular Film* (Bowling Green, OH: Bowling Green State University Popular Press, 1993).

7 Linda Wagner-Martin, *A Historical Guide to Ernest Hemingway* (London: Oxford University Press, 2000). Writing in Toronto's *Star*, Hemingway said, 'A trench coat will admit you into that camaraderie of returned men which is the main result we obtained from the war.' According to *The American Legion Monthly*, the trench coat allows a man to be taken as an officer. See vols 9 and 10 (1930).

8 See George Batson, *Design for Murder: A Mystery Thriller in Three Acts* (New York: French, 1960).

9 'I went over to the divan and peeled off my trench coat and pawed through the girl's clothes.' Raymond Chandler, *The Big Sleep*, originally published in 1939.

10 John G. Cawelti, *Adventure, Mystery, and Romance: Formula Stories as Art and Popular Culture* (Chicago, IL: University of Chicago Press, 1976).

11 An internet search supports the use of this description, as do other popular sources and news accounts. This is the definition from *Urban Dictionary*: ORIGIN: In 1994, a student (belonging to a group of computer gamers and loners who were often bullied by popular and athletic students of the school) – attending Columbine High School near Littleton, Colorado, US – was given a black duster (trench coat) as a gift from his mother, and he wore it to school. Soon after, the student's friend started wearing a black trench coat as well, because he liked the style, and it wasn't long before the others followed suit. They wore the long coats even when weather was warm outside. It also wasn't long before jocks in the school started to ridicule the group by calling them 'a trench coat mafia'. Available at http://www.urbandictionary.com/define.php?term=Trench%20Coat%20Mafia (accessed 5 January 2010). After this, the group of friends took on the name and wore it like a badge, adopting the name for themselves, 'The Trench Coat Mafia' (TCM) for short.

12 'Report from the trenches', photographed by Deborah Turbeville, *Interview* 30/1 (January 2000), pp. 74–83. Hollander writing about the trench coat says that the details of the fashionable trench no longer relate to function. Anne Hollander, *Seeing Through Clothes* (New York: Viking Press, 1978).

13 'Brief Encounter' American *Vogue,* February 2001. See note 1.

14 'Entrenched', American *Vogue*, February 2000.

15 Tal Sharon, identified as a filmmaker, is one among others interviewed on the streets regarding the trench coat. See Hallie Daily, 'Street trench', http://www.halliedaily.com/?p=2234 (2 September 2010).

16 In 2009, Burberry launched a website called 'Art of the Trench', which invites consumers to post pictures of themselves in their own Burberry trench coats. Angela Ahrendts has promoted the use of social media in connection with the Burberry brand. See also TheFedoraLounge.com as a site for posting images of trench-coated people.

17 Peter Falk in his raincoat or trench as the detective Columbo in the television series *Columbo* is illustrated in Foulkes' *The Trench Book*, 276. The book is a compendium of illustrations of the trench coat worn by actors, soldiers and so on as icons of popular culture.

18 Ibid., 41.

19 Smith, *The Classic Ten,* 146.

20 'What lies beneath', American *Vogue*, April 2007, p. 208; emphasis mine.

21 Perniola writes that in the figurative arts 'eroticism appears as a relationship between clothing and nudity'. See Katherine Frank, 'Body talk: Revelations of self and body in contemporary strip clubs', in Adeline Masquelier (ed.), *Dirt, Undress, and Difference: Critical Perspectives on the Body's Surface* (Bloomington, IN: Indiana University, 2005), pp. 96–121, p. 109.

22 Peggy Phelan, *Unmarked: The Politics of Performance* (Abingdon: Routledge, 1993).

23 Efrat Tseelon, 'From fashion to masquerade: Towards an ungendered paradigm', in Joanne Entwistle and Elizabeth Wilson (eds), *Body Dressing* (Oxford: Berg, 2001), pp. 103–18.

24 For Tolstoy, according to John Harvey, the amount of clothing worn to cover or uncover is a crucial insight into character. Tolstoy views fashion as 'a partial revelation of nakedness'. John Harvey, 'Showing and hiding: Equivocation in the relations of body and dress', *Fashion Theory* 11/1 (March 2007), pp. 65–94, p. 68.

25 Beverly Gordon, 'Material culture in a popular vein: Perspectives on studying artifacts of mass culture', in Ray B. Browne and Marshall W. Fishwick (eds), *Symbiosis: Popular Culture and Other Fields* (Bowling Green, OH: Bowling Green State University Popular Press, 1988), pp. 170–6.

26 Caroline Evans, *Fashion at the Edge: Spectacle, Modernity and Deathliness* (New Haven, CT: Yale University Press, 2007). Rebecca Arnold views fashion as 'inherently contradictory, revealing both our desires and anxieties and constantly pushing at the boundaries of acceptability'. Rebecca Arnold, *Fashion, Desire and Anxiety: Image and Morality in the Twentieth Century* (London: I.B. Tauris).

27 Craik writes that the uniform for a woman inscribes 'the formation of a modern self that is normatively male and transgressively female'. Jennifer Craik, 'The cultural politics of the uniform', *Fashion Theory* 7/2 (June 2003), pp. 143–4. By reconfiguring the trench, fashion struggles with classic cultural forms.

Chapter 14

1   Imogen Tyler, *Revolting Subjects Social Abjection and Resistance in Neoliberal Britain* (London: Zed Books, 2013), p. 3.

2   Lloyd Boston, *The Style Checklist: The Ultimate Wardrobe Essentials for You* (New York: Simon and Schuster 2010), p. 39.

3   Gary Younge, 'The man who raised a black power salute at the 1968 Olympic Games', *The Guardian*, 30 March 2012.

4   Oliver Brown, 'London 2012 Olympics: Tommie Smith and John Carlos' famous Black Power salute still resonates 44 years on', *The Telegraph*, 12 July 2012.

5   Teri Agins, *Hijacking the Runway* (London: Penguin, 2014).

6   Cheryl Buckley, *Designing Modern Britain* (London: Reaktion Books, 2007), p. 193.

7   Neil Spencer, 'Menswear in the 1980s', in Juliet Ash and Elizabeth Wilson (eds), *Chic Thrills* (London: Pandora, 1992), pp. 40–8, p. 44.

8   Jim Fixx, *The Complete Book of Running* (New York: Random House, 1979).

9   Lawrence K. Altman and MD, 'The doctor's world: A reformer's battle', *New York Times*, 24 July 1984. Available at https://www.nytimes.com/1984/06/12/science/the-doctor-s-world-a-reformer-s-battle.html (accessed 9 April 2015).

10 See a discussion of US athlete Carl Lewis, in Antony Easthope, *What a Man's Gotta Do: The Masculine Myth in Popular Culture* (London: Paladin Grafton Books, 1986), p. 52.

11 Rosalind Gill, Karen Henwood and Carl McLean, 'Body projects and the regulation of normative masculinity', *Body and Society* 11/1 (2005), pp. 37–62, p. 38.

12 Ibid., p. 39.

13 Tim Edwards, 'Sex, booze and fags: Masculinity, style and men's magazines', *Sociological Review* 51/1 (2003), pp. 132–46, p. 135.

14 Sean Redmond and Su Holmes, *Stardom and Celebrity* (London: Sage Publications, 2007), p. 197.

15 Garry Whannel, *Media Sports Stars: Masculinities and Moralities* (London: Routledge, 2002), p. 132.

16 Ibid., pp. 131–2.

17 Ingrid Loschek, *When Clothes Become Fashion: Design and Innovation Systems* (London: Bloomsbury, 2009), p. 119.

18 Ibid., p. 120.

19 Roland Barthes, *The Fashion System* [1967], trans. Matthew Ward and Richard Howard (Berkeley, CA: University of California Press, 1983).

20 Pierre Bourdieu, *Distinction: A Social Critique of the Judgement of Taste* (London: Routledge, 1984).

21 Brenda Polan and Roger Tredre, *The Great Fashion Designers* (Oxford: Berg, 2009), p. 125.

22 Pamela Skaist-Levy and Gela Nash-Taylor, with Booth Moore, *The Glitter Plan: How We Started Juicy Couture for $200 and Turned it into a Global Brand* (New York: Gotham Books, 2014).

23 Tyler, *Revolting Subjects*, pp. 3–4.

24 Ibid., pp. 7–9.

25 Ibid., p. 19.

26 William Miller, cited in Tyler, *Revolting Subjects*, p. 21.

27 Fred Davis, *Fashion, Culture and Identity* (Chicago, IL: University of Chicago Press, 1994); Malcolm Barnard, *Fashion as Communication*, 2nd edn (Abingdon: Routledge, 2002); Alison Lurie, *The Language of Clothes* (London: Bloomsbury, 1992).

28 Diana Crane, *Fashion and It's Social Agendas: Class, Gender, and Identity in Clothing* (Chicago, IL: University of Chicago, 2001), p. 2.

29 Joanne Turney, *The Culture of Knitting* (Oxford: Berg, 2009).

30 'Deindustrialisation' is a term used to describe the decline of manufacturing industries and its replacement with service-based economies, whilst manufacturing is outsourced to the developing world. This began in the US and the UK in the 1970s and continued throughout the US and Western Europe into the twenty-first century. In the UK, manufacturing jobs decreased from 8 million in 1971 to 5.5 million in 1984, with unemployment at its peak in 1976, with 6.4 per cent (1.5 million) of the population out of work. See Gerd Bayer (ed.), *Heavy Metal Music in Britain* (Farnham: Ashgate, 2009), p. 146.

31 Margaret Maynard, *Dress and Glabalisation* (Manchester: Manchester University Press, 2004).

32 Pierre Bourdieu, *The State Nobility: Elite School in the Field of Power* [1969], trans. Lauretta C. Clough (Cambridge: Polity Press, 1996).

33 Sally Robinson, *Marked Men: White Masculinity in Crisis* (New York: Columbia University Press, 2000). p. 86, quoted in Richard A. Rogers, 'Beasts, burgers, and hummers: Meat and the crisis of masculinity in contemporary television advertisements', *Environmental Communication*, 1/3 (November 2008), pp. 281–301, p. 286.

34 Bill Lancaster, 'Newcastle – capital of what', in Robert Colls and Bill Lancaster (eds), *Geordies: Roots of Regionalism* (Edinburgh: Edinburgh University Press, 1992), pp. 53–70, quoted in Anoop Nayak, *Race, Place and Globalization: Youth Cultures in a Changing World* (Oxford: Berg, 2003), p. 649.

35 Sarah Nettleton and Jonathan Watson (eds), *The Body in Everyday Life* (London: Routledge, 1988), quoted in Gill et al., 'Body projects and the regulation of normative masculinity', p. 38.

36 Larry J. Siegel, *Criminology: The Core* (Boston, MA: Cengage Learning, 2007), p. 264; Edward J. Maggio, *Private Security in the 21st Century: Concepts and Applications* (Sudbury, MA: Jones & Bartlett Publishers, 2011), p. 137; Bill Sanders, *Youth Crime and Youth Culture in the Inner City* (London: Routledge, 2004).

37 Jeff Ferrell and Clinton Sanders, *Cultural Criminology* (Boston, MA: Northeastern University Press, 1995), p. 221, Susan Talburt and Shirley R. Steinberg (eds), *Thinking Queer Sexuality, Culture, and Education* (London: Peter Lang, 2000), p. 185.

38 Derrick Watkins and Richard Ashby, *Gang Investigations: A Street Cop's Guide* (Burlington, MA: Jones and Bartlett, 2007), p. 45; Paul Fussell, *Uniforms: Why We Are What We Wear* (New York: Houghton Mifflin, 2002), p. 122.

39 Raewyn Connell, *Maculinities* (Cambridge: Polity Press, 1995) cited in Rosalind Gill, Karen Henwood and Carl McLean, 'Body projects and the regulation of normative masculinity' (London: LSE Research Articles Online, 2005). Available at: http://eprints.lse.ac.uk/archive/00000371/

40 'Sexual assault against a girl, 15: Detectives launch appeal', North Yorkshire Police website, 19 February 2018. Available on https://northyorkshire.police.uk/news/assault-appeal/ (accessed on 29 July 2018).

41 Michael Kimmel, *The History of Men: Essays on the History of American and British Masculinities* (New York: State University of New York Press, 2012), p. 66.

REFERENCES

Introduction

Arnold, Rebecca, *Fashion, Desire and Anxiety* (London: I.B. Tauris, 2001).

Barnard, Malcolm, *Fashion as Communication* (Abingdon: Routledge, 1996).

Barthes, Roland, *Mythologies*, trans. Annette Lavers (London: Paladin, 1973).

Barthes, Roland, *The Fashion System* (Oakland, CA: University of California Press, 1983).

Benjamin, Walter, *The Arcades Project* [1982] (Cambridge, MA: Harvard University Press, 1999).

Cohen, Stanley, *Folk Devils and Moral Panics*, 3rd edn (London: Routledge, 2002).

Crane, Diana, *Fashion and Its Social Agendas* (Chicago, IL: University of Chicago Press, 2000).

Davis, Fred, *Fashion, Culture, and Identity* (Chicago, IL: University of Chicago Press, 1992).

Dugdale, John, 'The most borrowed library books of 2010', *The Guardian*, 19 February 2011, Available at https://www.theguardian.com/books/2011/feb/18/library-most-borrowed-books (accessed 19 May 2017).

Ericson, Richard V., Patricia M. Baranek and Janet B. L. Chan, *Representing Order: Crime, Law, and Justice in the News Media* (Toronto: University of Toronto Press, 1991).

Evans, Caroline, *Fashion at the Edge: Spectacle, Modernity and Deathliness* (New Haven, CT: Yale University Press, 2003).

Flügel, John C., *The Psychology of Clothes* [1930] (New York: AMS Press, 1976).

Frost, Vicky, 'The Killing, a slow-moving drama with subtitles, is a hit for BBC', *The Guardian*, 4 March 2011. Available at https://www.theguardian.com/tv-and-radio/2011/mar/04/the-killing-bbc-danish-crime-thriller (accessed 19 May 2017).

Gerbner, George, 'Cultural indicators: The case of violence in television drama', *Annals of the American Academy of Political and Social Science* 338/1 (2007), pp. 69–81.

Goddard, Victoria A. (ed.), *Gender, Agency and Change: Anthropological Perspectives* (London: Routledge, 2000).

Goodrum, Alison, *Fashion and Identity* (Oxford: Berg, 2008).

Harvey, John, *Men in Black* (Chicago, IL: University of Chicago Press, 1995).

Hebdige, Dick, *Subculture: The Meaning of Style* (London: Taylor and Francis, 1979).

Henry, Stuart and Mark M. Lanier, *The Essential Criminology Reader* (Boulder, CO: Westview Press, 2006).

Kaiser, Susan B., *The Social Psychology of Clothing: Symbolic Appearances in Context* (London: Fairchild Publications, 1997).

Kuchler, Susanne and Daniel Miller (eds), *Clothing as Material Culture* (Oxford: Berg, 2005).

Lawrence, Regina G., *The Politics of Force: Media and the Construction of Police Brutality* (Berkley, CA: University of California Press, 2000).

Livingstone, Sonia, 'On the continuing problem of media effects research', in James Curran and Michael Gurevich (eds), *Mass Media and Society* (London: Arnold, 1996).

Lombroso, Cesare, *Criminal Man* [1876], trans. Mary Gibson (Durham, NC: Duke University Press, 2006).

Loschek, Ingrid, *When Clothes Become Fashion* (Oxford: Berg, 2009).

MacLin, M. Kimberley and Vivian Herrera, 'The criminal stereotype', *North American Journal of Psychology* 8/2 (June/July 2006), pp. 197–208.

Pearson, Geoffrey, *Hooligan: A History of Respectable Fears* (Basingstoke: Macmillan, 1983).

Pidd, Helen, 'Bid to impose asbo for wearing low-slung trousers dropped', *The Guardian*, 4 May 2010. Available at https://www.theguardian.com/society/2010/may/04/asbo-low-slung-trousers-dropped (accessed 5 July 2010).

Rawlings, Philip, *Drunks, Whores and Idle Apprentices: Criminal Biographies of the Eighteenth Century* (London: Routledge, 1998).

Ribeiro, Aileen, *Dress and Morality* (Oxford: Berg, 2003).

Salecl, Renata, *On Anxiety* (London: The Psychology Press, 2004).

Tarlo, Emma, *Clothing Matters: Dress and Identity in India* (Chicago, IL: University of Chicago Press, 1996).

Williams, Paul and Julie Dickinson, 'Fear of crime: Read all about it?: The relationship between newspaper crime reporting and fear of crime', *The British Journal of Criminology* 33/1 (Winter 1993), pp. 33–56.

Chapter 1

Barnard, Malcolm, *Fashion Theory: A Reader* (London: Routledge, 2007).

Baudrillard, Jean, *Simulations*, trans. Paul Foss, Paul Patton and Philip Beitchman (New York: Semiotext(e), 1983).

Bruzzi, Stella, *Undressing Cinema: Clothing and Identity in the Movies* (London: Routledge, 1997).

Debord, Guy, *The Society of the Spectacle*, trans. Donald Nicholson-Smith (Detroit, MI: Red & Black, 1973).

Dyer, Richard, *The Matter of Images: Essays on Representations* (London: Routledge, 1993).

Gage, John, *Colour and Culture* (London: Thames & Hudson, 1993).

Harvey, John, 'Showing and hiding: Equivocation in the relations of body and dress', *Fashion Theory* 11/1 (2007), pp. 65–94.

Lehmann, Ulrich, 'The language of the PurSuit: Cary Grant's clothes in Alfred Hitchcock's "North by Northwest"', *Fashion Theory* 4/4 (2000), pp. 467–86.

Wigley, Mark, *White Walls, Designer Dresses* (Cambridge, MA: MIT Press, 2001).

Chapter 2

Abbas, Mohammed and Kate Holton, 'London rioters point to poverty and prejudice', *Reuters*, 9 August 2011. Available at www.reuters.com/article/2011/08/09/britain-riot-contrast-idUSL6E7J91RM20110809 (accessed 11 August 2011).

Braddock, Kevin, 'The power of the hoodie', *The Guardian*, 9 August 2011. Available at https://www.theguardian.com/uk/2011/aug/09/power-of-the-hoodie (accessed 11 August 2011).

Craik, Jennifer, *The Face of Fashion: Cultural Studies in Fashion* (London: Routledge, 1994).

Garner, Richard, 'Hoodies, louts, scum: How media demonises teenagers', *The Independent*, 13 March 2009.

Graham, Jane, 'Hoodies strike fear in British cinema', 5 November 2009. Available at https://www.theguardian.com/film/2009/nov/05/british-hoodie-films (accessed 20 February 2010).

Knight, India, 'Let them wear hoodies', *The Sunday Times*, 15 May 2002. Available at https://www.thetimes.co.uk/article/india-knight-let-them-wear-hoodies-6vznmrml0lv (accessed 25 May 2007).

Oliver, Kelly (ed.), *The Portable Kristeva* (New York: Columbia University Press, 2002).

Ribeiro, Aileen, *Dress and Morality* (London: Bloomsbury Academic, 1986).

Shaw, Michael, 'From hooligans to hoodies', *TES*, 8 October 2010. Available at https://www.tes.com/news/hooligans-hoodies (accessed 11 August 2011).

The Telegraph, 'London riots: Eric Pickles blames looting on "criminal sub-culture"', 9 August 2011. Available at https://www.telegraph.co.uk/news/uknews/crime/8691598/London-riots-Eric-Pickles-blames-looting-on-criminal-sub-culture.html (accessed 11 August 2011).

Chapter 3

Alford, Holly, 'The zoot suit: Its history and influence', *Fashion Theory* 8/2 (2004), pp. 225–36.

Amaral, Matt, 'Latino boys in the red white and blue', *Teach 4 Real*, 2007. Available at http://www.teach4real.com/2010/07/07/latino-boys-in-the-red-white-and-blue/ (accessed 30 January 2011).

Associated Press, 'Florida judge rules saggy pant law unconstitutional after teen spends night in jail', *Fox News* [online] 17 September 2008. Available at http://www.foxnews.com/story/02933,424123,00.html (Accessed 10 November 2010).

Baker, Lee D., 'Saggin' and braggin'', in Alisse Waterston and Maria D. Vesperi (eds), *Anthropology Off the Shelf: Anthropologists on Writing* (Chichester: Wiley-Blackwell, 2009), pp. 46–59.

Calvin Klein History [online] (2011). Available at http://www.buycalvinkleinunderwear.com/calvin_klein.com (accessed 30 January 2011).

Chavis, Clarence, 'Men are looking like a fool with your pants on the ground', Part 2, *SF Men's Issues Examiner*, 9 February 2010. Available at http://www.examiner.com/men-s-issues-in-san-francisco/men-you-are-looking-like-a-fool-with-your-pants-on-the-ground-part-two?render=print (accessed 12 January 2011).

Daniel, Mike, 'Rap about saggin' pants upsets gay groups', *McClatchy-Tribune Business News*, 2 November 2007, Proquest. Available at URL? (accessed 12 December 2010).

East, Darlene F., 'Baggy, baggier, baggiest! Young males are "glad bags"': From "Fauntleroy" to rap', *NCAT Journalism Magazine*, 2002. Available at http://worldlymind.org/baggy.htm (accessed 12 January 2011).

Florin, Hector, 'A saggy-pants furor in Riviera Beach', *Time*, 1 October 2008. Available at http://www.time.com/time/world/article/0,8599,1846205,00.html#ixzz1Mf1sG0NO (accessed 10 November 2010).

Graff, Laura, 'March will protest sagging', *Winston Salem Journal*, 8 October 2010. Available at http://www2.journalnow.com/news/2010/oct/08/march-will-protest-sagging-ar-442768/ (accessed 14 December YEAR?; not available outside US).

Haberman, Clyde, 'Can Obama help kill baggy pants look?', *New York Times*, 13 November 2008. Available at https://www.nytimes.com/2008/11/14/nyregion/14nyc.html (accessed 10 November 2010).

Hatfield, Julie, 'Hip hop gets the bounce', *Boston Globe*, 30 November 1993, Section 3, p. 61.

Heaggans, Raphael, *The 21st Century Hip Hop Minstrel Show: Are We Continuing the Black Face Tradition?* (San Diego, CA: University Readers, 2009).

Hill, Marc Lamont, 'Sagging pants: Hip hop trend or prison culture?' *MarcLamontHill* [online] 21 April 2010. Available at http://www.marclamonthill.com/sagging-pants-fashion-trend-or-prison-culture-7651 (accessed 21 April 2011).

Johnson-Elie, Tannette, '*Milwaukee Journal Sentinel* Tannette Johnson-Elie column', *Knight Ridder/Tribune Business News*, 16 February 2005. Available at http://www.accessmylibrary.com/coms2/summary_0286-8288840_ITM (accessed 12 December 2010).

Kim, Serena, 'Style council', *Vibe* 9/9 (2001), pp. 206–10.

Koppel, Niko, 'Are your jeans sagging? Go directly to jail', *New York Times*, 30 August 2007. Available at http://www.nytimes.com/2007/08/30/fashion/30baggy.html (accessed 14 December 2010).

Lah, Kyung, 'Olympic snowboarder's "street" style offends Japanese', *CNN*, 18 February 2010. Available at http://www.cnn.com/2010/SPORT/02/18/japan.kokubo.olympics/index.html (accessed 18 February 2010).

MC Lyte, 'Paper thin', *Lyte as a Rock*, Track 6 (First Priority Music/Atlantic Records, 1988).

Montgomery, Eric, 'Is gangsta rap irrelevant?' *Riverside, CA* [online] 22 July 2010. Available at http://www.examiner.ca.riverside/is-gangsta-rap-irrelevent (accessed 8 May 2011).

O'Connell, Brian, 'Tighten your belt, or at least wear one', *The Irish Times* [online] 11 May 2010. Available at http://www.irishtimes.com/newspaper/features/2010/0511/1224270124758.html (accessed 12 December 2011).

Orlando Sentinel, 'Baggy pants: Baggy pants trip up teen suspected in robberies', *Orlando Sentinel*, 26 January 2007. Available at http://articles.orlandosentinel.com/2007-01-26/news/MUSNEWS26_6_1_baggy-pants-covington-caught (accessed 13 May 2011).

The Outdoor World, 'Ben Davis work pants', *The Outdoor World* [online]. Available at http://www.theoutdoorworld.com/bendavispants.cfm (accessed 7 January 2011).

Saggerboys.com (2011). Available at http://www.saggerboys.com/ (accessed 7 January 2011).

Schneiderman, R. M., 'Ad campaign asks Queens bus riders to pull up their pants', *Wall Street Journal*, 17 May 2010. Available at http://blogs.wsj.com/metropolis/2010/05/17/ad-campaign-asks-queens-bus-rider-to-pull-of-their-pants/ (accessed 12 December 2010).

Smith, Joshua, 'The legend of baggy pants', *Metro Spirit*, 19, http://www.metrospirit.com/index.php?cat=1211101074307265&ShowArticle_ID=1102200508 (accessed 3 June 2010).

TransWorld SKATEboarding, 'Roots, rock, reggae, skateboarding', July 2003. Available at http://skateboarding.transworld.net/1000012446/photos/roots-rock-reggae-skateboarding/ (accessed 13 May 2010).

Urban Dictionary, website http://www.urbandictionary.com/

Westbury, Anthony, 'Saggy pants symbolize what's gone wrong in black community, kids say', TCPalm, 21 October 2010. Available at http://archive.tcpalm.com/news/columnists/anthony-westbury-saggy-pants-symbolize-whats-gone-wrong-in-black-community-kids-say-ep-389105840-345689782.html/ (accessed 15 May 2011).

Williams, Onika K., 'The suppression of a saggin' expression: Exploring the "saggy pants" style within a First Amendment context', *Indiana Law Journal* 85/3 (2010), pp. 1188–96.

Wright, Pierre, interview, 3 February 2011.

Chapter 4

Benson, Peter, 'El Campo: Faciality and structural violence in farm labor camps', *Cultural Anthropology* 23/4 (2008), pp. 589–629.

Cheng, Anne, 'Wounded beauty: An exploratory essay on race, feminism, and the aesthetic question', *Tulsa Studies in Women's Literature* 19/2 (2000), pp. 191–217.

Dwyer, Claire and Philip Crang, 'Fashioning ethnicities: The commercial spaces of multiculture', *Ethnicities* 2/3 (2002), pp. 410–30.

Finn, Jonathan M., *Capturing the Criminal Image: From Mug Shot to Surveillance Society* (Minneapolis, MN: University of Minnesota Press, 2009).

Frosh, Paul, *The Image Factory: Consumer Culture, Photography and the Visual Content Industry* (New York: Gates, 2006).

Gates, Kelly, 'Identifying the 9/11 "faces of terror"', *Cultural Studies* 20/4–5 (2006), pp. 417–40.

Goodwin, Charles, 'Professional vision', *American Anthropologist* 96/3 (1994), pp. 606–33.

Hall, Rachel, 'Of Ziploc bags and black holes: The aesthetics of transparency in the War on Terror', in Shoshana Magnet and Kelly Gates (eds), *The New Media of Surveillance* (New York: Routledge, 2009), pp. 41–68.

Kingsolver, Ann, 'Contested livelihoods: "Placing" one another in "Cedar", Kentucky', *Anthropological Quarterly* 65/3 (1992), pp. 128–36.

Lynch, Kevin, *The Image of the City* (Cambridge, MA: MIT, 1960).

Maguire, Mark, 'The birth of biometric security', *Anthropology Today* 25/2 (2009), pp. 9–14.

Michaelson, Mark and Steven Kasher, *Least Wanted: A Century of American Mugshots*, 1st edn (New York: Steven Kasher Gallery, 2006).

Noble, Greg, 'The face of evil: Demonising the Arab Other in contemporary Australia', *Cultural Studies Review* 14/2 (2008), pp. 14–33.

Poole, Deborah, 'An excess of description: Ethnography, race, and visual technologies', *Annual Review of Anthropology* 34 (2005), pp. 159–79.

Sadre-Orafai, Stephanie, 'Fashion's other images', in Æsa Sigurjónsdóttir, Michael Langkjær and Joanne Turney (eds), *Images in Time* (Bath: Wunderkammer, 2011), pp. 123–30.

Segal, Daniel A., 'Can you tell a Jew when you see one? Or thoughts on meeting Barbra/Barbie at the museum', *Judaism* (Spring 1999), pp. 234–41.

Sekula, Allan, 'The body and the archive', *October* 39 (1986), pp. 3–64.

Sontag, Susan, 'An argument about beauty', *Daedalus* 131/4 (2002), pp. 21–6.

Stewart, Kathleen, *A Space on the Side of the Road: Cultural Politics of an 'Other' America* (Princeton, NJ: Princeton University Press, 1996).

Tagg, John, *The Burden of Representation: Essays on Photographies and Histories* (Minneapolis, MN: University of Minnesota Press, 1993).

Chapter 5

Asian Women's Foundation (AWF), *1997 Survey*, March 1998.

Bell, Shannon, *Reading, Writing, and Rewriting the Prostitute Body* (Bloomington, IN: Indiana University Press, 1994).

Cawaii!, 'Kagai burando namaiki gōman', May 1996.

Cawaii!, July 1997, pp. 15–16.

Dower, John W., *Embracing Defeat: Japan in the Wake of World War II* (New York: W.W. Norton and Company The New Press, 1999).

H, 'Watashitachi no orutanatibu weii', April 2003.

Harootunian, Harry, *Overcome by Modernity: History, Culture and Commodity in Interwar Japan* (Princeton, NJ: Princeton University Press, 2000).

Hayami, Yukiko, 'Toragyaru osorubeki enjo kōsai: Joshikōsei saisentan rupo', *AERA* 9/16 (15 April 1996), pp. 62–5.

Hirota, Masaki, 'Notes on the "Process of Creating Women"', in Wakita Haruko, Anne Bouchy and Ueno Chizuko (eds), *Gender and Japanese History*, vol. 2 (Osaka: Osaka University Press, 1999), pp. 197–219.

Hoggart, Richard, *The Uses of Literature* (Harmondsworth: Penguin Books, 1957).

Hume, Marion, 'Tokyo glamorama', *Harpers Bazaar*, 1 October 2000, pp. 311–15 and 338.

Kinsella, Sharon, 'What's behind the fetishism of Japanese school uniforms?', *Fashion Theory* 6/2 (May 2002), pp. 215–37.

Kinsella, Sharon, 'Black faces, witches, and racism against girls', in Laura Miller and Jan Bardsley (eds), *Bad Girls of Japan* (New York: Palgrave Macmillan, 2005), pp. 143–58.

Lott, Eric, *Love and Theft: Blackface Minstrelsy and the American Working Class* (London: Oxford University Press, 1993).

Maruta, Kōji, 'Giji-ibento to shite no enjo kōsai' [Compensated dating as a pseudo event], *Osaka jogakuin tankidaigaku kiyō*, dai 30 (2000), pp. 209–22.

McVeigh, Brian J., *Wearing Ideology* (London: Berg, 2000).

Miller, Laura, 'Graffiti Photos: Expressive Art in Japanese Girls' Culture', *Harvard Asia Quarterly* 3 (Summer 2003), pp. 31–42.

Miyadai, Shinji, *Seikimatsu no sahō: Owarinaki nichijō o ikiru chie* [*Millenial Etiquette: The Art of Living a Never-ending Everyday Life*] (Tokyo: Recruit, 1997).

Ohnuma, Shōji, *Minzoku* [*Tribe*] (Tokyo: Kawade Shobō Shinsha, 2001).

Popteen, 12, 1993, p. 175.

Sato, Barbara, *The New Japanese Woman: Modernity, Media and Women in Interwar Japan* (Durham, NC: Duke University Press, 2003).

Satō, Ikuya, *Kamikaze Biker: Parody and Anomy in Affluent Japan* (Chicago, IL: University of Chicago Press, 1991).

Silverberg, Miriam, 'The modern girl as militant', in Gail Lee Bernstein (ed.), *Recreating Japanese Women 1600–1945* (Berkeley, CA: University of California Press, 1999), pp. 239–66.

Spa!, 'Kogyaru no yūwake', 9 June 1993.

Tamanoi, Mariko Asano, *Under the Shadow of Nationalism: Politics and Poetics of Rural Japanese Women* (Honolulu: University of Hawaii Press, 1998).

Tokyo Street News, December 2002, pp. 34–41.

Valverde, Mariana, 'The love of finery: Fashion in nineteenth-century social discourse', *Victorian Studies* 32/2 (Winter 1989), pp. 169–88.

Winge, Theresa, 'Undressing and dressing loli: A search for the identity of the Japanese Lolita', *Mechademia* 3 (2008), pp. 47–63.

Chapter 6

Amnesty International UK, 'UK: New poll finds a third of people believe women who flirt partially responsible for being raped', press release, 2005. Available at https://www. amnesty.org.uk/press-releases/uk-new-poll-finds-third-people-believe-women-who-flirt-partially- responsible- being (accessed 3 January 2010).

Bailey, Reg, 'Letting children be children: Report of an independent review of the commercialisation and sexualisation of childhood', Department for Education, June 2011. Available at https://assets.publishing.service.gov.uk/government/uploads/attachment_data/file/175418/Bailey_Review.pdf (accessed 5 January 2010).

Brown, Foxy, 'Stylin", *The Source Presents: Hip Hop Hits, Vol. 6*, Def Jam Records, Track 13, 2002.

Casadei, Marta, 'New Burberry models', *Vogue Italia*, 4 February 2011. Available at http://www.vogue.it/en/magazine/daily-news/2011/02/burberry-spring-summer-2011-adv (accessed 5 January 2010).

Cent, 'P. I. M. P', *Get Rich or Die Tryin'*, Aftermath Entertainment/Shady Records/Interscope Records, Track 11, 2003.

Coates, Ta-Nehisi, 'Hip-hop's down beat', *Time*, 17 August 2007. Available from: http://www.time.com/time/magazine/article/0,9171,1653639,00.html (accessed 6 January 2010).

Fredrickson, Barbara L. and Kristen Harrison, 'Throwing like a girl: Self-objectification predicts adolescent girls' motor performance', *Journal of Sport and Social Issues* 29/1 (2005), pp. 79–101.

Harlow, John, 'Bubbly bursts as bling crowd desert Cristal over "racism"', *Sunday Times*, 9 July 2006. Available at https://www.thetimes.co.uk/article/bubbly-bursts-as-bling-crowd-desert-cristal-over-racism-cwxnmg60brm (accessed 6 January 2010).

International Federation of the Phonographic Industry (IFPI), 'Recording Industry in Numbers 2010', 28 April 2010. Available at http://www.snepmusique.com/wp-content/uploads/2014/01/rin2010.pdf (accessed 2 February 2015).

Latifah, Queen, 'U.N.I.T.Y.', *Black Reign*, Motown/PolyGram Records, Track 12, 1993.

Ludacris, 'Ho', *Incognegro*, Disturbing the Peace, Track 12, 1999.

Lyte, MC, 'Paper Thin', *Lyte as a Rock*, First Priority Music/Atlantic Records, Track 6, 1988.

Mulvey, Laura, 'Visual pleasure and narrative cinema' [1975], in Leo Braudy and Marshall Cohen (eds) *Film Theory and Criticism*, 5th edn (New York: Oxford University Press, 1999), pp. 833–44.

Orbach, Susie, *Bodies* (London: Profile Books, 2009).

Packaged Facts, 'The Young Urban Consumer: How hip-hop culture affects the lifestyle and buying decisions of 12- to 34-year olds', 1 May 2008. Available at http://www.marketresearch.com/product/display.asp?productid=1692747 (accessed 7 January 2010).

Perec, Georges, *Species of Spaces and Other Pieces* (London: Penguin, 1999).

Rouzaud, Frederic, *The Economist*, 8 May 2006.

Thomas, Lesley, 'The sobering subject of consent', *The Telegraph*, 28 March 2007. Available at http://www.telegraph.co.uk/comment/personal-view/3638785/The-sobering-subject-of-consent.html (accessed 9 January 2010).

Chapter 7

Allan, Jay, *Bloody Casuals: Diary of a Football Hooligan* (Ellon: Framedram Publishers, 2004).

Armstrong, Gary, *Football Hooligans: Knowing the Score* (Oxford: Berg, 1998).

Armstrong, Nancy and Leonard Tennenhouse (eds) *The Violence of Representation: Literature and the History of Violence* (Abingdon: Routledge, 1989).

Bakhtin, Mikhail, *Rabelais and His World* (Bloomington, IN: Indiana University Press, 1984).

Bale, John, *Sport, Space and the City* (London: Routledge, 1993).

Beaven, Brad, *Leisure, Citizenship and Working-Class Men in Britain, 1850-1945* (Manchester: Manchester University Press, 2005).

Benwell, Bethan, *Masculinity and Men's Lifestyle Magazines* (Oxford: Wiley-Blackwell, 2003).

Brown, Lorne and Nick Harvey, *A Casual Look: A Photo-diary of Football Fans, 1980s–2001* (Brighton: Football Culture UK, 2002).

Bruzzi, Stella, *Undressing Cinema: Clothing and Identity in the Movies* (Abingdon: Routledge, 1997).

Campbell, Beatrix and Adam L. Dawson, 'Indecent exposures: Men, masculinity and violence', in Mark Perryman (ed.), *Hooligan Wars: Causes and Effects of Football Violence* (Edinburgh: Mainstream, 2001), pp. 62–76.

Cohen, Stanley, *Folk Devils and Moral Panics*, 3rd edn (London: Routledge, 2002).

Craik, Jennifer, *The Face of Fashion* (London: Routledge, 1994).

Dunning, Eric, *Sport Matters: Sociological Studies of Sport, Violence and Civilisation* (London: Taylor & Francis, 1999).

Easthope, Antony, *What a Man's Gotta Do: The Masculine Myth in Popular Culture* (London: Paladin Grafton Books, 1986).

Edwards, Tim, *Men in the Mirror: Men's Fashion, Masculinity, and Consumer Society* (London: Continuum International Publishing Group Ltd., 1997).

Eitzen, D. Stanley, *Sport in Contemporary Society: An Anthology* (Oxford: Oxford University Press, 2014).

Entwistle, Joanne, *The Fashioned Body* (London: Polity Press, 2000).

Foucault, Michel, *Discipline and Punish: The Birth of the Prison* (New York: Random House Publishing, 1975).

Gall, Caroline, *Zulus: Black, White and Blue; The Story of the Zulu Warriors Football Firm* (London: Milo Books, 2005).

Gilbert, Francis, *Yob Nation: The Truth About Britain's Yob Culture* (London: Portrait Press, 2006).

Giulianotti, Richard, *Football: A Sociology of the Global Game* (Oxford: Blackwell, 1999).

Harvey, Adrian, *Football: The First 100 Years* (London: Routledge, 2005).

Hebedige, Dick, *Subculture: The Meaning of Style* (London: Taylor and Francis, 1979).

Hewitt, Paolo and Mark Baxter, *The Fashion of Football* (Edinburgh: Mainstream Publishing, 2006).

Hough, Ian, *Perry Boys: The Casual Gangs of Manchester and Salford* (Wrea Green: Milo Books, 2007).

King, Martin and Martin Knight, *Hoolifan: 30 Years of Hurt* (Edinburgh: Mainstream Publishing, 1999).

Knight, Martin, *Common People* (Edinburgh: Mainstream Publishing, 2000).

Lunt, Peter Kenneth and Sonia Livingstone, *Mass Consumption and Personal Identity: Everyday Economic Experience* (Buckingham: Open University Press, 1992).

Martin, Richard and Harold Koda, *Jocks and Nerds: Men's Style in the Twentieth Century* (New York: Rizzoli, 1989).

Millie, Andrew, *Securing Respect: Behavioural Expectations and Anti-social Behaviour in the UK* (Bristol: Policy Press, 2009).

Mort, Frank, *Cultures of Consumption: Masculinities and Social Space in Late Twentieth Century Britain* (London: Routledge, 1996).

Murphy, Patrick J., John Williams and Eric Dunning, *Football on Trial: Spectator Violence and Development in the Football World* (London: Routledge, 1990).

Nixon, Sean, *Hard Looks: Masculinities, Spectatorship and Contemporary Consumption* (New York: Palgrave Macmillan, 1996).

Osgerby, Bill, *Youth in Britain since 1945* (Oxford: Wiley-Blackwell, 1998).

Redhead, Steve, 'Terrace terrors and glamorous hooligans', Mobile Accelerated Nonpostmodern Culture (MANC) 8, 2009.

Rivers, Dan, *Congratulations, You Have Just Met the Casuals* (London: John Blake Publishing Ltd., 2007).

Sabo, Donald F. Jr and Ross Runfola, *Jock: Sports and Male Identity* (Englewood Cliffs, NJ: Prentice Hall Inc., 1980).

Shields, Rob, *Places on the Margin: Alternative Geographies of Modernity* (London: Psychology Press, 1992).

Spencer, Neil, 'Menswear in the 1980s', in Juliet Ash and Elizabeth Wilson (eds), *Chic Thrills* (London: Pandora, 1992), pp. 40–8.

Thornton, Phil, *Casuals: Football, Fighting and Fashion* (London: Milo Books, 2003).

Waddington, David, *Contemporary Issues in Public Disorder* (London: Routledge, 1992).

Wagg, Stephen, *The Football World: A Contemporary Social History* (London: Harvester Press, 1984).

Whannel, Garry, *Media Sports Stars: Masculinities and Moralities* (London: Routledge, 2002).

Willmott, Michael and William Nelson, *Complicated Lives: Sophisticated Consumers, Intricate Lifestyles, Simple Solutions: The Malaise of Modernity* (London: Wiley, 2003).
Wilson, Elizabeth, *Adorned in Dreams: Fashion and Modernity* (London: Virago, 1985).
Winlow, Simon, *Badfellas: Crime, Tradition and New Masculinities* (Oxford: Berg, 2001).
Woodward, Sophie, *Why Women Wear What They Wear* (Oxford: Berg, 2007).

Chapter 8

Barnard, Malcolm, *Fashion as Communication* (Abingdon: Routledge, 1996).
Bartlett, Djurdja, *Fashion East: The Spectre that Haunted Socialism* (London: MIT Press, 2010).
Burucs, K., 'Újrakezdés', *História* 5/3 (1983), pp. 26–8.
Foucault, Michel, *Discipline and Punish: The Birth of the Prison*, trans. Alan Sheridan (London: Allen Lane, 1977).
Laver, James, *A Concise History of Costume* (London: Thames & Hudson, 1979).
Lipovetsky, Gilles, *The Empire of Fashion: Dressing Modern Democracy*, trans. Catherine Porter (Princeton, NJ: Princeton University Press, 1994).
Medvedev, Katalin, 'Socialism, dress and resistance', in Donald Clay Johnson and Helen Bradley Foster (eds), *Dress Sense: The Emotional and Sensory Experience of Clothes* (Oxford: Berg, 2007), pp. 23–35.
Medvedev, Katalin, 'Ripping up the uniform approach: Hungarian women piece together a new communist fashion', in Regina Lee Blaszczyk (ed.), *Producing Fashion: Commerce, Culture, and Consumers* (Philadelphia, PA: University of Pennsylvania Press, 2008), pp. 389–418.
Mesterházi, Lajos, *Férfikor* (*The Age of Men*) (Budapest: Kossuth, 1967).
Simonovics, Ildikó and Tibor Valuch (eds), *Öltöztessük fel az Országot! Divat és Öltözködés a Szocializmusban* (*Let's Dress the Country! Fashion and Clothing in Socialism*) (Budapest: Argumentum, 2009).
Valuch, Tibor, *Magyarország Társadalomtörténete a XX. Század Második Felében* (*The Social History of Hungary in the Second Half of the 20th Century*) (Budapest: Osiris Kiadó, 2001).
Valuch, Tibor, *A Lódentől a Miniszoknyáig* (*From the Loden Coat to the Miniskirt*) (Budapest: Corvina Kiadó/1956-os Intézet, 2004).

Chapter 9

Ahmed, Sara, *Queer Phenomenology: Orientations, Objects, Others* (Durham, NC: Duke University Press, 2006).
Butler, Judith, 'Critically queer', *GLQ: A Journal of Lesbian and Gay Studies* 1/1 (1993), pp. 17–32.
Butler, Judith, *Gender Trouble: Feminism and the Subversion of Identity* (New York: Routledge, 1999).
Goffman, Erving, *Relations in Public: Microstudies of the Public Order* (New York: Transaction Publishers, 2010).
Grosz, Elizabeth, *Volatile Bodies: Toward a New Corporeal Feminism* (Bloomington, IN: Indiana University Press, 1994).

Halberstam, Judith, *In a Queer Time and Place: Transgender Bodies, Subcultural Lives* (New York: New York University Press, 2005).

Halberstam, Judith, 'The anti-social turn in Queer Studies', *Graduate Journal of Social Science* 5/2 (2008), pp. 140–56.

Latour, Bruno, *Pandora's Hope: Essays on the Reality of Science Studies* (Cambridge, MA: Harvard University Press, 1999).

Latour, Bruno, *Reassembling the Social: An Introduction to Actor-Network-Theory* (Oxford: Oxford University Press, 2007).

Merleau-Ponty, Maurice, 'The experience of the body and classical psychology' [2002], in Mariam Fraser and Monica Greco (eds), *The Body: A Reader* (London: Routledge, 2005).

Weiss, Gail, *Body Images: Embodiment as Corporeality* (New York: Routledge, 1999).

Chapter 10

Attwod, Feona, *Mainstreaming Sex: The Sexualization of Western Culture* (London: I.B. Tauris, 2014).

Barnard, Malcolm, *Fashion as Communication*, 2nd edn (Abingdon: Routledge, 2002).

Benjamin, Walter, *The Arcades Project* [1982] (Cambridge, MA: Harvard University Press, 1999).

Berger, John, *Ways of Seeing* (London: Fontana, 1972).

Calhoun, Lawrence G., James W. Selby, Arnie Cann and G. Theodore Keller, 'The Effects of victim attractiveness and sex of respondents on social relations to victims of rape', *British Journal of Social and Clinical Psychology* 12/2 (1978), pp. 191–2.

Cunningham, F. and D. Weiss, 'Perceptions of sexy clothing by college females', Association of College Professors of Textiles and Clothing Proceedings: Combined Central, Eastern and Western Regional Meetings, Monument, CO (1985).

Davis, Fred, *Fashion, Culture and Identity* (Chicago, IL: University of Chicago Press, 1994).

Debord, Guy, *The Society of the Spectacle*, trans. Donald Nicholson (Detroit, MI: Red & Black, 1970).

Denfield, Rene, *The New Victorians: A Young Woman's Challenge to the Old Feminist Order* (New York: Warner Books, 1996).

Dion, Karen, Ellen Berscheid and Elaine Walster, 'What is beautiful is good', *Journal of Personality and Social Psychology* 24/3 (1972), pp. 285–90.

Eco, Umberto, *A Theory of Semiotics* (Bloomington, IN: Indiana University Press, 1976).

Edmonds, Ed M. and Delwin Cahoon, 'Female clothes preference related to male sexual interest', *Bulletin of the Psychonomic Society* 22/3 (1984), pp. 171–3.

Edmonds, Ed M. and Delwin Cahoon, 'Attitudes concerning crimes related to clothing worn by female victims', *Bulletin of the Psychonomic Society* 24/6 (1986), pp. 444–6.

Evans, Caroline, *Fashion at the Edge: Spectacle, Modernity and Deathliness* (New Haven, CT: Yale University Press, 2003).

Flugel, John C., *The Psychology of Clothes* (London: Hogarth Press, 1930).

Grubb, Amy and Emily Turner, 'Attribution of blame in rape cases: A review of the impact of rape myth acceptance, gender role conformity and substance use on victim blaming', *Aggression and Violent Behaviour* 17/5 (2012), pp. 443–52.

Jacobson, Marsha B., 'Effects of victim's and defendant's physical attractiveness on subject's judgements in a rape case', *Sex Roles* 7/3 (1981), pp. 247–55.

Jacobson, Marsha B. and Paula M. Popovich, 'Victim attractiveness and perceptions of responsibility in an ambiguous rape case', *Psychology of Women Quarterly* 8/1 (1983), pp. 100–4.

Johnson, Kim K. P., 'Attributions about date rape: Impact of clothing, sex, money spent, date type, and perceived similarity', *Family and Consumer Sciences Research Journal* 23/3 (March 1995), pp. 292–310.

Kanekar, Suresh and Maharukh Kolsawalla, 'Factors affecting responsibility attributed to rape victims', *Journal of Social Psychology* 113/2 (1981), pp. 285–6.

Kelley, Harold and John Michela, 'Attribution theory and research', *Annual Review of Psychology* 31 (1980), pp. 457–501.

Lerner, Melvin and Dale T. Miller, 'Just world research and the attribution process: Looking back and ahead', *Psychological Bulletin* 85/5 (1978), pp. 1030–51.

Levy, Ariel, *Female Chauvinist Pigs: Women and the Rise of Raunch Culture* (New York: Simon & Schuster, 2006).

Lewis, Lacinda and Kim K. P. Johnson, 'Effect of dress, cosmetics, sex of subject, and casual inference on attribution of victim responsibility', *Clothing and Textiles Research Journal* 8/1 (Fall 1989), pp. 22–7.

Lipovetsky, Gilles, *The Empire of Fashion: Dressing Modern Democracy*, trans. Catherine Porter (Princeton, NJ: Princeton University Press, 1994).

Mathes, Eugene and Sherry Kempher, 'Clothing as non-verbal communicator of sexual attitudes and behaviour', *Perceptual and Motor Skills* 43/2 (1976), pp. 495–8.

Mazelan, Patti, 'Stereotypes and perceptions of the victims of rape', *Victimology: An International Journal* 5/2 (1980), pp. 121–32.

McCaul, Kevin D., Lois G. Veltum, Vivian Boyechko and Jacqueline J. Crawford, 'Understanding Attributions of victim blame for rape: Sex, violence and foreseeability', *Journal of Applied Social Psychology* 20/1 (1990), pp. 1–26.

McDowell, Colin, *The Anatomy of Fashion: Why We Dress the Way We Do* (London: Phaidon, 2013).

Moor, Avigail, 'She dresses to attract, he perceives seduction: A gender gap in attribution of intent to women's revealing style of dress and its relation to blaming the victims of sexual violence', *Journal of International Women's Studies* 11/4 (May 2010), pp. 115–27.

Paasonen, Susanna, Kaarina Nikunen and Laura Saarenmaa, *Pornification: Sex and Sexuality in Media Culture* (Oxford: Berg, 2008).

Rape, Abuse and Incest National Network (RAINN), 'Campus sexual violence: Statistics', n.d. Available at https://www.rainn.org/statistics/campus-sexual-violence (accessed 1 December 2017).

Ribeiro, Aileen, *Dress and Morality* (Oxford: Berg, 2003).

Schult, Deborah G. and Lawrence J. Schneider, 'The role of sexual provocativeness, rape history, and observer gender in perceptions of blame in sexual assault', *Journal of Interpersonal Violence* 6/1 (1991), pp. 94–101.

Scroggs, James, 'Penalties for rape as a function of victim provocativeness, damage and resistance', *Journal of Applied Social Psychology* 6/4 (1976), pp. 360–8.

Sterling, Alinor C., 'Undressing the victim: The intersection of evidentiary and semiotic meanings of women's clothing in rape trials', *Yale Journal of Law and Feminism* 7/1 (1995), pp. 87–132.

Terry, Roger and Suzanne Doerge, 'Dress, posture and setting as additive factors in subjective probability of rape', *Perceptual and Motor Skills* 48/3 (1979), pp. 903–6.

Van der Bruggen, Madeleine and Amy Grubb, 'A review of the literature relating to rape victim blaming: An analysis of the impact of observer and victim characteristics on attribution of blame in rape cases', *Aggression and Violent Behaviour* 19/5 (2014), pp. 523–31.

Warshaw, Robin, *I Never Called it Rape: The Ms Report on Recognizing, Fighting, and Surviving Date and Acquaintance Rape* (New York: Harper & Row, 1988).

Warwick, Alexandra and Dani Cavallaro, *Fashioning the Frame; Boundaries, Dress and the Body* (Oxford: Berg, 1998).

Whatley, Mark A., 'Victim characteristics influencing attributions of responsibility to rape victims: A meta-analysis', *Aggression and Violent Behaviour* 1/2 (1996), pp. 81–95.

Whelehan, Imelda, *Overloaded: Popular Culture and the Future of Feminism* (London: The Women's Press, 2000).

Chapter 11

Baur, Tori, 'Pirates invade ABC Television's "Wife Swap" in season opener', 5 September 2006. Available at http://www.keepthecode.com/2006/09/pirate-invade-abc-television-wifeswap.html (accessed 17 February 2007).

Clarke, John, Stuart Hall, Tony Jefferson and Brian Roberts, 'Subcultures, cultures and class', in Stuart Hall and Tony Jefferson (eds), *Resistance Through Rituals: Youth Subcultures in Post-war Britain* [1975] (London: Routledge, 1976), pp. 9–74.

Cordingly, David, *Under the Black Flag: The Romance and the Reality of Life Among the Pirates* (New York: Random House, 2006).

Croce, Pat, *Pirate Soul: A Swashbuckling Journey through the Golden Age of Pirates* (Philadelphia, PA: Running Press, 2006).

Hari, Johann, 'You are being lied to about pirates', *The Independent*, 5 January 2009.

Hebdige, Dick, *Subculture: The Meaning of Style* (London: Taylor and Francis, 1979).

Kuhn, Gabriel, *Life Under the Jolly Roger: Reflections on Golden Age Piracy* (Oakland: PM Press, 2010).

Kilpatrick, Kate, 'White riot', 6 June 2007. Available at http://www.philadelphiaweekly.com/view.php?id=14772&highlight=White (accessed 21 July 2007; not available outside US).

Land, Chris, 'Flying the black flag: Revolt, revolution and the social organisation of piracy in the "golden age"', *Management and Organizational History* 2/2 (2007), pp. 169–92.

Lefebvre, Henri, *Everyday Life in the Modern World* (New York: Harper and Row, 1971).

Marx, Jenifer G., 'The golden age of piracy', in David Cordingly (ed.), *Pirates: A Worldwide Illustrated History* (Edmonds, WA: J.B. Press, 1998), pp. 100–23.

Matthews, John, *Pirates* (New York: Atheneum Books for Young Readers, 2006).

Panethiere, Darrell, 'The persistence of piracy: The consequences for creativity, for culture, and for sustainable development', Global Alliance for Cultural Diversity, UNESCO (2005). Available at http://unesdoc.unesco.org/images/0014/001455/145517e.pdf (accessed 15 July 2007).

Rankin, Hugh F., *The Golden Age of Piracy* (New York: Holt, Rinehart and Winston, 1969).

Rediker, Marcus, *Between the Devil and the Deep Blue Sea: Merchant Seamen, Pirates and the Anglo-American Maritime World, 1700–1750* (Cambridge: Cambridge University Press, 1987).

Rediker, Marcus, *Villains of All Nations* (London: Beacon Press, 2005).

Richards, Keith, *Life* (London: Weidenfeld and Nicholson, 2010).

Sandoval, Greg, 'Feds raise questions about big media's piracy claims', *cnet*, 12 April 2010. Available at http://news.cnet.com/8301-31001_3-20002304-261.htm (accessed 25 July 2008).

Tharoor, Ishaan, 'How Somalia's Fishermen Became Pirates', *Time*, 18 April 2009.

Vahdati, Arash, 'Skull symbol', 23 June 2010 [online]. Available at http://www. kolahstudio.com/Underground/index.php?s= skull+crossbones&submit=GO (accessed 10 November 2010).

Wilczynski, Krzysztof, 'Jolly Roger', 18 March 2007. Available at http://www.pirateinfo. com/detail/detail.php?article_id=59 (no longer available)

Chapter 12

Andrewes, Janet, *Bodywork: Dress as Cultural Tool* (Leiden: Brill, 2005).

Blehr, Barbro, *En norsk besvärjelse : 17 maj-firande vid 1900-talets slut* (Nora: Bokförlaget Nya Doxa, 2000).

Bohn, Annichen Sibbern, *Norwegian Knitting Designs* (Olso:Grøndahl, 1929).

Brøgger, Waldemar, *Skikk og bruk* (Oslo: Cappelen 1960).

Colbun, Mae, Reading into Norwegian Wool an Annotated Bibliography for Textile Innovators and Entrepreneurs. http://www.hioa.no/Om-HiOA/Senter-for-velferds-og-arbeidslivsforskning/SIFO/Publikasjoner-fra-SIFO/Reading-into-Norwegian-Wool 2012.

Conell, Raewyn, *Masculinities* (Cambridge: Polity Press 2001).

Gau, Colleen, '*Conventional Work Dress*', in Joanne Eicher and Phyllis Tortora (eds), *Berg Encyclopedia of World Dress and Fashion*, vol. 10: *Global Perspective* (Oxford: Bergy, 2010), pp. 85–96.

Goffman, Erving, *The Presentation of Self in Everyday Life*, Monograph No. 2 (Edinburgh: University of Edinburgh Social Sciences Research Centre, 1958).

Hebdige, Dick, 1979, *Subculture: The Meaning of Style* (London: Taylor and Francis, 1979).

Hellesund, Tone, 'Dressen - det mandligste av alt"', in Liv Hilde Boe and Anne Sofie Hjemdahl (eds), *Kropp og Klær* (Oslo: Norsk Folkemuseum, 2000).

Hollander, Anne, *Sex and Suits* (Sparkford: Claridge Press, 1994).

Klepp, Ingun Grimstad, *Klær, kropp og velvære. Hva vil det si å føle seg velkledd*?. *In Modets metamorfoser. Den klädda kroppens identiteter och förvandlingar* (Stockholm: Carlsson Bokförlag, 2009).

Klepp, Ingun Grimstad, 'Patched, louse-ridden, tattered: Clean and dirty clothes', *Textile: The Journal of Cloth & Culture* 5 (2007). pp. 254–75.

Klepp, Ingun Grimstad and Silje Elisabeth Skuland, 'The rationalisation of consumption – reasons for purchasing outdoor recreational outfits', in Maria Vaccarella and Jacque Lynn Foltyn (ed.), *Fashion-Wise* (Oxford: Inter-Disciplinary Press, 2013), pp. 43–52.

Klepp, Ingun Grimstad and Tone S. Tobiasson (in press) *Norsk strikkehistorie* (Hugesund: Vormedal forlag, 2018).

Küchler, Susanne and Daniel Miller (eds), *Clothing as Material Culture* (Oxford: Berg, 2005).

Lennon, Sharron J., Johnson, Kim K.P. and Schulz, Theresa Lennon et al. 'Forging linkages between dress and law in the U.S., Part I: Rape and sexual harassment', *Clothing and Textiles Research Journal* 17/3 (June 1999), pp. 144–56.

Miller, Daniel, *Stuff* (Cambridge: Polity Press, 2010).

Pettersen, Kristine, *Dress med press – En studie av mannlig klesbruk i stortingssalen.* SIFO rapport 7-2004, http://www.hioa.no/Om-HiOA/Senter-for-velferds-og-arbeidslivsforskning/SIFO/Publikasjoner-fra-SIFO/Dress-med-press-En-studie-av-mannlig-klesbruk-i-stortingssalen, 2004.
Rubinstein, Ruth P. *Dress Codes* (Oxford: Westview Press, 2001).
Turney, Joanne, *The Culture of Knitting* (Oxford: Berg, 2009).

Chapter 13

Arnold, Rebecca, *Fashion, Desire and Anxiety: Image and Morality in the Twentieth Century* (London: I.B. Tauris).
Batson, George, *Design for Murder: A Mystery Thriller in Three Acts* (New York: French, 1960).
Cawelti, John G., *Adventure, Mystery, and Romance: Formula Stories as Art and Popular Culture* (Chicago, IL: University of Chicago Press, 1976).
Craik, Jennifer, 'The cultural politics of the uniform', *Fashion Theory* 7/2 (June 2003), pp. 143–4.
Evans, Caroline, *Fashion at the Edge: Spectacle, Modernity and Deathliness* (New Haven, CT: Yale University Press, 2007).
Foulkes, Nick, *The Trench Book* (New York: Assouline, 2007).
Frank, Katherine, 'Body talk: Revelations of self and body in contemporary strip clubs', in Adeline Masquelier (ed.), *Dirt, Undress, and Difference: Critical Perspectives on the Body's Surface* (Bloomington, IN: Indiana University, 2005), pp. 96–121.
Gordon, Beverley, 'Material culture in a popular vein: Perspectives on studying artifacts of mass culture', in Ray B. Browne and Marshall W. Fishwick (eds), *Symbiosis: Popular Culture and Other Fields* (Bowling Green, OH: Bowling Green State University Popular Press, 1988), pp. 170–6.
Harvey, John, *Men in Black* (Chicago, IL: University of Chicago Press, 1995).
Harvey, John, 'Showing and hiding: Equivocation in the relations of body and dress', *Fashion Theory* 11/1 (March 2007), pp. 65–94.
Hollander, Anne, *Seeing Through Clothes* (New York: Viking Press, 1978).
Loukides, Paul and Linda K. Fuller, *Beyond the Stars III: The Material World in American Popular Film* (Bowling Green, OH: Bowling Green State University Popular Press, 1993).
MacDonell Smith, Nancy, *The Classic Ten: The True Story of the Little Black Dress and Nine Other Fashion Statements* (London: Penguin Books, 2003).
Phelan, Peggy, *Unmarked: The Politics of Performance* (Abingdon: Routledge, 1993).
'Report from the trenches', photographed by Deborah Turbeville, *Interview* 30/1 (January 2000), pp. 74–83.
Tseelon, Efrat, 'From fashion to masquerade: Towards an ungendered paradigm', in Joanne Entwistle and Elizabeth Wilson (eds), *Body Dressing* (Oxford: Berg, 2001), pp. 103–18.
Tynan, Jane, '"Tailoring in the trenches": The making of First World War British Army uniform', in Jessica Meyer (ed.), *British Popular Culture and the First World War* (Boston, MA: Leiden, 2008), pp. 71–94.
Wagner-Martin, Linda, *A Historical Guide to Ernest Hemingway* (London: Oxford University Press, 2000).
Wilcox Putnam, Nina, *Believe You Me!* (New York: George H. Doran Company, 1919).

Chapter 14

Agins, Teri, *Hijacking the Runway* (London: Penguin, 2014).

Altman, Lawrence K. and MD, 'The doctor's world; a reformer's battle', *New York Times*, 24 July 1984. Available at https://www.nytimes.com/1984/06/12/science/the-doctor-s-world-a-reformer-s-battle.html (accessed 9 April 2015).

Barnard, Malcolm, *Fashion as Communication*, 2nd edn (Abingdon: Routledge, 2002).

Barthes, Roland, *The Fashion System* [1967], trans. Matthew Ward and Richard Howard (Berkeley, CA: University of California Press, 1983).

Bayer, Gerd (ed.), *Heavy Metal Music in Britain* (Farnham: Ashgate, 2009).

Boston, Lloyd, *The Style Checklist: The Ultimate Wardrobe Essentials for You* (New York: Simon and Schuster 2010).

Bourdieu, Pierre, *The State Nobility: Elite School in the Field of Power* [1969], trans. Lauretta C. Clough (Cambridge: Polity Press, 1996).

Bourdieu, Pierre, *Distinction: A Social Critique of the Judgement of Taste* (London: Routledge, 1984).

Brown, Oliver, 'London 2012 Olympics: Tommie Smith and John Carlos' famous Black Power salute still resonates 44 years on', *The Telegraph*, 12 July 2012.

Buckley, Cheryl, *Designing Modern Britain* (London: Reaktion Books, 2007).

Crane, Diana, *Fashion and Its Social Agendas: Class, Gender and Identity in Clothing* (Chicago, IL: University of Chicago, 2001).

Connell, Raewyn, *Masculinities* (Cambridge: Polity Press, 1995).

Davis, Fred, *Fashion, Culture and Identity* (Chicago, IL: University of Chicago Press, 1994).

Easthope, Antony, *What a Man's Gotta Do: The Masculine Myth in Popular Culture* (London: Paladin Grafton Books, 1986).

Edwards, Tim, 'Sex, booze and fags: Masculinity, style and men's magazines', *Sociological Review* 51/1 (2003), pp. 132–46.

Ewing, Elizabeth, *History of 20th Century Fashion* (London: Pavilion Books, 2014).

Farrell, Jeff and Clinton Sanders, *Cultural Criminology* (Boston, MA: Northeastern University Press, 1995).

Fixx, Jim, *The Complete Book of Running* (New York: Random House, 1979).

Fussell, Paul, *Uniforms: Why We Are What We Wear* (New York: Houghton Mifflin, 2002).

Gill, Rosalind, Karen Henwood and Carl McLean, 'Body projects and the regulation of normative masculinity', *Body and Society* 11/1 (2005), pp. 37–62.

Kimmel, Michael, *The History of Men: Essays on the History of American and British Masculinities* (New York: State University of New York Press, 2012).

Lancaster, Bill, 'Newcastle – capital of what', in Robert Colls and Bill Lancaster (eds), *Geordies: Roots of Regionalism* (Edinburgh: Edinburgh University Press, 1992), pp. 53–70.

Loschek, Ingrid, *When Clothes Become Fashion: Design and Innovation Systems* (London: Bloomsbury, 2009).

Lurie, Alison, *The Language of Clothes* (London: Bloomsbury, 1992).

Maggio, Edward J., *Private Security in the 21st Century: Concepts and Applications* (Sudbury, MA: Jones & Bartlett Publishers, 2011).

Maynard, Margaret, *Dress and Glabalisation* (Manchester: Manchester University Press, 2004).

Nayak, Anoop, *Race, Place and Globalization: Youth Cultures in a Changing World* (Oxford: Berg, 2003).

Nettleton, Sara and Jonathan Watson (eds), *The Body in Everyday Life* (London: Routledge, 1988).

Polan, Brenda and Roger Tredre, *The Great Fashion Designers* (Oxford: Berg, 2009).

Redmond, Sean and Su Holmes, *Stardom and Celebrity* (London: Sage Publications, 2007).

Robinson, Sally, *Marked Men: White Masculinity in Crisis* (New York: Columbia University Press, 2000).

Sanders, Bill, *Youth Crime and Youth Culture in the Inner City* (London: Routledge, 2004).

Siegel, Larry J., *Criminology: The Core* (Boston, MA: Cengage Learning, 2007).

Skaist-Levy, Pamela and Gela Nash-Taylor, with Booth Moore, *The Glitter Plan: How We Started Juicy Couture for $200 and Turned it into a Global Brand* (New York: Gotham Books, 2014).

Spencer, Neil, 'Menswear in the 1980s', in Juliet Ash and Elizabeth Wilson (eds), *Chic Thrills* (London: Pandora, 1992), pp. 40–8.

Talburt, Susan and Shirley R. Steinberg (eds), *Thinking Queer: Sexuality, Culture, and Education* (London: Peter Lang, 2000).

Turney, Joanne, *The Culture of Knitting* (Oxford: Berg, 2009).

Tyler, Imogen, *Revolting Subjects: Social Abjection and Resistance in Neoliberal Britain* (London: Zed Books, 2013).

Watkins, Derrick and Richard Ashby, *Gang Investigations: A Street Cop's Guide* (Burlington, MA: Jones and Bartlett, 2007).

Whannel, Garry, *Media Sports Stars: Masculinities and Moralities* (London: Routledge, 2002).

Younge, Gary, 'The man who raised a black power salute at the 1968 Olympic Games', *The Guardian*, 30 March 2012.

INDEX

www.ingramcontent.com/pod-product-compliance
Lightning Source LLC
Chambersburg PA
CBHW050418280326
41932CB00013BA/1909